ROGER DOMMERGUE

TRUTH AND SYNTHESIS
THE END OF SHAMS

ROGER-GUY POLACCO DE MENASCE
(1924-2013)

Roger Dommergue was a Franco-Luxembourg professor of philosophy best known for his controversial positions on the Holocaust. Dommergue supported revisionist theories of the Holocaust, questioning the number of Jewish victims and claiming that the Nazi gas chambers were a myth. He gave lectures and interviews in which he denied the extent of the crimes committed by the Nazi regime during the Second World War.

TRUTH AND SYNTHESIS

THE END OF SHAMS

Vérité et synthèse – La fin des impostures

2000

Translated and published by

OMNIA VERITAS LTD

*Ø*MNIA VERITAS.

www.omnia-veritas.com

© Omnia Veritas Limited – 2025

All rights reserved. No part of this publication may be reproduced by any means without the prior permission of the publisher. The intellectual property code prohibits copies or reproductions for collective use. Any representation or reproduction in whole or in part by any means whatsoever, without the consent of the publisher, the author or their successors, is unlawful and constitutes an infringement punishable by articles of the Code of Intellectual Property.

PREFACE 17
  The Jew is the main enemy 24
PART ONE 25
WHAT THE JEWS SAID ABOUT THEMSELVES 25
  FUNDAMENTAL FOREWORD 25
A RABBI PLEADS GUILTY 28
WHAT JEWS SAY ABOUT JEWS 35
  Baruch Lévy, Jewish 38
  The glands of humanity 38
  "Jewish World 39
  Walter Ratheneau, Jewish 40
  Benjamin Disraeli, Jewish 40
  Benjamin Disraeli, Jewish 42
  Marcus Éli Ravage, Jewish 42
  Isidore Loeb, Jewish 44
  "La Revue des Études Juives 44
  The Protocols of the Elders of Zion 46
  Werner Sombart, Jewish 47
  The Coadjutor of the Chief Rabbi of Jerusalem 47
  Henri Barbusse, Jewish 47
  Adolphe Crémieux, Jewish 47
  Adolphe Crémieux, Jewish 49
  René Groos, Jewish 50
  Blumenthal, Jewish 50
  The Central Conference of American Rabbis 50
  Statements made within B'nai B'rith 51
WHAT THE JEWS THEMSELVES SAY ABOUT COMMUNISM
.... 56
  Rabbi Judah L. magnes 56
  Mr Cohan, Jewish 56
  Nahum Sokolow, Jewish 57
  Rabbi Lewis Brown 57
  Professor Reinhold Niebuhr, Jewish 57
  "The American Hebrew 57

Hermalin, Jewish 58
"Jewish Chronicle 58
Rabbi Judah L. Magnes 58
Otto Weininger, Jewish 58
"Towards Moscow 59
Angelo Rappoport, Jewish 59
Moritz Rappoport, Jewish 59
"Jewish tribune 59
Kadmi Cohen, Jewish 59
"The Maccabean 60
Maurice Samuel, Jewish 61
Angelo Rappoport, Jewish 61
Bernard Lazare, Jewish 61
"The Israelite world 61
"Israelite Archives 62
"New York Time 62
Elie Eberlin, Jewish 62
"Jewish Chronicle 63
Rabbis' Manifesto 63
Louis Fisher, Jewish 64
"The Maccabean 64
"Jewish World 65
"Canadian Jewish Chronicle 65
Maurice Murrey, Jewish 65
"Novy mar 65
J. Olgin, Jewish 66
Bernard Lazare, Jewish 66
Angelo Rappoport, Jewish 71
Alfred Nossig, Jewish 71

COMMUNISM SUPPORTED AND FINANCED BY JEWISH HIGH BANKING 73

Here is the text and the analyses by Father Fahey. 73
US Secret Service report 74
Jewish capitalists 76
The Russian Revolution was a Jewish investment 77
The symbolism of the red flag 77

Jews and liberalism **79**
An interesting British document about the Jews **79**
Unavoidable findings **80**
A leading Jewish banker makes a sensational confession **81**
Here is an atrocious document: **90**
Big property destroys small property **90**
History's true genocides **90**
Interesting document on the conversion of Chief Rabbi Neofit **94**
Two interesting quotes from Zinovieff, a Jew **95**
Jewish gold, master of the world **95**
The Tsar in the Rothschild castle **101**
"Tag **101**
"Jews must live **101**
An unbridgeable chasm **108**
The Jews are the most racist of all peoples **110**
The Society of Nations, a Jewish organisation **110**
Dr Klee, Jewish **110**
Jesse E. Sampter, Jewish **111**
Max Nordau, Jewish **111**
Nahum Sokolov, Jewish **111**
Lucien Wolf, Jewish **111**
Lennhorr, Jewish **111**
"Judische Rundschau **112**
Sir Max Waechter, Jewish **112**
Lenin, Jewish **112**
Emil Ludwig, Jewish **112**
At the Grand International Masonic Convent **113**
At the Grand Orient convent **113**
At the American Jewish Committee Congress **114**
The Peace Conference **114**
Freemasonry, a Jewish instrument **114**
Benjamin Disraeli, Jewish **116**
"The Israelite Truth **116**
Bernard Shillmann, Jewish **116**
Bernard Lazare, Jewish **116**
Ludwig Blau, Jewish **117**
Isaac Wise, Jewish **117**

Bernard Lazare, Jewish 117
"The Jewish Historical Society 117
"The free Mason Guide 117
"Encyclopedia of freemasonry 118
Rudolph Klein, Jewish 118
Rev. S. Mac Gowan 118
"Symbolism 118
"The text book of free-masonry 118
"Alpina 119
"The Anderson Constitutions 119
Samuel Untermeyer, Jew and Freemason 119
Findel, Jew and Freemason 119
"The Jewish tribune 120
"The Jewish Encyclopaedia 120
"B'nai B'rith magazine 120

WHY CAN'T JEWS EVER BE THE NATIONALS OF ANY COUNTRY? 121

UNLIMITED PROOF OF THIS 121

Dr Chaïm Weizman, Jewish 121
Ludwig Lewinsohn, Jewish 121
"Israel messenger 121
Jesse E. Sempter, Jewish 122
"Jewish Encyclopedia 122
"New York tribune 122
Max Nordau, Jewish 122
"Jewish Chronicle 122
"Israelite Archives 123
Lévy-Bing, Jewish 123
Bernard Lazare, Jewish 123
"Pro-Israel 123
Max Nordau, Jewish 123
Nahum Sololow, Jewish 124
S. Rokhomovsky, Jewish 124
"The Israelite world 124
"Israelite Archives 124

"Jewish Chronicle 125
Wodislawski, Jewish 125
"Sunday Chronicle 125
"Jewish World 125
Theodore Herzl, Jewish 126
Léon. Lévy, Jewish 126
"Jewish World 127
"Jewish World 127
Rabbi Morris Joseph 127
Arthur D. Lawis, Jewish 127
Léon Simon, Jewish 127
Moses Hess, Jewish 128
"Jewish Chronicle 128
"Jewish Courrier 128
G. B Stern, Jewish 128
S. Gerald Soman, Jewish 128
The Kol Nidre prayer 133
Consequences of this psychopathology 133
Klatskin, Jewish 134
Jacob Braffmann, Jewish 134
Marcus Éli Ravage, Jewish 134
James Darmesteter, Jewish 134
Kurt Munzer, Jewish 135
Otto Weininger, Jewish 135
Bernard Lazare, Jewish 135
René Groos, Jewish 136
Mr J Olgin, Jewish 136
Medina Ivrit, Jewish 136
Koppen, Jewish 136
Baruch Lévi, Jewish 137
Dr Ehrenpreis, Chief Rabbi 137

THE COLLAPSE OF RUSSIA 139

"British Israel Truth 139
Is totalitarian Judeopathy tolerable? 139
"Jewish Encyclopedia 140
Bernard Lazare, Jewish 141

- Dr Hugo Ganz, Jewish 141
- Théodore Reinach, Jewish 141
- Dr Rudolf Wasserman, Jewish 142
- Cerfbeer from Medelsheim, Jewish 142
- Usury gave the Jews half of Alsace 142
- Oscar Frank, Jewish 143
- Graetz, Jewish 143
- Dr Rudolf Wasserman, Jewish 144
- Dr M. J. Guttmann, Jewish 144
- Kreppel, Jewish 144
- The French flag as seen by the Jew Jean Zay 144
- Symbolism of the closed fist and raised arm, open hand 149
- Danger! 150
- Communism and Jewishness in Canada 151
- A vital interest 152
- Karl Marx, founder of Communism 153
- Systematic boycott of all works that are not pro-Jewish, as far back as 1895 153
- Russia's fate was decided in 1913 153
- About the Bible 154
- About Japan 154

WHAT THEY HAVE DONE FOR HUMANITY 157

- Latzis, Jewish 157
- Dr. Fromer, Jewish 157
- Some significant statements by Jews 158
- Fundamental corruption 159
- The Jewish Chronicle comments on the work of an Irish theologian 162
- The Judeo-Communists of the Spanish Popular Front and 1837 .. 163
- Unanimous testimony from Jews and Goyim alike 164

TRAGIC CONCLUSION 168
WHAT DID THE JEWS SAY IN THIS FIRST PART OF THE BOOK? 169

- A thousand years! Next to the eternal Zion! 181

PART TWO 189

WHAT THE GOYIM SAY ABOUT THE JEWS 189
Winston Churchill 189
Mohammed 191
Erasmus 191
Luther 191
Ronsard 192
Voltaire 192
Emmanuel Kant 192
Benjamin Franklin 192
Malesherbes 193
Fichte 193
Napoleon 193
Charles Fourier 193
Schopenhauer 194
Alfred de Vigny 194
Honoré de Balzac 194
Alphonse Toussenel 194
Proudhon 194
Michelet 195
Ernest Renan 195
Bakunin 195
Dostoyevsky 195
Victor Hugo 195
Wagner 196
Édouard Drumont 196
Edmond de Goncourt 197
Guy de Maupassant 197
Jules Verne 197
Adolphe Hitler 198
Georges Simenon 198
Jean Giraudoux 198
Lucien Rebatet 198
Paul Morand 199
Marcel Aymé 199
Pierre-Antoine Cousteau 199
Louis Ferdinand Céline 199

THE SHERLOCKHOLMIZED HOLOCAUST ... **203**

Additional information about the UN ... **209**
General secretariat ... **210**
Information centre ... **211**
International Labour Office (ILO) ... **211**
Food and Agriculture Organisation (FAO) ... **211**
Educational, Scientific and Cultural Organization (Unesco) ... **212**
World Bank for Reconstruction and Development ... **212**
International Monetary Fund (IMF) ... **213**
World Refugee Organization ... **213**
World Health Organization (who) ... **213**
World Trade Organisation (WTO) ... **214**
International Telecommunication Union (ITU) ... **214**

PART THREE ... **216**
AN OVERWHELMINGLY TRUE TEXT ATTRIBUTED TO A JEW ... **216**

The right of the superior race ... **217**

OURS FOR FRANCE! ... **245**
TOTALITARIAN GLOBALIST JUDEOPATHY ... **260**
CONCLUSION ... **265**
OTHER TITLES ... **267**

PREFACE

"Everything will end with the scoundrel". Nietzsche

Attached to their community, Jews cannot be assimilated. The genius of the Jewish people is to have presented the Jewish problem in its religious aspect alone. According to the Jew, there are French people of the Jewish faith, just as there are French people of the Catholic faith. Many goyim (strangers to the Jewish people) have fallen into this trap. Monsignor Lustiger is a typical example of a Catholic Jew.

First of all, Semites are not of European origin; they are ethnically close to Arabs, not Gauls.

Secondly, the Jew belongs first and foremost to the people of Israel, which is his national community.

Finally, Judaism religiously endorses the oldest form of racism the world has ever known. Only the chosen people belong to the very essence of God, the rest of mankind are likened to animals. Rabbis don't proselytise, converting animals to Judaism is pointless.

Proof of his treachery, the Jew calls himself a Frenchman of Romanian origin (François Copé, Pierre Moscovici), a Frenchman of Hungarian origin (Nicolas Sarkozy), a Frenchman of Luxembourg origin (Stéphane Bern), a Frenchman of Spanish origin (David Pujadas) ...

When they don't call themselves French, Jews call themselves European, Corsican, Breton... Citizens of the world.

But never, oh never, does he call himself a Jew.

Where there's gold, there's our homeland - this typically Jewish saying is true everywhere. Jews are concentrated in the richest regions of the richest nations. No Jews in Mozambique, many Jews in America. The Paris region and Alsace, the two richest regions of France, concentrate most of the Jewish population.

Money rules the world and the Jews are the kings of finance: Soros, Barclay, Rothschild, Rockefeller ...

Even the usurer Moses urged his people to lend money, but never to borrow it.

Borrowing with interest between Jews is religiously forbidden.

This passion for gold is confirmed by the names of our most famous economists: Marc Touati, Elie Cohen, Alain Minc, Guy Sorman...

Nine times out of ten our finance minister belongs to the wandering race. Whereas the Jewish population of our country is one per cent.

For the record, the first lyrics of Jean-Jacques Goldman's commercial hit (in French: *L'homme en or*) were "*Un jour j'aurai tout ce qui brille entre mes mains*" ("*One day I'll have everything that shines in my hands*"). More than a symbol, a prophecy.

Every year at the CRIF (Representative Council of Jewish Institutions in France) meeting, all the political leaders are summoned and asked to publicly pledge allegiance to the Jewish community. With the exception of the National Front, which was excluded from French political life following an order issued by B'naï B'rith (exclusively Jewish freemasonry) in 1986.

Jacques Chirac (the most Jewish of the French) owes his position to the promise he made to the community that, once elected, he would officially denounce the French state and its anti-Jewish national preservation measures.

In 2002, the swindler was re-elected with over 80% of the vote, defending the most important value that the Jewish people demand from others: Tolerance.

The Jewish dream of a world without borders involves the dissolution of nations into Europe, and then the dissolution of Europe into the world. Remember the dismay of the Jewess Christine Ockrent when France said no to the Euro-globalist referendum in 2005.

Jews are the most fanatical supporters of Turkey's entry into the European Union:

Daniel Cohn-Bendit, Pierre Lellouche, Gilles Martin-Chauffier, Pierre Moscovici, Alexandre Adler...

Their dream must become our nightmare. The argument is that Turkey has always been the protector of the Jews, even in the darkest hours of our history.

Jews in the United States are fighting just as hard for Mexico's entry into the American union.

Always this Jewish desire to annihilate the white man who could once again threaten the little-people-who-are-suffering.

As the Front National has always maintained, it is not immigrants who should be blamed, but those responsible for immigration policy.

From Marek Halter to Elie Wiesel, here in France Jews dream of immigration, of interbreeding, of opening up to the world, of welcoming the Other - with a capital A.

The driving force behind this obsession is revenge. The Jewish people want to make us pay for the reprisals, which they believe to be unjust, that they have suffered throughout the history of our country.

The Jewish people are constantly reminding us of our duty to remember. At best to extract money from us, at worst to make us accept the unacceptable: the replacement of a French population of European origin by another of African origin. The staging of the Holocaust and its political exploitation prevent us from taking any steps towards national salvation.

The most rabid supporters of the undocumented immigrants belong to the Judas race: the Jewish beast Emmanuelle Béart, the Jewish beast Stéphane Hessel, the Jewish beast Alain Krivine, the Jewish beast Patrick Gaubert, the Jewish beast Mathieu Kassovitz, the Jewish beast Arno Klarsfeld ...

For 30 years the Jewish supported the Arabisation and Islamisation of France. Jews and Arabs marched hand in hand against the sincere representatives of the French people. Ranting against the National Front and its president. The Jewish Bernard Stasi hammered home his slogan *'Immigration is a chance for France'*. Those were the halcyon days of S.O.S. racisme, founded by the Jew Julien Dray.

Since the outbreak of violence in the Middle East between Jews and Arabs. We have seen a reversal of the situation, and now these two communities are at war on our own soil. Even the black community is calling to account the Jews who profited from the slave trade (Jewish families from Nantes, including the Mendès-France family). The Jewish people are now turning to the French, seeking their support through the voice of Alain Finkielkraut, who is now denouncing anti-white racism.

Islamophobia, Philippe de Villiers' hobbyhorse, is first and foremost a sign addressed to the Jewish community. It is a sign of allegiance and rallying to the lobby that does not exist.

After Iraq, the Jews are preparing public opinion for a war against Iran. The preventive war so dear to Bernard Kouchner is first and foremost the possibility of preventively destroying any country that might threaten the State of Israel.

After the Jewish victory in 1945, anti-racism, multiculturalism and miscegenation became the founding values of Judeo-Western society.

Sarkozy's partner Cécilia, a full-blooded Jew, boasts that she has not a single drop of French blood in her veins. While her husband explains the decline of civilisations by the lack of interbreeding.

For the Jewish Madame de Fontenay, organiser of the miss-France elections, the prettiest women are found in the most mixed regions.

Officially, races don't exist, but they have to mix, and it's vital to mix what doesn't exist!

The dominant people claim to love justice. Closer to the murderers than to their victims, the Jew Robert Badinter had the death penalty abolished.

The Jew André Gluksmann constantly denounces the mistakes made in Chechnya, but systematically ignores the crimes committed by the Jewish people in Palestine.

The guardian of the temple of memory, Claude Lanzmann, has publicly stated that if revisionist historians were allowed to express themselves freely, within 2 or 3 years nobody would believe in the Holocaust any more.

It's true that for a people who claim to have been exterminated, there are plenty of them in the media: the Druckers, the Arthurs, the Fogiel, the Castaldi, the Moati, the Okrent, the Millers, the

Benamou, the Schonberg, the Pujadas, the Attals, the Veils, the Abikers, the Beigbeders, the Namias, etc.

These were the same media that organised spontaneous demonstrations against the FN in the run-up to the 2002 presidential elections.

Anti-Semites are said to suffer from paranoia, to see Jews everywhere. Let's take a random example. The Socialist Party candidates for the 2007 presidential election are :

Laurent Fabius: *Jewish*

Dominique (*Gaston*) Strauss-Kahn: *Jewish*

Jack Lang: *Jewish*

François Hollande: *Jewish*

Bernard Kouchner: *Jewish*

Ségolène Royal: *A Frenchwoman at last!*

Anti-Semites are said to overestimate the influence of the Jew. But who is it that dictates US foreign policy? To such an extent that it is no longer clear whether it is the United States that is Israel's ally or vice versa.

From Voltaire to Shakespeare to Dostoyevsky, the most brilliant minds in European culture are anti-Semitic.

As for the philosemites, they want to convince us that all men are equal. However, the real attack on a French person generally arouses little interest; it's just another news item, a triviality, a point of detail. Whereas the real (*Halimi affair*) or fictitious (*RER affair*) attack on a Semite immediately triggers an outcry, the emotion aroused is at its peak and the highest authorities issue their call to order: '*Attacking a Jew is attacking the whole of France*'.

We are urgently reminded that the life of a single Jew is worth the lives of 60 million French people.

This Jewish France is morally embodied by the billionaire Bernard Henry Levy. In his rag-tag book *L'idéologie française*, he vomits out la France profonde, French France.

Civilisations are born and die, but the Jew is always there, eternal to himself. Scattered across the world, a minority everywhere, they have survived the millennia.

When France, which has been Africanised to death, finally joins the Third World. The Jews will pack their bags and head for more prosperous lands (*probably Asia*) to continue their business. Jacques Attali has always shown his contempt for sedentary peoples attached to their land.

Immigration for repopulation and the encouragement of abortion (*inaugurated by the Jew Simone Veil*) are the 2 pillars of Jewish policy against the native French. No doubt we should not generalise about the guilt of Jews in the extermination of the French people. There may have been a few innocents among them.

For a long time, our kings protected us from Jewish financial power. The monarchy even succeeded in expelling the Jewish people from the kingdom of France.

As for the Catholic Church, it has betrayed its primary mission: to protect us from the perfidy of the deicidal people.

Today, the Jewish beast is pinning all its hopes on stateless capitalism. The whole world seen as one big open market, with no borders, no nations, no identities, no traditions. A one-colour world populated by consumers all wearing Levis jeans.

Nothing now seems to stand in the way of the Jewish people's ascent towards the world government of the Wise Men.

Does that mean we should give up all hope, lie down and die the slow death that is the Jew's secret?

In the past, the Jewish people believed they would achieve their goal of world domination through communism (*the ideology of the Jew Marx, the revolution of the Jew Trotsky*). Communism gave rise to fascism and Nazism.

Each time the Jewish beast approaches its supreme goal, it shows itself to be too sure of itself; it becomes reckless; it reveals its haughty arrogance. Causing the non-Jew to spring to life.

THE JEW IS THE MAIN ENEMY

To convince yourself of this, read the Jewish press, particularly the LICRA's *Droit de vivre* magazine.

Take the example of the RECONQUISTA, the 5-century-long struggle against the Arab occupation of Spain, which would never have been possible without the prior expulsion of the Jewish people.

G. S.

Summer Solstice 2006

PART ONE
WHAT THE JEWS SAID ABOUT THEMSELVES

"The kings of the age we are about to enter will be those who know best how to seize wealth. The sons of Israel possess this aptitude to a degree that has not yet been equalled, and in the general movement that is taking shape everywhere against them, we must see the precursory symptoms of the fearsome struggles that will have to be waged against them in order to escape their threatening power".[1] Gustave le Bon, *late 19th century*

FUNDAMENTAL FOREWORD

The word anti-Semitic means absolutely nothing.

A Jew is only Semitic if geographical circumstances force him to be, and then only in the same way as other Semites. A tall, blond, blue-eyed Jew whose family has lived in Poland for seven centuries is in no way Semitic. A short, stocky Jew from South America has nothing in common with this Polish Jew, apart from a constant particularism in time and space, which this book will deal with at length.

Apart from the white, black, yellow and red races, races do not exist: there are only ethnic groups that are the result of hormonal adaptation to a fixed environment, over at least eight to ten

---

[1] The unfortunate fact is that, a century later, in 1999, totalitarian Judeopathy has completed its hegemonic work, with the consequences of moral, physical and ecological pollution which, being unnatural, can only be resolved by multiform cataclysms.

centuries. The Jews have never lived in a fixed geographical location for a thousand years, not even in Palestine: they can in no way constitute an ethnic group.

The caricatural traits they often display, as well as their unparalleled speculative abilities, but lacking in moral sense and spirit of synthesis, as we see in profusion in the news of this century, and in History, are exclusively due to the effects of circumcision on the 8th day, the first day of the twenty-one days of the first puberty.[2]

So there are no Goyim like Soros, Warburg, Hammer, Marx or Freud (finance, dismasted logic, system dreams).

It is therefore possible to be "anti-Jewish" for obvious reasons, proven by implacable arguments and facts.

Famous Jews exposed them. Famous Goyim like Benjamin Franklin, who wanted to deny them American citizenship, confirmed them.

Any truth about the Jews is automatically labelled "anti-Semitic" and henceforth punishable by law, since the Jews have had racist "anti-racist" laws enacted (thought crime according to Orwell) which forbid disclosure of their manoeuvres, their actions, their monstrous importance in Western governments where, as in the United States, they dominate everything.

In this book, we will study the truths expressed by very famous Jews and confirmed by famous Goyim.

---

[2] The problem of Jewish circumcision is dealt with in my book *"Secret Files of the 21st Century"*. This discovery is due to Dr Jean Gautier, who explained the functional anteriority of the hormonal system over the nervous system. I defended a doctoral thesis at the Sorbonne based on his work: *"Le dandysme, hyperthyroïdie physiologique"*.

In this day and age, such a study is confidential, since in the year 2000 there is still no freedom of expression, apart from that profusely granted to drugs, pornography, homosexuality, abortion, the pathogenic and teratogenic pill, food and pharmaceutical chemtrails, paedophilia, ecological destruction and economic horror in general...

I'm often asked: "Why do you, a Jew, choose to reveal the truth that can only harm your 'race'?

My answer to that is that, first of all, it's not a question of race but of extra-dimensional pathology and that just because you have the plague doesn't mean that you should claim that the plague is a health criterion.

What's more, the symbiosis of Jewish perversity and goyish stupidity (there's no other word for it) is leading the whole world to nothingness, to its end.

I would like, insofar as I am able, to prevent the realisation of Hitler's prediction in *Mein Kampf*: "If the Jews, with their Marxist profession of faith, take over the reins of humanity, then the earth will be deprived of its inhabitants and will start spinning again, alone in the ether, as it did millions of years ago".

The following text: "*A Rabbi Pleads Guilty*", is of such importance that I have deliberately put it at the beginning of this book. With implacable lucidity, Rabbi Manfred Reifer gives a masterly overview of the Jewish necrosis that preceded Hitler, demystifying Hitler's demonisation and highlighting Jewish demonisation.

Never has a Goy 'anti-Semite' written with such implacable lucidity, not even Céline...

A RABBI PLEADS GUILTY

This document, which is now impossible to find, was destroyed en masse by the Jews.

It's easy to see why. Eight months after Hitler came to power, the *Czernowitz Allgemeine Zeitung* published this article by Rabbi Manfred Reifer on 2 September 1933.

"The current situation of the Jews in Germany is the culmination of a historical process. It is a development whose beginning can be traced back to the time of Bismarck. It had to be this way if we are to understand the profound historical importance of this anti-Semitic movement, of which Hitler is the strongest expression. Anyone who could not foresee this was blind.[3]

We tried to close our eyes to events and acted according to the vulgar axiom: "what we don't want, we don't believe in". *It was a convenient way of avoiding fundamental questions, of looking at the world through rose-coloured glasses. The preachers of Jewish assimilation tried to throw a veil over the reality of things and played Liberalism, long dead, as their last card. They didn't understand the course of history and thought they could escape it by declaring themselves* "Germans of the Mosaic faith", *denying the existence of a Jewish*

---

[3] Ten years before Nazism, the Jewish philosopher Henri Bergson warned Jews that if they did not change their behaviour, they would experience the greatest anti-Semitic demonstration in history.

But today, when the parameters of anti-Semitism are as concentrated as they have ever been in history, I say exactly the same thing to them: they won't listen to me because you can't even tell them without being charged, whether you're a Jew or a Goy. This superb analysis will be supplemented by my own in the second part of the book.

nation, cutting all the wires that linked them to Jewry, erasing the word "Zion" from their prayer books, and inaugurating the "Sunday Service". They saw anti-Semitism as a passing phenomenon that could be eliminated by intensive propaganda and the organisation of societies founded to combat it.[4]

These were the thoughts of a large number of German Jews. Hence the immense disappointment, the profound resignation in the face of Hitler's victory, hence the nameless despair, the growing psychosis, culminating in suicide, the complete demoralisation. But anyone who judges events in Germany according to the principle of causality will judge the National Socialist movement as the culmination of a natural development.

He will also understand that history knows no accidents, that each era is the result of the era that preceded it. This is the key to understanding the present situation. In Germany, the fight against Jewishness has been waged with great intensity and German precision for half a century. Scientific anti-Semitism has taken root in the very soil of Germany.

All this the Jews of Germany refused to see. They fed on false hopes, ignored reality and dreamt of cosmopolitanism, of the era of Dohm, Lessing and Mendelssohn. The uprooted Jews indulged in fantasies and deluded themselves with cosmopolitan dreams. This manifested itself in two ways: either they acclaimed general liberalism or they became the standard-bearers of Socialism. Both fields of activity provided fresh fodder for anti-Semitism. In good faith, wishing to serve the cause of humanity, the Jews began to infiltrate actively into the life of the

---

[4] They are making the same mistake again: they imagine that the creation of MRAP, LICRA, SOS Racisme, etc. will prevent them from being completely out of date, even if they reach the Stalinist level of the Gayssot law.

They won't be able to escape a terrible explosion because that's not the problem. It's in themselves. The only radical solution is to abolish circumcision on the 8th day, because they are incapable of changing their behaviour: on the contrary, they are making it worse by geometric progression.

German people. With their characteristic Jewish passion, they threw themselves into all fields of knowledge. They took over the press, they organised the masses of workers and they endeavoured to influence the whole of spiritual life in the direction of liberalism and democracy. This naturally provoked a profound reaction in the people who sheltered them. When the Jews, for example, took control of the so-called international disciplines, when they distinguished themselves in the fields of physics, chemistry, medicine, astronomy and, to a certain extent, philosophy, they could at best inspire envy in their Aryan colleagues, but not a general hatred of the whole nation. People did not like to see Jews winning Nobel Prizes, but they accepted it in silence. But when it comes to national disciplines, it's quite a different matter.

In this field, every nation strives to develop its original strengths and to pass on to present and future generations the fruits of the spiritual labours of the race. It is not a matter of indifference to the people to know who is writing about Christmas, who is celebrating Mass, who is asking to attend Church. Every people in every nation wants its children to be educated in its own spirit. But while large sections of the German people were struggling to maintain their species, we Jews filled the streets of Germania with our clamour.

We posed as world reformers and thought we could influence public life with our ideas.

We rang the bells and called for silent prayer, we prepared the Lord's Supper and celebrated his Resurrection.

We played with the most sacred possessions of the people and made a mockery of everything that was sacred to the nation.

We relied on the imperishable rights of democracy and felt ourselves to be equal citizens of the state in the German community . We posed as censors of the people's morals and poured out cups full of satire on the German Michael.

We wanted to be prophets in the pagan fields of Germania and we forgot ourselves to the point of forgetting that all this would bring destruction upon us.

We made revolutions and, like eternal seekers of God, we rushed to the head of the masses.

We have given a second Bible to the international proletariat, a Bible in tune with the times, and we have aroused the passions of the Third Estate.

> ➢ *From Germany, the Jew Karl Marx declared war on capitalism.*
> ➢ *The Jew Lassalle organised the masses of people in Germany itself.*
> ➢ *The Jewish Édouard Bernstein popularised the idea.*
> ➢ *The Jews Karl Liebknecht and Rosa Luxembourg gave life to the Spartakist movement.*
> ➢ *Kurt Eistner, a Jew, founded the Bavarian Soviet Republic and was its first president.*

Against all this, the German nation rose up and revolted. It wanted to forge its own destiny, to determine for itself the future of its children. It should not be blamed for wanting this.

What I have never agreed with is the idea of world citizenship and cosmopolitanism, with Jews at the forefront of their troops. These uprooted people⁵ imagined that they possessed the strength to transplant the ideas of Isaiah to the plains of Germania and to storm Walhalla with Amos. At times they succeeded, but they swallowed themselves up

---

[5] Simone Weil used this term again: "The Jews, this handful of *'uprooted people'*, caused the uprooting of the entire globe".

with the entire Jewish people under the ruins of a world that had collapsed.

We need to look at the Hitler regime's struggle from a different angle from the one we impose and learn to understand it. Didn't we Jews revolt and wage bloody wars against everything foreign?

What were the wars of the Maccabees if not a protest against a foreign, non-Jewish way of life? And what did the eternal battles of the prophets consist of? Nothing other than the elimination of foreign elements and the sacred preservation of the original nature of Jewishness. Did we not rebel against the racially mixed kings of the house of the Idumeans? Did we not exclude the Samaritans from our community because they practised mixed marriages?

Why shouldn't German nationalists do as we have done, when Kurt Eisner personally appropriates the prerogatives of the Wittelsbachs?

We must learn to look the truth in the face and draw our own conclusions.

I'd like to be a false prophet, but dismissing the tangible facts won't solve the problem.

What is happening today in Germany will happen tomorrow in Russia. For all the crimes which have resulted from the Communist system the Jews of Soviet Russia will have to suffer one day. We shall have to pay dearly for the fact that Trotsky, Joffe, Sinovieff, etc. played leading roles in Soviet Russia.

Did we not sin more seriously against democracy in Soviet Russia than in Germany? Whereas in Germany Hitler was elected by the majority, nothing of the sort happened in Russia. In that country a small minority, which today numbers barely four million people, after 15 years of organisation, proclaimed the dictatorship of the proletariat.

In Soviet Russia, the Jews also tried to be the precursors and proclaimers of a new absolute truth. They stepped up their efforts to interpret the Bolshevik Bible and to influence the thinking of the Russian people.

This process calls for the strongest resistance and leads to anti-Semitism. What will happen when the Soviet government falls and democracy celebrates its solemn entry into Russia?

Will the Jews be better off than they are today in Germany?[6] Behind the Trotskys, the Kameneffs, the Sinovieffs, etc., will the Russian people not discover their old Jewish names and make their children suffer for the crimes of their fathers? Will the Russian people not discover their old Jewish names and make their children suffer for the crimes of their fathers? Or will the regime last so short that the fathers themselves will have to atone?[7]

Are there not examples of this? Didn't thousands of Jews lose their lives in Hungary because Bela Kuhn established a Soviet republic in the land of Saint Stephen? The same Bela Kuhn who had 25,000 Christian massacred in less than a hundred days! The Jews of Hungary paid dearly for playing the prophet.

Within the Internationales, the Jews appeared to be the most radical elements.

The Germans, the French, the Poles and the Czechs have a homeland and their internationalism resides in Germany, France, Poland and Czechoslovakia. They are natives under a national power. In 1914, the

---

[6] This analysis is all the more topical given that on 17 November 1998, Russian anti-Semitism, even Communist anti-Semitism, had just erupted, going so far as to lead to pogroms. This underlines the lucidity of this analysis, of which no Goy, to my knowledge, has been capable.

[7] In a historical programme on the French channel La Cinq, we learnt that Stalin, just before his death, had planned a national pogrom which did not take place because of his death.

Germans burned the red flag in the Berlin zoo and ran off to war with patriotic refrains on their lips. The Polish socialist Daszinski was at the forefront of the struggle to resurrect Poland and the Czech socialists enthusiastically sang their patriotic song (Kde domov muj).

Only the Jews didn't want to hear anything about homeland. They fell as conspicuous prophets on the battlefield of freedom. Karl Liebnecht, Rosa Luxembourg, Kurt Eisner, Gustave Landauer: no Kaddosh will be recited,[8] no mass will be said. They, and to a certain extent the children of Liberalism, all these poets, authors, artists, journalists (Jews) have prepared the present times, nourished anti-Jewry, provided the basis and materials for Nazism. They all wished for the best and only achieved the opposite.

The curse of blindness had struck them.[9]

They did not see the catastrophe approaching. They did not hear the footsteps of time, the heavy footsteps of their destiny, the very heavy footsteps of History's nemesis."

---

[8] They were all killed during the unrest caused by the revolutions they had organised.

[9] And will always strike them until they have destroyed humanity by destroying themselves. Only the radical abolition of circumcision on the 8th day could save the Jews and humanity.

WHAT JEWS SAY ABOUT JEWS

In its issue of 1 July 1880, "*Le Contemporain*", a leading Parisian journal, published a long article entitled "*Compte rendu de Sir John Readcliff sur les événements politico-historiques survenus dans les dix dernières années*". It was a speech given in Prague by Rabbi Reichhorn in 1869 at the tomb of Chief Rabbi Simeon Ben Jehuda. This document was reproduced in the book "*La Russie juive*", by Calixte de Volsky, then in "*The Britons*" in London, then in "*La Vieille France*" (No. 214), and other newspapers. *La Vieille France*" reported that Readcliff had been killed shortly before the publication of this document and that the Jew who had provided it (a certain Lassalle) had been killed in a duel.

These were the words of Rabbi Reichorn:

"Every hundred years, we, the Sages of Israel, are accustomed to meet in the Sanhedrin to examine our progress towards the dominion promised to us by Jehovah, and our conquests over the enemy Christianity.

This year, gathered at the tomb of our venerated Simeon Ben Jehouda, we can proudly say that the past century has brought us closer to our goal, and that this goal will soon be reached. Gold has always been and always will be the irresistible power. Handled by expert hands, it will always be the most useful lever for those who possess it and the object of envy for those who do not. Gold is used to buy the most rebellious consciences, to fix the rate of all securities, the price of all products, and to subsidise the loans of governments, which are thus at our mercy.

Already the main banks, the world's stock exchanges and claims on all governments are in our hands. The other great power is the press. By relentlessly repeating certain ideas, the press makes them accepted as truths. The theatre performs similar services. (The cinema did not exist at the time and it would become their monopoly).

Everywhere the press and the theatre obey our directives. By tirelessly praising the democratic regime, we will divide Christians into political parties, destroy the unity of their nations and sow discord. Powerless, they will submit to the law of our bank, always united, always devoted to our cause. We will drive Christians to war, exploiting their pride and stupidity. They will slaughter each other and clear the way for us to push our own people. The possession of land has always brought influence and power. In the name of social justice and equality, we will break up the great estates, we will give fragments of them to the peasants who want them with all their might and who will soon be in debt because of the exploitation. Our capital will make us masters of them. We, in turn, will become the great landowners, and possession of the land will guarantee us power.

Let us strive to replace gold in circulation with paper money. Our coffers will absorb gold and we will regulate the value of paper, which will make us masters of all lives. We have among us orators capable of feigning enthusiasm and persuading crowds. We will spread them among the peoples to announce the changes that must bring happiness to the human race. With gold and flattery, we will win over the proletariat who will take it upon themselves to destroy Christian capitalism. We will promise the workers wages they have never dared to dream of, but we will then raise the price of necessary things to such an extent that our profits will be even greater. In this way, we will prepare for the revolutions that Christians themselves will make, and we will reap all the rewards.

By our mockery, by our attacks, we will make their priests ridiculous and odious, and their religion as ridiculous and odious as their clergy. We will thus be masters of their souls. For our pious attachment to our religion and our worship will prove the superiority of our souls.

We have already placed our men in all the important positions. Let us endeavour to provide the Goyim with lawyers and doctors. The lawyers are aware of all the interests; the doctors, once in the house, become confessors and directors of conscience.

But, above all, let's take over education. By doing so, we will spread the ideas that are useful to us from childhood and we will mould brains to our liking. If one of our own falls by misfortune into the clutches of Christian justice, let us run to his aid. Let us find as many testimonies as we need to save him from his judges, until we ourselves become judges.

The monarchs of Christendom, swollen with ambition and vanity, surround themselves with luxury and numerous armies. We will provide them with all the money their folly demands and we will keep them on a leash. We must be careful not to prevent the marriage of our men with Christian daughters, for through them we penetrate the most closed circles. If our daughters marry Goyim, they will be no less useful to us because the children of a Jewish mother are ours. Let us propagate the idea of free union to destroy Christian women's attachment to the principles and practices of their religion.

For centuries, the despised and persecuted sons of Israel have been working their way to power. They control the economic life of the accursed Christians; their influence is predominant over politics and morals. At the desired hour, fixed in advance, we shall unleash the revolution which, ruining all the classes of Christendom, will enslave us Christians once and for all.

This is how God's promise to his people will be fulfilled.[10]

---

[10] The Jews can only deny the authenticity of such texts: there is no point, because these simple lines are a perfect account of the politics of the century as I have observed them and as they have come to pass.

Baruch Lévy, Jewish

A friend of Adolphe Crémieux and the Rothschilds, Baruch Lévy wrote the following letter to Karl Marx. This little-known letter was nevertheless reproduced in numerous books and newspapers, including the "*Revue de Paris*" of 1 June 1928, page 574: "*In the new organisation of humanity, the children of Israel will spread over the entire surface of the globe and will become everywhere without the slightest opposition the leading element, especially if they succeed in imposing on the working class the firm control of a few of them. The governments of the nations forming the Universal Republic will pass effortlessly into Jewish hands under cover of the victory of the proletariat.*

Private property will then be abolished by the Jewish rulers, who will control public funds everywhere. This will fulfil the promise of the Talmud that when the time of the Messiah arrives, the Jews will possess the property of all the peoples of the earth.

Saint Paul himself said: "*The Jews do not please God and are the enemies of mankind*" (First Epistle). All that is reported here, perfectly realised in the year 2000, does not prove Saint Paul wrong...

The Glands of Humanity

Text composed by Louis Lévy in 1918, published by "*Nytnordisk Forlag*" in Copenhagen. It was read by the Jewish actor Samuel Basekow at a party in support of Karen Hajesad in Copenhagen on

---

They also said that "*The Protocols of the Elders of Zion*" was a forgery. I have no trouble believing that, but alas, everything in that book is absolutely true, and far removed from the horrors of the present day (globalism, economic ruin, pornography, drugs, homosexuality, ecological collapse, etc.).

8 December 1935, according to the *Berlingske Tidende* of 9 December 1935, before a delirious Jewish audience.

"The times have come - and only one thing matters now - and that is that we show ourselves for what we are: a nation among nations - the princes of money and intelligence. A sigh will rise from all the earth and the crowds will tremble as they listen attentively to the wisdom that resides in the Jews.

Who does not know what the glands of the human body mean? Well, now, by a judicious instinct of self-preservation, the Jews have fixed themselves in the glands of the modern community of peoples. The glands of this community of nations are the Stock Exchanges, the Banks, the Ministries, the major daily newspapers, the publishing houses, the arbitration commissions, the insurance companies, the hospitals, the law courts.

There are a few publicans and a few sinners, scholars and professors who claim that there is no Jewish Question. Ask the first person who passes in the street, he knows better. Because of his belligerent jealousy, this lout will be anti-Semitic!

Naturally, the Jewish people would have to have international representation, a national territory of its own. Do not believe that the Jews of Western Europe will take a single step. On the surface, everything will remain unchanged, yet everything will be transformed. Jerusalem will become the new Papacy. Jerusalem will resemble a laborious spider's web, a web whose threads of electricity will shine on the whole world.

The centre of this golden network, from which all the threads will flow, will be Jerusalem.

"JEWISH WORLD

One of England's leading Jewish newspapers published the following on 9 February 1883: "*The dispersion of the Jews has made them a cosmopolitan people. They are the only truly cosmopolitan people, and in that capacity they must and do act as a dissolver of all distinctions of race and nationality.*

The great ideal of Judaism is not that the Jews should one day gather together in some corner of the earth for separatist purposes, but that the whole world should be imbued with Jewish teaching and that in a universal brotherhood of nations - a greater Judaism in fact - all separate races and religions should disappear.

As a cosmopolitan people, the Jews have gone beyond the stage that the national form of separatism represents in social life. They can never return to it. They have made the whole world their home, and are now extending their hands to the other nations of the world to follow their example. They are doing more. By their activity in literature and science, by their dominant position in all branches of public activity, they are gradually casting non-Jewish thoughts and systems in Jewish moulds."

WALTER RATHENEAU, JEWISH

Industrialist (AEG) and organiser of the Reich's war economy during the First World War, Walter Ratheneau, a Jew and German Foreign Minister, published the following comments in the "*Wiener Press*" in December 1921: "*Only three hundred men, each of whom knows all the others, govern the destinies of Europe. They choose their successors from their own circle. The German Jews have in their hands the means to put an end to any form of government they deem unreasonable.*"

BENJAMIN DISRAELI, JEWISH

Queen Victoria's Prime Minister wrote this in "*Coningsby*", a famous novel published in 1844: "*And at this very moment, in spite *of centuries or scores of centuries of degradation, the Jewish mind exerts a vast influence over the affairs of Europe. I am not talking about their laws, which you always obey, or their literature, with which your brains are saturated, but the Israelite intellect of today. You will never see a great intellectual movement in Europe in which the Jews have not played a major part. This mysterious Russian diplomacy that so alarms Europe is organised and conducted mainly by Jews. This great revolution, which will in fact be a second Reformation, more important than the first, and about which so little is known in England, is developing under the auspices of Jews who largely monopolise the professorial chairs in Germany.*

Neander, the founder of spiritual Christianity and Royal Professor of Theology at the University of Berlin, is Jewish. Benary, also famous, and from the same university, is also Jewish.

A few years ago, we were approached from Russia. The truth is that there have never been any ties of friendship between the Court of Saint Petersburg and my (Rothschild) family... However, circumstances tended towards a rapprochement between the Romanoffs and the Sidonias (Rothschilds). I decided to go to Saint Petersburg myself. On arriving, I had a meeting with the Russian Finance Minister, Count Cancrine. I found myself face to face with the son of a Lithuanian Jew. The loan was related to Spanish business. I made the journey in one go. As soon as I arrived, I was granted an audience with the Spanish minister, el Señor Mendizabel. I was face to face with a fellow Jew, the son of a "nuevo christiano", a Jew from Aragon.

As a result of what was transpiring in Madrid, I was going straight to Paris to consult the President of the French Council. I found myself face to face with a French Jew: a hero, a Marshal of the Empire, and there was nothing surprising in that, for where would military heroes be if not among those who worship the God of armies?

- And Soult, is he Jewish? - Yes, and many other French Marshals. The most famous of them is Masséna, whose real name is Manasseh.

But back to my anecdote. The result of our consultations was that it would be a good idea to call upon some northern power as a friend and mediator. We decided on Prussia, and the President of the Council approached the Prussian minister who attended our conference a few days later. Count Arnim entered the cabinet and I found myself face to face with a Prussian Jew. You can see, my dear Coningsby, that the world is governed by quite different characters than those who are not behind the scenes imagine...".

BENJAMIN DISRAELI, JEWISH

Benjamin Disraeli, (Lord Beaconsfield) published another book entitled "*The life of Lord George Bentinck, a political biography*". On page 357 of this book, he wrote: "*Let an insurrection break out against tradition and aristocracy, against religion and the right of property, then the natural equality of man and the abolition of the right of property will be proclaimed by secret societies which form provisional governments, for Jews are to be found at the head of each of these societies. The people of God collaborate with the atheists: the most skilful accumulators of wealth ally themselves with the Communists. The particular and chosen race gives its hand to all the dregs and scum of the underworld of Europe, and all because the Jews want to destroy this ungrateful Christendom which owes them even its name and whose tyranny they no longer wish to endure*".

Disraeli also wrote on the same page, about the revolution of 1848 which plunged several countries into chaos: "*Had it not been for the Jews, this undesirable disturbance would not have ravaged Europe*".

MARCUS ÉLI RAVAGE, JEWISH

This Jewish author wrote the following in the "Century Magazine" of January and February 1928:

"You're making a lot of noise about the undue influence of Jews in theatre and film. All right, then. Let's admit that your complaint is well-founded. But what is that compared with our penetrating influence in your churches, your schools, your laws, your everyday thoughts? You have not yet begun to appreciate the true depth of our guilt. We are intruders. We are troublemakers. We are subversives. We have taken your natural world, your ideals, your destiny and blurred them. We were at the root not only of the last great war, but of almost all your wars, not only of the Russian revolution, but of all the major revolutions in your history. We have brought discord, confusion and frustration into your personal and public lives. We are still doing it and no one can say how much longer we will do it.

Who knows what great and glorious destiny would have been yours if we had left you alone! But we didn't leave you alone. We took you in hand and tore down the beautiful and generous structure you had built, and we changed the course of your history. We conquered you in a way that none of your empires has ever conquered Africa or Asia. And we did it without weapons, without bullets, without bloodshed and without noise, by the sheer force of our spirit. We did it solely by the irresistible force of our spirit, our ideas and our propaganda.

Take the three main revolutions of modern times: the French, the American and the Russian. What are they if not the triumph of the Jewish idea over social, political and economic justice? We still dominate you... Is it any wonder you resent us? We put the brakes on your progress. We have simply divided your soul, confused your impulses and paralysed your desires. If we were in your shoes, we'd hate you more than we hate you. You call us subversives, agitators, fomenters of revolutions. And it's true. You can learn with the simplest effort and the slightest realisation of the facts that we have been at the heart of every major revolution in your history. Without doubt we played an important part in the Lutheran revolution, and it is a known fact that we were the main instigators of the bourgeois, democratic revolutions of the century before last in France and the

United States. If we had not been, we would have ignored our interests.

ISIDORE LOEB, JEWISH

In his book "*The Jewish Question*", Georges Batault quotes Isidore Loeb as follows: "*The nations will gather to pay their respects to the people of God: all the wealth of the nations will pass to the Jewish people. They will walk behind the Jewish people in chains like captives and bow down before them. Kings will raise their sons and princesses will nurse their children. The Jews will command the nations. They will call to them peoples they do not even know, and peoples who do not know them will come running to them. The riches of the sea and the wealth of the nations will come of themselves to the Jews. The people and the kingdom that do not serve Israel will be destroyed. The chosen people will drink the milk of the nations and suck at the breast of kings. They will eat the wealth of the nations and cover themselves with their glory. The Jews will live in abundance and joy. Their happiness will not end, their hearts will rejoice, they will grow like grass. The Jews will be a race blessed by God and the whole people will be a people of gods. The posterity of the Jews and their name will be eternal. The smallest of them will multiply into thousands and the smallest will become a great nation. God will make an eternal covenant with them. He will again reign over them and their power over men will be such that, as the saying goes, they will walk with great strides on the heights of the earth. Nature itself will be transformed into a kind of earthly paradise: it will be the golden age of mankind*".

"LA REVUE DES ÉTUDES JUIVES

Financed by James de Rothschild, this magazine published a previously unpublished document in 1880 showing the Elders of Zion at work in France from the 15th century onwards, directing the conquering action of the Jews.

On 13 January 1489, Chamor, rabbi of the Jews of Arles in Provence, wrote to the Great Sanhedrin sitting in Constantinople and asked for its advice in critical circumstances.

The French of Aix, Arles and Marseille, who were not betraying themselves at the time by electing a Léon Blum, threatened the synagogues: What could be done?

This was the reply: "*Beloved brothers in Moses, we have received your letter in which you tell us of the anxieties and misfortunes you are enduring. We were filled with as much sorrow as you were.*

The opinion of the great satraps and rabbis is as follows: to what you say is imposed on you, it is good to become a Christian. Do it because you have to, but keep the Law of Moses in your heart.

To what you say is a command to strip you of your possessions: Make your children merchants so that little by little they will strip the Christians of theirs. When you say that your lives are at stake, make your children doctors and apothecaries so that they can rob Christians of their lives.[11] *When you say they are destroying your synagogues, make your children canons and clerics so that they destroy their Church.*[12] *To*

---

[11] This statement seems exaggerated and even absurd. But the reality is much worse: the mandarinate of allopathic medicine is Jewish. This chemical medicine is pathogenic and teratogenic. The chemical therapy laboratories are radically linked to Jewish finance. It is not Christians that they are killing but Man as a whole at the chromosomal level. Simone Veil's abortion and Baulieu's pathogenic pill are both Jewish. Systematic vaccination, a financial boon, destroys immune systems and massively degenerates the human race. (500 cases of multiple sclerosis in 1995 following vaccination against hepatitis B).

[12] The most important French prelate at the dawn of the year 2000 is a Jew: Cardinal Lustiger, Archbishop of Paris. He is not the one who will support J.M. Le Pen, the holder of elementary Christian ideas, or simply the elementary ideas for a nation to be healthy, whatever its religious tradition.

what you say about other vexations being inflicted on you: make your children lawyers, notaries, and let them always meddle in the affairs of the States so that, by putting the Christians under your yoke, you will dominate the world and be able to take revenge on them.

Do not deviate from this order that we are giving you, because you will be lowered at a time when you will soon be at the pinnacle of power". (Signed; V.S.S.V.F.F., *Prince of the Jews*, 21st of Casleu, November 1489)

THE PROTOCOLS OF THE ELDERS OF ZION

Let us quote for the record this confounding text. The Canadian Jewish Congress tried to discredit this document by relying on an article in "*L'Ordre*" that the "*Patriote*" had confused in March 1934. In a pamphlet. The CJC claims that "*The Protocols of the Elders of Zion*" was first published in London in 1920, even though the British Museum had catalogued this work, Nilus edition, as early as 1906 (as 3926 D17, 10 August 1906, as mentioned by the publishers of the first English edition, "*Eyres and Spottishwoode, Limited*", the British government printer).

Once again, authenticity is , since in these texts is true. During my lifetime, throughout the 20th century, I have personally witnessed the realisation of all the watchwords in this book, and even much worse (Freudism, pornography, pathogenic and criminogenic music, drugs, ecological collapse, intellectual and aesthetic collapse, not to mention the supreme horror of Marxism).

Similarly, John Paul II's mother is Jewish. The Pope is therefore Jewish. Jewish penetration collapsed the Church, when a rabbi said: "If I were a Catholic, I would be a fundamentalist, because being a Jew, I am certainly a fundamentalist. It's not in a synagogue that you'd find the equivalent of a woman without a hat, in jeans, mass in front of the people, in French, with regressive music under the alibi of openness and tolerance. Nothing moved in the synagogue. Everything has become grotesque in Catholicism.

WERNER SOMBART, JEWISH

In his study "*The Jews and Economic Life*" (1926, page 51), the German economist and sociologist Werner Sombart tells us: "*To a certain extent, we are entitled to affirm that it is to the Jewish imprint that the United States owes what it is, i.e. its Americanism, for what we call Americanism is only the Jewish spirit having found its definitive expression. And in view of the enormous influence which America has exerted on the economic life of Europe and on the whole of European culture since its discovery, the role which the Jews have played in building the American world has become of capital importance for the whole development of our history*".

THE COADJUTOR OF THE CHIEF RABBI OF JERUSALEM

This report on the situation in Palestine (Source: *Agence Télégraphique Juive*, July 1920) stated: "*The Jew now appears to be the true monarch of the world. Empires like Russia, Germany and Austria are governed by Jews. The Jews are the leaders of the peoples. Other countries and nations will soon follow. The Jews will see their flag flying over the whole world.*"

HENRI BARBUSSE, JEWISH

In his book "*Jésus nous dit*", this admirer of Stalin says the following: "*We will treat the nations with a rod of iron. Justice is the restoration of the dynasty of David. Pity is the condition of the Jews. Faith is revenge. I say to you that we are the true and only fulfillers of the law of the final struggle for the kingdom of God and for eternal life, which is the eternal glory of the Jewish conqueror. Through you, may the word of the Lord roll over the cities like a scroll. I have in mind an uprising that resembles a revolution*".

ADOLPHE CRÉMIEUX, JEWISH

Adolphe Crémieux, who emancipated the Jews of Algeria, was Grand Master of the Grand Orient de France, President of the Alliance Israélite Universelle and twice Minister of Justice in 1848 and 1870, at the critical time of these two revolutions. The following statement was published in *The Morning Post* in London on 6 September 1920: "*The union we wish to found will not be a French, English, Irish or German union, but a universal Jewish union. Other peoples and races are divided into nationalities. We alone do not have citizens but co-religionists.*

Under no circumstances will a Jew become the friend of a Christian or a Muslim until the moment arrives when the light of the Jewish faith, the only religion of reason, will shine on the whole world. Dispersed among the other nations, which from time immemorial have been hostile to our rights and interests, we wish first of all to be and remain immutably Jews. Our nationality is the religion of our fathers, and we recognise no other nationality. We live in foreign lands and cannot worry about the changing ambitions of countries that are entirely foreign to us while our moral and material problems are crucial. Jewish education must extend to the whole earth.

Israelites! Wherever destiny leads you, scattered as you are all over the earth, you must always consider yourselves part of the chosen people.

If you realise that the faith of your fathers is your only patriotism, if you recognise that in spite of the nationalities you have adopted, you remain and form always and everywhere a single nation, if you believe that Judaism is the one and only religious and political truth, if you are convinced of this, Israelites of the universe, then come, hear our call, and send us your adhesion.

Our cause is great and holy, and its success is assured. Catholicism, our enemy of all time, lies in the dust, mortally wounded in the head. The net that Israel is now casting across the globe is widening and spreading, and the grave prophecies of our holy books will at last be fulfilled.

The time is drawing near when Jerusalem will become the house of prayer for all nations and peoples, when the unique banner of the God of Israel will be unfurled and raised to the farthest shores. Let us make the most of every opportunity.

Our power is immense: let's learn to adapt that power to our cause. What do you have to fear? The day is not far off when all the riches, all the treasures of the earth will become the property of the children of Israel."

ADOLPHE CRÉMIEUX, JEWISH

This man of influence declared in the review "*Les Archives israélites*" (issue no. 25, 1861):

"*The Jerusalem of a new order, a holy foundation between East and West, must replace the dual empire of popes and emperors. I make no secret of the fact that over the years I have devoted my thoughts to this one and only work. No sooner had it begun its work than the influence of the Alliance Israélite Universelle was felt far and wide.*

It is not restricted to our faith alone, but wants to penetrate all religions, just as it has penetrated all countries.

➢ *Nationalities must disappear, religions must be abolished.*
➢ *Israel must not disappear, because this small people is God's chosen one.*

In every country we must put isolated Jews in touch with the authorities so that at the first news of an attack we can rise up as one man. We want our voices to be heard in ministers' chambers, in the ears of princes, and come what may. So much the worse if we have to use laws of force incompatible with the progress of the time, we will then join all protesters.[13] *We are urged to forgive the past, but now is the time to build an immortal alliance on unshakeable foundations.*

RENÉ GROOS, JEWISH

In an article published in "*Le Nouveau Mercure*" in May 1927, he wrote: "*The two internationals of finance and revolution are working hard: they are the two faces of the Jewish international... There is a Jewish conspiracy against all nations.*"

BLUMENTHAL, JEWISH

This editor of the "*Judisk Tidskrift*" wrote the following (No. 57, 1929): "*Our race has given the world a new prophet, but he has two faces and two names: Rothschild, head of the great capitalists, and Karl Marx, the apostle of the enemies of the other*".

(These lines sum up world politics).

THE CENTRAL CONFERENCE OF AMERICAN RABBIS

The Chicago Jewish newspaper "*The Sentinel*", in its issue of 24 September 1936, reported the following remarks made during this conference: "*The most remarkable but also the most harmful of the consequences of the world war has been the creation of new nationalisms and the exaltation of existing ones.*

---

[13] At the dawn of the year 2000, all the racist protest organisations, disguised as anti-racism, are Jewish: SOS Racisme, LICRA, MRAP who, under the guise of anti-racism, are concocting a monstrous racism of juxtapositions of mutually unassimilable ethnic groups which would pose no problem if they lived according to the geographical, logical and natural norms which concern them. The anti-racist mystification inflicted by megalomaniacal Jewish racism is a supreme mystification which relies above all on the stupidity of the Goyim.

*Nationalism is a danger for the Jewish people. Today, as at all times in history, it has been proven that the Jews cannot remain in strong states where a high national culture has developed."*¹⁴

STATEMENTS MADE WITHIN B'NAI B'RITH

This exclusively Jewish Masonic sect is therefore forbidden to the Goyim. The following comments were quoted in "*Le Réveil du Peuple*" of February 1936: "*As long as a moral conception of the social order persists among the Goyim, and as long as faith, patriotism and dignity have not been uprooted, our reign over the world is impossible.*

We have already accomplished part of our task, but we cannot yet claim that all the work has been done. We still have a long way to go before we overthrow our main enemy: the Catholic Church. We must always bear in mind that the Catholic Church is the only institution that has survived, and as long as it survives, it will stand in our way.

The Catholic Church, through its methodical work and its edifying and moral teachings, will always keep its children in such a state of mind that they will have too much self-respect to bend before our domination and our future King of Israel.

This is why we have endeavoured to discover the best means of shaking the Catholic Church to its foundations. We have spread the spirit of rebellion and false liberalism among the nations of the Goyim so as to persuade them to abandon their faith and even to inspire in them the shame of professing the precepts of their religion and obeying the commandments of their Church. We have led many of them to boast of being atheists and, better still, to boast of being descendants of the ape!

---

¹⁴ Hence the need for the Jews to degrade nations by every means possible: secularism, Marxism, Freudianism, chemification, systematic vaccinations, the pornography of Benazareff et al, drugs managed by their High Finance, pathogenic and criminogenic music, etc...

We have provided them with new theories that are radically impossible to realise, such as communism, socialism and anarchism.

These myths serve our purposes. The stupid Goyim have accepted them with the greatest enthusiasm, without realising in the slightest that these theories come from us and that they are a powerful instrument against themselves.

We have blackened the Church with the most ignominious slanders. We have sullied its history and discredited its noblest activities. We have imputed to her the wrongs of her enemies and brought them closer to us. And so today we are satisfied witnesses to rebellions against the Church in many countries.

We have turned its clergy into objects of hatred and derision. We have exposed them to the scorn of the masses. We have made the practices of the Catholic religion seem old-fashioned and a waste of time.

The Goyim, to our amazement, have proved to be extraordinary dupes. We expected more intelligence and practical sense from them, but they are no better than a flock of sheep: let them graze in our fields until they are fat enough to be sacrificed to our future King of the World.

We have founded many secret associations that work to our ends, under our orders and direction. We have made it an honour for the Goyim to belong to them. They are flourishing more than ever thanks to our gold.

The Goyim who betray their most precious interests in this way must be unaware that these associations are our work and that they are working for us. One of the many triumphs of Freemasonry is that the Goyim do not even suspect that we are using them to build their own prison, and that they are forging the chains of their own servility to us.[15]

Up to now we have been attacking the Church from the outside. But that is not all. Let us now see how we have proceeded to hasten the ruin of the Church, how we have penetrated its innermost circles and induced a large part of its clergy to become preachers of our cause.

In addition to the influence of our philosophy, we took other steps to breach the Church. We induced some of our children to join the Catholic body, with the explicit intimation that they were to work even more effectively to disintegrate the Church by creating scandals within it. We obeyed the age-old order: "make canons of your children so that they can destroy the Church".

Unfortunately, not all converted Jews have been faithful to their mission.[16] *Many have betrayed us. But many have kept their promise and honoured their word.*

We are the fathers of all revolutions, even those that have sometimes turned against us. We are the supreme masters of peace and war. We can boast that we were the creators of the Reformation. Calvin was a Jew, the Jewish authorities trusted him and he had the help of Jewish finance to draw up his reform plan.

---

[15] It is not only Freemasonry that plays this role. Associations such as the CFR, the Club of Rome, the Bilderberg, the Trilateral Commission, etc., have enslaved politicians of all parties. Freemasonry makes no secret of its desire to destroy "race, nation and family" (see "*Juifs et Francs-Maçons constructeurs de temples*", Editions du Rocher, by Bérésniak).

[16] Today, the converted Jews are all faithful to this instruction to disintegrate the Church. Not a single famous prelate supports Jean Marie Le Pen, who is the only defender of the traditional values without which no nation can survive and which are fundamentally Catholic.

Martin Luther gave in to the influences of his Jewish friends and, thanks to Jewish authority and finance, his plot against the Church was crowned with success.

Thanks to our propaganda, our theories on Liberalism, our perverse definition of Freedom, the Goyim were ready to accept the Reformation. They broke away from the Church to fall into our nets. The Church was weakened, its authority over kings reduced to nothing.

We are grateful to Protestants for their loyalty to our purposes. But most of them have no idea that they are loyal to us. But we are grateful to them for the marvellous help they give us in our struggle against the stronghold of Christian civilisation and our preparations for the advent of our supremacy over the whole world and the kingdoms of the Goyim.

We have succeeded in overthrowing the majority of thrones in Europe. The others will follow in the near future. Russia already serves our domination. France, with its Masonic government, is entirely at our mercy. England, with her dependence on our finance, is under our heel and her Protestantism will destroy Catholicism in the country. Spain and Mexico are but toys in our hands.

Many countries are in our hands: the United States is one of them. But the Church is still alive. We must destroy it without further delay and without mercy.[17] *The world press is under our control. Let us promote hatred of the Catholic Church more violently. Let us intensify our*

---

[17] Today, the Church is destroyed. Its prelates are grotesque. Thirty Communist bishops have signed a *"repentance"* concerning a holocaust that is arithmetical-technical nonsense. But it is certain that Jews died during the Second World War, from acts of war, typhus and malnutrition in the camps.

But two or three hundred thousand Jews who died in the Second World War are a far cry from the fifteen million Germans who died in a war that the Jews declared on Hitler in 1933!

activities in poisoning the morals of the Goyim. Let us spread the spirit of revolution in the hearts of the people.

They must be led to despise patriotism and love of family, to regard their faith as nonsense, their obedience to the Church as degrading servility, so that they become deaf to the Church's call and blind to its cries of alarm against us.[18]

Above all, let us make it impossible for Christians outside the Church to join the Church and for non-Christians to join the Church. Otherwise, the greatest obstacle to our domination will be strengthened and our work will remain unaccomplished.[19] *Our plot would be exposed. The Goyim would turn against us in a spirit of revenge and our domination would become impossible.*[20]

As long as the Church has militants, we will not be the masters of the world. The Jews will not reign until the Pope of Rome is dethroned, like all the other monarchs of the earth."

---

[18] All this has been achieved perfectly in the year 2000.

[19] This policy has changed: today the Jews preach ecumenism, which is an asset in a Church that has disappeared.

[20] Given the goyish stupidity, there is no risk. They see nothing, understand nothing and demonstrate as soon as a Jew lifts a finger.

WHAT THE JEWS THEMSELVES SAY ABOUT COMMUNISM

RABBI JUDAH L. MAGNES

Speaking in New York in 1919, he declared: "*The radical qualities that are in the Jew go to the very bottom of things; in Germany, he becomes a Marx or a Lassalle, a Haas and an Edouard Bernstein. In Austria, he becomes a Victor Adler, in Russia, a Trotsky. Look at the current situation in Germany and Russia. The revolution is putting its creative forces into action; look at the large contingent of Jews who are immediately ready for battle. Revolutionary Socialists, Mensheviki, Bolsheviki, majority and minority Socialists, by whatever name they may be called, in all these parties there are Jews as their devoted leaders and as their regular workers.*"

MR COHAN, JEWISH

This statement was published in "*The Communist*", Kharkoff, No°72, 12 April 1919):

"*It can be said without exaggeration that the great Russian revolution was made by the hand of the Jews. It was precisely the Jews who led the Russian proletariat to the dawn of the International who not only led but still lead the cause of the Soviets, which remain in their reliable hands. It is true that there are no Jews in the Red Army as far as the soldiers are concerned, but the Jews bravely command as leaders of the Soviet committees and organisations, and lead the masses of the Russian proletariat to victory. The symbol of Jewry has become the symbol of the Russian proletariat. With this symbol will come the death of the parasites of the bourgeoisie who will pay in drops of blood for the Jewish tears.*"

Nahum Sokolow, Jewish

This great Jewish leader states in his book "*The history of Zionism*": "*Zionism played an important role in the Bolshevik activities in Russia*".

Rabbi Lewis Brown

This rabbi tells us, in his book "*How odd of God*": "*We want to remake the non-Jewish world, to do what the Communists are doing in Russia.*"

Professor Reinhold Niebuhr, Jewish

This famous Protestant theologian, speaking on 3 October 1934 before the *Jewish Institute of Religion* in New York: "*Marxism is a modern form of Jewish prophecy*".

"The American Hebrew

The following article appeared in the September 10, 1920 edition: "*Out of economic chaos the Jew conceived capital with its mechanism of application, the bank. One of the impressive phenomena of our modern times is the revolt of the Jews against this monster which his mind had conceived and his hands had fashioned. The Bolshevik revolution in Russia, that achievement destined to go down in history as the primordial result of the Great War, was to a large extent the result of Jewish thought, of Jewish discontent.*

What Jewish idealism and Jewish discontent have so powerfully helped to achieve in Russia, the same historic Jewish qualities of heart and mind tend to achieve in other countries.[21]

---

[21] There's no need to dwell on the universally tentacular Marxism and its 200 million victims...

Will America, like the Russia of the Tsars, accuse the Jew of being a destroyer and force him to be an irreconcilable enemy? Or will America take advantage of the Jewish genius? That is a question for the people of America to answer.

HERMALIN, JEWISH

This Jewish Communist declared in a speech in New York in 1917: "*The Russian revolution was made by the Jews. We formed secret societies. We imagined the reign of terror. We made the revolution succeed by our convincing propaganda and mass murder in order to form a government of our own.*"

"JEWISH CHRONICLE

In the April 4, 1919 edition of London's leading Jewish newspaper: "*There is much in the fact of Bolshevism itself, in the fact that so many Jews are Bolsheviks, in the fact that the ideals of Bolshevism merge on many points, with the highest ideals of Judaism.*"

RABBI JUDAH L. MAGNES

This rabbi from New York made the following statement at the US National Radical Conference in April 1918: "*I claim to be a true Bolshevik. I can say definitively that the President of the United States will shortly appeal to the Allied governments for an immediate peace. He will demand immediate peace on the simple basis advanced by the Bolshevists of Russia.*"

OTTO WEININGER, JEWISH

In "*Sex and Character*", published in Vienna in 1921, this Austrian Jew declares on page 406:

"The idea of property is indissolubly linked with individuality, with the particularity of character. This is one of the reasons why Jews flock to communism."

On page 413: *"The Jew is a Communist"*.

On page 407: *"The complete inability of the Jew to understand the idea of the State."*

"TOWARDS MOSCOW

In the September 1919 edition of this Jewish Bolshevik newspaper, we read: *"We must not forget that the Jewish people form the true proletariat, the true international which has no homeland"*.

ANGELO RAPPOPORT, JEWISH

The author of *"Pioneers of the Russian Revolution"* tells us: *"The Jews of Russia, as a whole, were responsible for the revolution"*.

MORITZ RAPPOPORT, JEWISH

The author of the following lines, commenting on the German revolution of 1918: *"The revolution reminds us once again of the importance of the Jewish Question, because the Jews are the leading element of the revolution"*.

"JEWISH TRIBUNE

In its edition of 5 July 1922: *"The German revolution is the work of the Jews. The liberal democratic parties have a large number of Jews at their head, and Jews play a predominant role in high government posts"*.

KADMI COHEN, JEWISH

In his book "Nomads", published in 1928, the Jew Kadmi Cohen declared: "The very instinct of ownership, moreover resulting from attachment to the soil, does not exist among the Jews who have never possessed the soil, who have never wanted to possess it. Hence their undeniable communist tendency from the earliest times. (page 85) Is it not enough to recall the names of the great Jewish revolutionaries of the nineteenth and twentieth centuries, the Karl Marxs, the Lassalle, the Kurt Eisners, the Bela Kuhns, the Trotskys, the Léon Blums, for the names of the theoreticians of modern socialism to be mentioned?

Although it is not possible to declare Bolshevism, taken as a whole, as a Jewish nation, it is nevertheless true that the Jews provided several leaders of the maximalist movement and that, in fact, they played a major role. The tendencies of Jews towards communism, apart from any material collaboration in party organisations, are strikingly confirmed by the profound aversion which a great Jew, a great poet, Henri Heine, felt for Roman Law.

The subjective causes, the passionate causes of the revolt of Rabbi Aquiba and Bar Kocheba in 70 AD against the Pax romana and the Jus romanum, understood and felt subjectively, passionately by a nineteenth century Jew, who apparently had retained no ties with his race. And are the Jewish revolutionaries and Jewish communists who attack the principle of private property, whose most solid monument is the Codex Juris Civilis of Justinian and Vulpian, doing anything different from their ancestors who resisted Vespasian and Titus? In reality, it is the dead who are speaking". (page 86).

"THE MACCABEAN

In November 1905, this New York Jewish newspaper published a resounding article under the title

"A Jewish Revolution" - *"The 1905 revolution in Russia is a Jewish revolution, a crisis in Jewish history. It is a Jewish revolution because Russia is home to almost half of the world's Jews and the overthrow of its despotic government will have a very great influence on the destinies of millions of Jews living in that country and thousands who have emigrated from all over. But the Russian revolution is a Jewish revolution because the Jews are the most active revolutionaries in the Czar's empire"*.

MAURICE SAMUEL, JEWISH

In his book *Moi, le Juif (I, the Jew)*, published in 1923, the author declared: "*We Jews are revolutionaries. God has so made us and constituted us that if we were given the opportunity to achieve some of our goals, which are the object of our avowed desires, we would immediately set to work, on simple principle, to try to demolish what has just been built.*"

ANGELO RAPPOPORT, JEWISH

In "*Pioneers of the Russian Revolution*", published in 1918, on page 100: "*Throughout history, the spirit of the Jews has always been revolutionary and subversive, but subversive with the idea of building on ruins.*"

BERNARD LAZARE, JEWISH

In his book published in Paris in 1894, "*L'antisémitisme et ses causes*", the author tells us: "*The Jew plays a part in revolutions and participates in them as a Jew or, more correctly, as long as he remains a Jew. The Jewish spirit is essentially revolutionary and, consciously or otherwise, the Jew is a revolutionary*".

"THE ISRAELITE WORLD

In the issue of 5 September 1867: "*The revolution with its equality and fraternity is the star of Israel*".

"ISRAELITE ARCHIVES

In the issue of 6 July 1889: "*The year 1789 is a new Easter, the French Revolution has a very pronounced Hebraic character.*"

"NEW YORK TIME

In the edition of 24 March 1917: "*Kennan rewrites history. He tells how Jacob Schiff, a Jewish banker, financed revolutionary propaganda in the Tsar's army. Mr Kennan spoke of the work done for the revolution by the friends of Russian liberty. He said that during the Russo-Japanese War he was in Tokyo and was allowed to visit the 12,000 Russian prisoners in Japanese hands. He had conceived the idea of imbuing the Russian army with revolutionary ideas. He brought all the Russian revolutionary propaganda he could get from America. He said that one day Dr Nicholas Russell came to meet him in Tokyo and told him that he had been sent to help him in his work.*

The movement was financed by a New York banker whom you all know and love," *he said, referring to Mr Schiff. Soon we were receiving a ton and a half of revolutionary propaganda in Russian. By the end of the war, 50,000 Russian officers and soldiers were returning home as ardent revolutionaries. The friends of Russian freedom had planted 50,000 seeds of freedom in 100 regiments. I do not know how many of these officers captured the fortress of Petrograd last week, but we do know what part the army has just played in the revolution. Then a telegram from Jacob Schiff was read to the assembly, which read in part as follows: Tell those who are here this evening for me how much I regret not being able to celebrate with the 'friends of Russian liberty' the tangible reward for what we have hoped for and done over these long years*".

ELIE EBERLIN, JEWISH

This Jew, in his book *"The Jews of Today"*, published in 1928, wrote the following: *"The People of Zionism continues its task in Russia, Palestine and elsewhere. At the present time, it appears to be the only international proletarian party. One of its fractions adheres to the Communist International, the other to the Socialist International* (page 24). *In the course of its autonomous existence, the Jewish people has passed through many forms of government. But neither the paternal dictatorship of the great Moses, nor the power of kings governed by a religious constitution, nor the republic of the faithful under the presidency of the high priests, nor the despotism of the last kings leaning on Rome were accepted by this people of dreamers. The Jews have always had a government, but they have always been subject to it* (page 134). *As a result, the Jews have not been able to maintain their state among the states of Antiquity and have inevitably had to become the revolutionary leaven of the universe* (page 143). *What is still Jewish in Bolshevism is the renunciation of the rewards of the hereafter, in the other world, and the pursuit of happiness on earth. This idea, which marks the triumph of Jewish values over mystical-Christian values, is common to all peoples today"*. (page 155).

"JEWISH CHRONICLE

The London Jewish newspaper published the following in its edition of 6 January 1933: *"More than a third of all Jews in Russia have become Soviet officers"*.

RABBIS' MANIFESTO

Manifesto of 25 February 1930, signed by the rabbis Menahem Gluskin of Minsk, Osée L. Zimbalist, Herz Mazel, Gabriel Gabrielow, Oscher Kerstein and Mendel Jarcho, and published by the Jewish communist Michael Sheimann in *"Krestobyl Pokhod Protiv"* USSR, Moscow, 1930, pages 103 and 104 :

"It is not possible for us to separate our destiny from that of the Jewish people, in respect of whom the government of the USSR can be

proclaimed the only one which openly combats all manifestations of anti-Semitism. From a world point of view it is a fact of the utmost importance that the leader of the Communist Party and head of the Soviet State, Lenin, issued a decree declaring anti-Jews to be the enemies of the people. And while bloody conflicts were still possible under British rule, and pogroms and other anti-Jewish demonstrations were still taking place in Romania and many other countries, in the USSR all the means of propaganda were mobilised against anti-Semitism and the apparatus of the law was even put into action.[22] Under the Soviet regime we were never subjected to any persecution because of our religious convictions[23]

LOUIS FISHER, JEWISH

This correspondent in Russia of the *"Nation"* newspaper wrote in the *"New York Jewish Tribune"* of 18 January 1924 as follows: *"If we judge the Bolsheviks by what the Jews have gained by them in the field of education the verdict is certainly in their favour. Jewish children, tens of thousands of them, attend official public schools where Yiddish is the language of instruction. The government has set up special Jewish pedagogical seminaries where teachers are trained to give instruction in Jewish schools in Yiddish. There are even sections in universities where Yiddish is the language of instruction. Before the revolution under the Tsar, the proportion of Jewish students was limited to 4%. Now there is no limit. In some universities, 50% of students are Jewish. In Minsk (White Russia) the percentage is even higher.*

"THE MACCABEAN

Extract from an article by the Jew Haas published in this newspaper: *"The Russian revolution is a Jewish revolution because it marks a*

---

[22] This is now the case in France with the Stalino-Orwellian *"Fabius-Gayssot"* law.

[23] It should be noted that this is not the case for other religions: at the time this text was written, 42,800 high dignitaries, priests and ministers of the Christian confessions had suffered martyrdom and death...

milestone in Jewish history. It is also a Jewish revolution because Jews were the most active revolutionaries in the Russian Empire."

"JEWISH WORLD

Article published on 8 August 1922: *"Business is picking up in Russia and under the new regime the Jews are rapidly becoming the captains of industry. There are now 100,000 Jews in Moscow and kosher butcher shop signs can be seen in many streets. However, anti-Semitism grew in the city as the Jewish population increased.*

"CANADIAN JEWISH CHRONICLE

Edition of 10 August 1923, quoted by the *Jewish Correspondence Bureau*: *"The number of Jewish bandits in Moscow is increasing alarmingly. Hardly a day goes by when attacks on the public highway or violent burglaries are not committed by gangs whose members are mainly Jews. They are the masters of the underworld, including the Mafia, and to better involve the Italians, they change their Jewish names for Italian ones"*.

MAURICE MURREY, JEWISH

In his book *L'Esprit juif (The Jewish Spirit)*, this French Jew wrote: *"By blood and tradition, Karl Marx belongs body and soul to Judaism. Karl Marx and Rothschild represent the two extremes, but as we often say, "extremes touch".*

Marx and Rothschild both personify the Jewish ideal raised to its highest power. The further the masses move away from Christianity, the more visibly Jewish they become. Jewish regenerative idealism may be preparing a disastrous revolution for the twentieth century. Every intense manifestation of properly Jewish idealism in Europe has coincided with uprisings, murders and rebellions."

"NOVY MAR

On 16 March 1922, this Bolshevik press organ published an appeal to Jewish workers and citizens throughout the world, which read: "*Our Soviet government has spent billions to help Jews who have suffered pogroms. But today our republic is destitute. You must put pressure on your governments to repair the devastated Jewish districts at their own expense and to compensate the Jews who have suffered in Russia. All the Jewish organisations of the world are invited to submit this request to the Genoa Conference through the Soviet delegation. It is your sacred duty to bring pressure to bear on your governments, whether or not they are represented at Genoa, to compel them to support the demands of the Jews of Russia. You must insist that the delegates of your respective countries in Genoa support the demands which the Jews will have presented by their representatives, the delegates of the Soviets.*"

J. OLGIN, JEWISH

This Communist leader, in his New York newspaper "*Morning Freiheit*" published the following lines: "*Every Jew must support the Popular Front because it is the bulwark defending the rights of the Jewish people*".

BERNARD LAZARE, JEWISH

In his book "*L'antisémitisme et ses causes*", published in Paris in 1894, the Jewish historian tells us: "*In the midst of all the nations of Europe, the Jews exist as a denominational community with its own nationality, having preserved a particular type, special aptitudes and a spirit of their own*". (page 297)

"*The Jew is a confessional type as he is; it is the law and the Talmud that have made him stronger than blood and climatic variations; they have developed in him characters that imitation and heredity have perpetuated."* (page 283)[24]

"No religion has been as good a kneader of souls and minds as the Jewish religion". (page 283)

[The Jewish religion is] *"older, more immutable, narrower, and more strictly adhered to than any other."* (page 281)

"Animated by that old Hebraic materialism which perpetually dreamed of a paradise realised on earth and always repelled the distant and problematic hope of an Eden after death." (page 346)

"The Jew's philosophy was simple. Having only a limited number of years to devote to himself, he wanted to enjoy them, and it was not moral pleasures that he asked for, but material pleasures to embellish his existence and make it sweet. As heaven did not exist, he could only expect tangible favours from God in return for his fidelity and piety, not vague promises good for seekers of the hereafter, but formal achievements, resolving themselves into an increase in well-being. With no hope of future compensation, the Jew could not resign himself to the misfortunes of life; it was only very late that he was able to console himself for his misfortunes by thinking of heavenly bliss. He did not respond to the scourges that befell him with Muslim fatalism or Christian resignation, but with revolt". (page 307)

"So the Jews' conception of life and death provided the first element in their revolutionary spirit. Starting from the idea that goodness, i.e. righteousness, should be realised not beyond the grave since beyond the

---

[24] We know that all this is false, or at any rate negligible, especially as the majority of bourgeois Jews are completely ignorant of their religion, as any Jew who has lived in the Western upper middle class knows. Jewish particularism stems exclusively from circumcision on the 8th day. It is obvious that *the "Jewish sociological atmosphere"* reinforces it, but is not at all decisive. (see *Secret Files of the 21st Century*).

grave there is sleep until the resurrection of the bodies, but during life they sought justice and never finding it, perpetually insatiable, they agitated to obtain it." (page 314)

"Without the law, without Israel to practise it, the world would not exist. God would turn it into nothingness, and the world will know happiness only when it is subjected to the universal empire of this law, that is, to the empire of the Jews." (page 8)

"Happiness will be achieved through freedom, equality and justice. However, although Israel was the first nation to think about these ideas, other peoples at various times in history supported them and were not therefore rebellious like the Jewish people. Why not? Because although these peoples were convinced of the excellence of justice, equality and freedom, they did not consider their full realisation as possible, at least in this world, and consequently did not work solely for their advent. On the contrary, not only did the Jews believe that justice, liberty and equality could be the sovereigns of the world, but they also believed that they had been specially commissioned to work for this regime. All the desires and hopes that these three ideas gave rise to ended up crystallising around a central idea: that of the messianic times, of the coming of the Messiah who was to be sent by Yahweh to establish his sovereign earthly power". (page 322)

"As he was, with his dispositions, with his tendencies, it was inevitable that the Jew would play a part in the revolutions: he did." (page 329)

"The Jews have always been discontented. I do not mean to suggest that they were simply rebellious or systematic opponents of any government, but they were not satisfied with the way things were. They were perpetually worried, waiting for something better that they never found. (page 305)

"The causes which gave rise to this agitation, which sustained and perpetuated it in the souls of some modern Jews, are not external causes

such as the effective tyranny of a prince, a people, or a fierce code. They are internal causes, i.e. they have to do with the very essence of the Hebrew spirit. We must ask what were the reasons for the feelings of revolt that animated the Jews in their idea of God and their conception of life and death[25]

"During the second revolutionary period, which began in 1830, they showed even more ardour than during the first, because in most of the States of Europe they did not enjoy the fullness of their rights. Even those of them who were not revolutionaries by reason or temperament were revolutionaries by interest, and by working for the triumph of liberalism, they worked for themselves. There is no doubt that with their gold, their energy and their talent they supported and seconded the European revolution. During those years, their bankers, their industrialists, their priests, their writers and their tribunes, motivated by very different ideas, were all working towards the same goal". (page 341)

"They are to be found mixed up in the movement of the young Germany; they were numerous in the secret societies, which formed the revolutionary fighting army in the Masonic lodges, in the groups of the Charbonnerie, in the Roman High Sales, everywhere in France, Germany, Switzerland, Austria and Italy".

---

[25] Bernard Lazare understood very well that this rebellious mentality has an internal cause: it's their hormonal nature. When interstitial insufficiency is total, it leads to dementia. There is therefore a lack of control, a lack of reason, which is aggravated by a thyroid potential much higher than that of the Goyim.

The thyroid is the gland of intelligence and sensitivity, but also of pride and temptation.

This hormonal configuration, to which is added an equally tenfold hypophyseal possibility (analytical speculation, finance, science, ideologies), constitutes the determinism of the nature of the Jews and their speculation. The Jews are not the masters of their speculative-parasitic nature or of their subversive nature: all this comes exclusively from the circumscription on the 8th day.

"On the one hand, they were among the founders of industrial and financial capitalism and are actively collaborating in this extreme centralisation of capital, which will undoubtedly facilitate its socialisation.

"On the other, they are among the most ardent opponents of capital. The gold-digging Jew, the product of exile, Talmudism, legislation and persecution[26] is opposed by the revolutionary Jew, the son of the biblical and prophetic tradition, the tradition that animated the libertarian German Anabaptists of the sixteenth century and the Puritans of Cromwell." (page 393)

"To Rothschild correspond Marx and Lassalle. To the fight for money the fight against money and the cosmopolitanism of the agioteur becomes proletarian and revolutionary internationalism." (page 343)

"The emancipated Jews entered the nations as foreigners. They entered modern societies not as guests, but as conquerors. They were like a herd of cattle. Suddenly, the barriers fell and they rushed into the open field. But they were not warriors: they made the only conquest for which they were armed: the economic conquest they had been preparing for many years." (page 223)

"The French Revolution was above all an economic revolution. If it can be seen as the outcome of a class struggle, it must also be seen as the outcome of a struggle between two forms of capital: property capital and movable capital, landed capital and industrial and agency capital. With the supremacy of the nobility, the supremacy of landed capital disappeared, while the supremacy of the bourgeoisie brought with it the supremacy of industrial and agency capital. The emancipation of the Jews is linked to the history of the preponderance of this industrial capital". (page 224)

---

[26] The gold-digging Jew is a product of the 8th day circumcision, like the revolutionary Jew immediately mentioned.

Angelo Rappoport, Jewish

On page 25 of his book "*Pioneers of the Russian Revolution*", published in 1918: "*There was not a single political organisation in this vast Russian country which was not influenced by the Jews or directed by them. The Social Democratic Party, the Socialist Revolutionary Party and the Polish Socialist Party all had Jews among their leaders. Perhaps Plehve was right when he said that the struggle for political emancipation in Russia and the Jewish question were virtually identical. The Bund, or General Union of Jewish Workers, was founded in 1897. It is a political, economic association of the Jewish proletariat, at first opposed to all nationalist distinctions, then gradually imbued with Jewish nationalist sentiments.*"

On page 288: "*More than the Poles, the Latvians, the Finns, or indeed any ethnic group in the vast empire of the Romanofs, the Jews were the supporters of the 1917 Revolution.*"

Alfred Nossig, Jewish

For the author of "*Integrales Judentum*", published in Berlin in 1922: "*The modern socialist movement is, for the most part, the work of the Jews. It was Jews who stamped their brains on it. It was also Jews who played a leading role in the leadership of the first socialist republics.*

However, most of the Jewish socialist leaders were far removed from Judaism. Despite this, the role they played did not depend on them alone. In them the old eugenic principle of Mosaicism operated unconsciously; the blood of the old apostolic people lived in their brains and in their social temperament. Today's world socialism is the first stage in the fulfilment of Mosaicism, the beginning of the realisation of the future world foretold by our prophets.

Only when there is a League of Nations, only when its allied armies are effectively employed in the protection of all the weak, can we hope that the Jews will be able to develop their national State in Palestine without hindrance, and only a League of Nations imbued with the socialist spirit will make it possible for us to enjoy our international as well as our national necessities.

That is why all Jewish groups, whether Zionist or dispersalist, have a vital interest in the victory of socialism. They must demand it not only because of its identity with Mosaicism, but also as a tactical principle."

COMMUNISM SUPPORTED AND FINANCED BY JEWISH HIGH BANKING

Nobody doubts this any more, but it is interesting to look at some documents on the subject. It was the big Jewish bankers in New York who financed Bolshevism in Russia. The United States Secret Service sent the following document to all the embassies of the Allied countries. This prodigious document was reproduced in 1929 in many patriotic newspapers in various countries. It was also reprinted in a Catholic journal "*The Mystical Body of Christ in Modern Times*" with the imprimatur of a bishop, by Father Denis Fahey, Professor of Theology at Black Rocks College, Dublin, Ireland.

HERE IS THE TEXT AND THE ANALYSES BY FATHER FAHEY.

The main document dealing with the way in which the Russian revolution was financed is the one published by the American secret service and forwarded by the French High Commissioner to his government. It was published by "*Documentation Catholique*" in Paris on 6 March 1920, preceded by the following remarks: "We guarantee the authenticity of this document. The American Secret Service takes responsibility for the accuracy of the information it contains. This document was published in 1920 in a supplement to the Paris newspaper "*La Vieille France*", which added: "All the governments of the Entente were aware of this memorandum, drawn up on the basis of information from the American Secret Service and sent to the French High Commissioner and his colleagues".

This memoir can also be found in Monseigneur Jouin's book "*Le péril judéo-maçonnique*", part III, pages 249-351, with the additional remark that the Jews obstructed its publication, so that the majority of the public ignored its existence. Although the Jewish origin of Kerensky, who brought about the first Russian revolution in 1917, has been questioned, it seems certain that he was the son of the Jew Aaron Kerbis and the Jewess Adler.[27] The document is divided into eight sections. Sections I to IV and VI to VIII are reproduced below.

US SECRET SERVICE REPORT

Section I: *In February 1916 it was first discovered that a revolution was being fomented in Russia. It was discovered that the following persons, together with the banks mentioned, were engaged in this work of destruction. Jacob Schiff, Jew, Guggenheim, Jew, Max Breitung, Jew, Kuhn, Loeb & C° Jewish bank whose directors were: Jacob Schiff, Felix Warburg, Otto Kahn, Mortimer Schiff, S.H Hanauer, all Jews.*

There can be no doubt that the Russian Revolution which broke out a year after the above information was leaked was fomented and declared by specifically Jewish influences. Indeed, in April 1917, Jacob Schiff made a public statement to the effect that it was he and his financial help that had led to the success of the Russian Revolution.

Section II: *In the spring of 1917, Jacob Schiff began to provide Trotsky (a Jew) with funds to bring about social revolution in Russia. The "New Cork Daily Forward", a Judeo-Bolshevik organ, made a subscription for the same purpose. In Stockholm, the Jew Max Warburg also provided Trotsky & Co° with funds. They also received funds from the Rhenish Westphalian Syndicate, which is an important Jewish banking company . Similarly, another Jew, Olaf Aschberg of the Nya bank in*

---

[27] This detail really doesn't matter, since everyone knows that the Bolshevik revolution was, on the whole, Jewish: ideologists, financiers, politicians, administrators, prison and concentration camp executioners. We'll talk about that later.

Stockholm, and Givotovsky, a Jew whose daughter was married to Trotsky.

Section III: *In October 1917, revolution broke out in Russia. Thanks to this revolution, the Soviet organisations took over the leadership of the Russian people. Among the Soviets, the following individuals, all Jews, became famous:*

Lenin (*Ulyanov*)	Garine (*Garfeld*)	Trotsky (*Bronstein*)
Zinovieff (*Apfelbaum*)	Kameneff (*Rosenfeld*)	Dan (*Gourevitch*)
Ganetzki (*Furstenberg*)	Parus (*Helphand*)	Uritsky (*Pademilsky*)
Larine (*Lurge*)	Bohrine (*Nathanson*)	Martinoff (*Zibar*)
Bogdanoff (*Zilberstein*)	Suchanoff (*Gimel*)	Kamnleff (*Goldmann*)
Sagersky (*Krochmann*)	Riazanoff (*Goldenbach*)	Solutzeff (*Belichmann*)
Pianitsky (*Ziwin*)	Axelrod (*Orthodox*)	Glasunoff (*Schultze*)
Zuriesain (*Weinstein*)	Lapinsky (*Lowensohn*)	

It should be added that Lenin's mother was Jewish, so Jewish tradition considered him to be a Jew in his own right. Lenin studied with Jewish students in Switzerland. Victor Marsden, an English correspondent in Russia, declared that Lenin was a Kalmyk Jew married to a Jewess (Kroupskaya) whose children spoke Yiddish. Hervert Fitch, a Scotland Yard detective who had spied Lenin as a waiter, declared that Lenin was a typical Jew.

Section IV: *At the same time the Jew Paul Warburg, who had been one of the founders of the Federal Reserve Board, became known for his active support of certain notorious Bolsheviks in the United States. These circumstances, and a report made about him, prevented him from being elected director of the Federal Reserve.*

Section VI: *the other hand, Judas Magnes, who receives subsidies from Jacob Schiff, is in close contact with the world Zionist organisation Poale-Sion, of which he is the de facto director. The ultimate aim of this organisation was to establish the international supremacy of the*

Jewish Labour Movement. Judas Magnes was then a rabbi in New York. He was then sent to Jerusalem to run the Jewish University. Poale-Sion, a militant Marxist organisation, has an active and powerful branch in Montreal.

Section VII: *The social revolution had scarcely broken out in Germany when the Jew Rosa Luxembourg automatically took over its political leadership. One of the main leaders of the international Bolshevik movement was the Jew Haase. At this time the social revolution in Germany was developing in parallel with the social revolution in Russia.*

Section VIII: *If we take into account the fact that the Jewish bank Kuhn, Loeb et Cie, is in contact with the syndicate Westphalien-Rhénan, a German Jewish bank, and with Lazare Frères, a Jewish bank in Paris, as well as with the Jewish house Gunsbourg of Petrograd, Tokyo and Paris, if in addition we note that all the Jewish houses mentioned above, are in close correspondence with the Jewish firm Speyer et Cie of London, New York and Frankfurt am Main, as well as with the Nya Banken, a Judeo-Bolshevik establishment of Stockholm, it becomes evident that the Bolshevik movement is the expression of a general Jewish movement and that large Jewish banks are interested in the organisation of this movement.*

This is how American intelligence established the collusion between Jewish capitalist multimillionaires and Jewish Bolshevik revolutionaries.

JEWISH CAPITALISTS

A few additional remarks about the people mentioned above seem interesting. According to *the "Écho de Paris"* of 28 April 1920, Max Warburg was the Managing Director of Banque Max Warburg & Cie in Hamburg. He was also the main shareholder in the Hamburg-America Line and Deutscher-Lloyd. His two brothers, Paul and Félix, one of whom was married to the sister-in-law and the other to the daughter of Frankfurt-born Jacob Schiff, were with Schiff at the head of Banque Kuhn, Loeb & Cie. In the "*German-Bolshevik Conspiracy*" page 27, published by the Committee of Public Information, Washington D.C. in October 1918, we learn that Max Warburg advanced money to the Bolsheviks.

Here is a revealing message: "*Stockholm, 21 September 1917. Mr Raphael Scholak, Haparand*": "*Dear comrade, in accordance with a telegram from the Westphalian-Rhineland Syndicate, the Bank Max Warburg & Cie informs us that a credit facility has been opened for Comrade Trotsky's company. Signed: Furstenberg.*

According to French sources, Jakob Schiff paid $12,000,000 for the Russian Revolution of 1917. If we now read Nesta Webster's book *The Surrender of an Empire*, pages 74, 79, we find further information on the rise of Bolshevism.

THE RUSSIAN REVOLUTION WAS A JEWISH INVESTMENT

It seems that the real name of the person mentioned in Section III as Parvus is Israel Lazarevitch Hellphand, a Jew from the province of Minsk in White Russia. Towards the end of the last century he took part in revolutionary work in Odessa. In 1886 he went abroad and eventually, after many wanderings, arrived in Copenhagen where he amassed a large fortune as chief agent for the distribution of German coal in Denmark, working through the Danish Socialist Party. Dr Ziv, in his "*Life of Trotsky*", relates that when he was in America in 1916, he asked Trotsky: "How is Parvus? Trotsky replied: "*He is in the process of completing his twelfth million*". It was this Jewish multimillionaire who, after Karl Marx, was Lenin's greatest inspiration. It was thanks to Parvus that Lenin was sent to Russia. Bolshevik Russia is not the triumph of the workers, but seems to be nothing more than a gigantic investment by Jewish capitalists for their own ends.

THE SYMBOLISM OF THE RED FLAG

The red flag has always been a symbol of danger. At the back of a train, on the edge of a precipice, on a broken road, on the outskirts of a quarry or mine, wherever there a danger of death or ruin, the red flag is unfurled to warn. Today, this flag, so perfectly symbolic, is unfurled and imposed on the ignorant masses by those who dream of taking over the world to lead it to planetary massacres and nothingness.

It is therefore the emblem of ruin, riots, disruption, chaos, social upheaval and human misery: two hundred million corpses of international Communism follow this flag. It is in fact the banner of international Jewish finance and was first flown by Rothschild. It was unfurled by Karl Marx as the banner of Judeo-Proletarian world politics.

The first Rothschild was Amschel Mayer. He lived in Frankfurt am Main, Germany, where he had a coin collecting and changing shop. When he wanted to indicate that his shop was having a special sale, he would display a red flag in front of the shop. People who went there would say: "I'm off to the red flag". When a passer-by mocked the flag, the Jew Amschel Mayer is said to have replied: "*This flag will one day dominate the world*".

The founder of international finance soon changed his name to Rothschild, which means "*red flag*" (or "*red banner*"). Once they had control of the world from above, through finance, the Jews decided to obtain control from below too, through the proletariat. They launched Karl Marx with his socialist and communist bible and financed the great international movements that grew out of it. So the red flag of high finance also became that of the international proletariat. Whether the conquest of peoples is carried out by Jewish finance or by the Internationals under Jewish control, it is always the Jews who win and it is always the red flag of Jewish domination that replaces the flags of the Nations.

And legions of Goyim, whom the Jews consider to be *"vile cattle seed"* (Zohar), ecstatically follow this red flag of their degradation and slavery, like sheep foolishly following their butchers. Leaders are trained to lead them towards what they believe to be their "freedom", i.e. the radical and absolute antithesis of true freedom.

The red flag of the Rothschilds is the banner of the Golden Calf, of the destroyers of countries, of the mass murderers of Spain, Russia and Hungary, the flag of the Trotskys, the Bela Kuhns, the Litvinoffs, the Kaganoviches (who led the Jewish prison and concentration camp executioners in the USSR: Frenkel, Yagoda, Firine, Apetter, Rappaport, Jejoff, Abramovici and fifty or so other Jewish executioners).

JEWS AND LIBERALISM

"The sentinel

In this Jewish newspaper of 9 June 1936, Rabbi Louis I. Newmann wrote: "*Jews must always be on the side of liberalism now and always. Even if liberalism suffers temporary setbacks. Judaism has nothing in common with reaction (Nationalism) but everything in its tradition is liberal.*"

AN INTERESTING BRITISH DOCUMENT ABOUT THE JEWS

In April 1919 in London, by order of Her Majesty, a White Paper was printed entitled "*Russia N°1*", published in 1919, "*A Collection of Reports on Bolshevism in Russia*". (A Collection of Reports on Bolshevism in Russia".) This official document was submitted to the House of Commons. This document, on page 6, contained a report from His Excellency Mr Oudendyk, Minister of the Netherlands in Petrograd, who was at the same time acting in an official capacity as protector of British subjects and interests, in place of the British representative, Captain Cromie, who had been murdered by the Bolsheviks.

Extract from this official report, dated 6 September 1918, and received by Balfour on 18 September 1918:

"In Moscow I had repeated meetings with Chichérine and Karachan. The whole Soviet government has fallen to the level of a criminal organisation. The Bolsheviks have embarked on a veritable criminal folly. The danger is now so great that I feel it my duty to draw the attention of the British Government and of all other Governments to the fact that the whole of world civilisation is greatly endangered if Russian Bolshevism is not immediately eradicated. I regard the immediate suppression of Bolshevism as the greatest problem now confronting the world, not excepting the war now raging. Unless Bolshevism is nipped in the bud without delay, it will spread in one form or another in Europe and throughout the world because it is organised and built up by Jews without nationality whose sole aim is to destroy the existing order of things for their own particular ends. The only way to avert this danger would be collective action by all the powers".

UNAVOIDABLE FINDINGS

➤ The Chinese Communist General Chen was called Cohen.
➤ The organiser of communism in China was called Crusenberg, alias Borodin.
➤ The leader of the Marxists in Italy was the Jew Claudio Trèves.
➤ In Russia, Lenin, Trotsky, Kerensky, Zinoviev, Radomilisky, Konstantinovitch, Abramovici, Rosenblum, Litvinov, Lindé, Ravitch and thousands of other Soviet leaders were Jews.
➤ In Hungary, the revolutionary movement of 1919 was led by the Jews Bela Kuhn, Kunsi, Agoston, Peter Grunbaum, Weinstein and others.
➤ In Bavaria, the 1918 revolution was led by Jews: Kurt Eisner, Loewenberg, Rosenfeld, Koenigberg, Birbaum, Kaiser and Hoch.

➢ In Berlin in 1918, it was the Jews Lundsberg, Riesenfeld, Lewisohn, Moses, Rosa Luxembourg, Cohen, Reuss and Hodenberg.

➢ In Munich, in April 1919, the leaders were Levine, Levien and Axelrod.

➢ In Hamburg in 1923, the Jew Sobelsohn (Karl Radek).

➢ In Brazil, in 1936, a Marxist insurrection broke out. The ringleaders were the Jews Rosenberg, Gardelsran, Gutnik, Képlanski, Goldberg, Sternberg, Jacob Gria, Weiss and Friedmann.

➢ In Spain in 1936, Bela Kuhn, Neumann, Ginsburg, Julius Deutch, the Jewess Nelken, Rosenberg, the USSR ambassador, and the Jew Del Vayo, the SDN delegate, reappeared.

➢ A whole host of Jews from Spain presided over the massacres and atrocities.

Exactly as in Russia... The fact is that all these communist revolutions, launched in favour of the proletariat, actually result in massacres of peasants and workers sacrificed to the Jewish cause.

A LEADING JEWISH BANKER MAKES A SENSATIONAL CONFESSION

At the end of 1936, the Count of Saint-Aulaire, the French ambassador, published a book entitled "*Genève contre la Paix*" *(Geneva against Peace)* (Edition Plon). In it he reported statements made to him by a leading Jewish banker from New York in a café in Budapest, the capital of Hungary, which the Jew Bela Kuhn had just bloodied with a dreadful Communist revolution. The bank referred to here is the Kuhn, Loeb & Co. Bank of New York, whose directors were Jacob H. Shiff, Otto H. Kahn and the brothers Paul and Félix Warburg.

This is what the book says on page 85 and following:

"This situation explains how Bela Kuhn's masked allies had remained in Budapest after his rout and how they could be found at the table of the Allied missions, some of whom were members, which was very convenient for them for the accomplishment of their other mission. They were just as happy drinking Tokay with the Allies as they were with Bela Kuhn, and when they had drunk more than small children drink milk, their tongues were loosened. Many of the Jewish revolutionaries expelled from Hungary had returned there after the armistice, in American uniform, and it was their reports to Wilson that inspired the Supreme Council's policy in Central Europe.

I remember the words of one of those augurs who sat next to me at one of those international dinners that are the best school and most dangerous pitfall of diplomacy. He had become a director of a major New York bank, one of those that financed the Bolshevik revolution. But he was not one of those bankers who, in the words of Louis Philippe about Casimir Perrier, were sealed to the floor like a safe. He had a 'ceiling' in his speciality and was happy to break it to reach higher regions.

As a good Oriental, he expressed himself through images to which, as a cerebral person, he gave intellectual extensions. A guest asked him "how High Finance could protect Bolshevism, the enemy of real estate property, a condition of the banking industry, as well as of the real estate wealth which is no less necessary to it", and our man in charge of supplying the breadless emptied a large glass of Tokay, took a moment to puff on his enormous five-franc gold cigar, and said: "Those who are astonished at our alliance with the Soviets forget that the people of Israel are the most nationalistic of all peoples, because they are the oldest, the most united, the most exclusive. They forget that its nationalism is the most heroic because it has withstood the most terrible persecutions.

They also forget that it is the hardest nationalism, the most intangible, since it has survived through the centuries in spite of all obstacles without the support of a territory. It is ecumenical and spiritual like the papacy. But it looks to the future instead of the past, and its kingdom is here on earth. That's why it is the salt of the earth, which doesn't prevent it from being, as they say on the boulevard, the most desalted of nationalisms, in other words, the most decanted, the most stripped bare...".

When some of the guests had greeted these last words with an ill-repressed smile, this Sage of Zion responded with this gloss: "When I say the most stripped down, I mean that our nationalism is the most drinkable of all, the one with the most bottle, the one that other peoples absorb most easily with delight and without hurting their hair. Turning to salt, do you know the precept of the cod salters? I learned it on the shoal in Newfoundland. Here it is: Too much salt burns the flesh, not enough corrupts it. The same goes for the mind and for people. We apply this precept wisely, as is appropriate, salt being the emblem of wisdom.

We mix it discreetly with the bread of men: we administer it in corrosive doses only in exceptional cases when it is necessary to burn the debris of an impure past, as for example in the Russia of the Tsars. That already goes some way to explaining why we like Bolshevism: it's an admirable salting-ground for burning, not preserving. But apart from and above this particular case, we are in communion with integral Marxism in the International, our religion, because it is the weapon of our nationalism, a weapon in turn defensive and offensive, the shield and the sword.

You might say that Marxism is the antithesis of capitalism, which is also sacred to us. It is precisely because they are poles apart that they give us the two poles of the planet and allow us to be its axis. These two opposites, like Bolshevism and us, find their identity in the International. What's more, these two opposites, which are poles apart in terms of both society and doctrine, are united in the identity of the same end: the renewal of the world from above, in other words through the control of wealth, and from below, in other words through revolution.

For centuries, Israel was separated from Christianity, driven back into the ghetto in order to show the faithful what were called the witnesses of the ancient faith, in a humiliation that, it was said, was the atonement for deicide. This is what saved us and, through us, will save humanity. We have thus preserved our genius and our divine mission. Today, we are the truly faithful. Our mission is to promulgate the new law and to create a God, in other words to purify the notion of God and to bring it to fruition when the time is past. We purify it by identifying it with the notion of Israel becoming its own Messiah, which will facilitate its advent through our definitive triumph. This is our New Testament.

In it we reconcile kings and prophets, like David the prophet-king or king-prophet, bringing them together in his person. We are kings so that the prophecies may be fulfilled, and we are prophets so that we may never cease to be kings".

With that, the king-prophet drank another glass of Tokay.

A sceptic objected: "This Messiah of whom you are prophets and apostles, are you not in danger of also being martyrs? After all, however deprived your nationalism may be, it sometimes deprives other peoples. If you despise wealth you do not despise it, if only as a means not of enjoyment but of power. How can the triumph of the universal revolution, which destroys and negates capitalism, pave the way for the triumph of Israel, the holy ark of that same capitalism?

"I am not unaware that Jeroboam founded the cult of the Golden Calf in Dan and Bethel. Nor am I unaware that the revolution is, in modern times, the high priestess of this cult, the most diligent purveyor of its tabernacles. If the Golden Calf is still standing, its most comfortable pedestal is the tomb of the Empires, for two reasons: firstly, revolution is never more than a displacement of privileges, and therefore of wealth. But what feeds our Golden Calf is not the creation of wealth, or even its exploitation, it is above all its mobilisation, the soul of speculation.

The more it changes hands, the more remains in ours. We are couriers who receive commission on all exchanges, or if you prefer, toll collectors who control the crossroads of the globe and collect tax on all movements of anonymous and vagrant wealth, whether these movements are transfers from one country to another, or oscillations between prices. Instead of the calm, monotonous song of prosperity, we prefer the passionate, alternating voices of rise and fall. To arouse them, nothing beats revolution if not war, which is a form of revolution. Secondly, revolution weakens peoples and makes them less resistant to foreign companies. The health of our Golden Calf requires the sickness of Nations, those that are capable of developing themselves. On the contrary, we are in solidarity with the great modern States such as France, the United States, England and Italy, represented at this table, which have given us generous hospitality and with whom we are collaborating for the progress of civilisation.[28]

But take pre-war Turkey for example, "the sick man" as the diplomats called him. This sick man was a factor in our health, because he lavished us with concessions of all kinds - banks, mines, ports, railways, etc. - and we had to make do with him.

His entire economic life was entrusted to us: we looked after him so well that he died, at least in Europe. Looking at it from the down-to-earth point of view of accumulating wealth in order accomplish our mission, we need another sick man. Apart from any higher considerations, this would have been reason enough to inoculate the old Russia with Bolshevism. It is now the sick man of the post-war period, much more nourishing than the Ottoman Empire and defending itself even less.

---

[28] This magnificent collaboration has not prevented Rothschild, Freud, Marx, Einstein, Picasso and their ilk from reducing the Christian West to the most extreme degeneracy and super-crimes of lèse-humanité: unemployment, drugs, pornography, youth suicide, food and therapeutic chemification, ecological collapse, extinction of species, Aids, Hiroshima, Chernobyl, and so on.

Now it is ready for another feast. It will soon be a corpse, and all we will have to do is skin it.

At the other end of the table, a co-religionist, an enfant terrible of the synagogue, was waiting for the moment to say his piece: "They think we're birds of prey, but we're more like scavengers".

Yes, if you insist," replied the confessor of the new law. But add that we do it for the good of humanity, for its moral health, just as other birds do it for public health in countries with rudimentary roads. Add also that our essential dynamism uses the forces of destruction and creation, but uses the former to fuel the latter. What were countries like the old Turkey, the old Russia, and even to a lesser extent the old Hungary with its feudal system and its latifundia? They were paralysed limbs that impeded all the world's movements; they were embolisms of Europe that could die from them, blood clots obliterating vital vessels. By dissolving them, we restore them to the circular current of the entire body. If a few drops of liquefied blood squirt out during the operation, why should we be moved? It's a tiny price to pay for an immense benefit. Someone once said that "we are revolutionary because we are self-preservationists".

In shaping the new world, we are proving our organisation for revolution and for conservation by this destruction, Bolshevism, and by this construction of the League of Nations, which is also our work, the one being the accelerator, the other the brake of the mechanism of which we are the engine and the direction. The goal? It is marked by our mission. Israel is a synthetic and homogeneous nation. It is made up of elements scattered all over the world but melted together by the flame of our faith in ourselves. We are an SDN that sums up all the others. That is what qualifies us to gather them around us. We are accused of dissolving them. We are dissolvers only on those points that are resistant to this synthesis, of which ours is the example and the means. We dissociate the surface only to reawaken in the depths the affinities that are ignored. We are the greatest common divider of peoples only to become their greatest common unifier. Israel is the microcosm and the seed of the future city.

This text deserves deep meditation. It is simply mind-boggling.

Dr. Oscar Lévy, Jewish :

"We Jews have led the Goyim into a new hell.

In 1920, the English writer Pitt-Rivers of Worcester College, Oxford, published a pamphlet entitled "The *World Significance of the Russian Revolution"*. The publisher was Basil Blackwell, Oxford. Dr Oscar Lévy, highly regarded in literary circles, wrote a preface to the book.

I have never come across an incredible and perfect confession written by a Jew. No Goy, not even a Céline, would be capable of reaching such a level of lucidity. This is to say that everything is Jewish, even the most perfect and complete form of anti-Semitism (anti-Jewishness, we should say).

Only the great Simone Weil, in her book "*La pesanteur et la Grâce" (Weight and Grace),* in the chapter on Israel, offered a remarkable critique of unparalleled metaphysical height. No goy has reached such a level of anti-Jewishness...

Here's the gist of it:

"Bolshevism is a religion and a faith. How could these half-converted believers dream of defeating the 'true' *and* 'faithful' *of their own faith, those holy crusaders who had rallied around the red flag of the prophet Karl Marx and who had fought under the bold guidance of those experienced officers of the last revolutions: the Jews?*

There is no race in this world more enigmatic, more fatal and therefore more interesting than that of the Jews. Any writer who, like you, is oppressed by the appearance of the present and embarrassed by the anguish of the future, must seek to elucidate the Jewish question and its impact on our time.[29]

For the Jewish question and its influence on the ancient and modern world goes to the very root of everything and must be discussed by every honest thinker, no matter how great the difficulties involved, no matter how complex the subject, no matter how many individuals of this race.[30]

*You reveal, and with great fervour, the links that exist between the collectivism of immensely rich international finance - the democracy of money values, as you call it - and the international collectivism of Karl Marx and Trotsky. And all these evils and miseries, both economic and political, you trace back to a single source, a single "*fons et origo malorum*": the Jews.*

Well then! Other Jews could outrage you and crucify you for this energetic expression of your opinion. For my part, I will refrain from adding to the chorus of condemnation they would inflict on you.

First of all, I must say this: hardly an event has occurred in modern Europe without being traced back to the Jews. All the ideas and movements of modern times have sprung from a Jewish source, and this for the simple reason that the Semitic idea has finally conquered and completely subjugated our universe. There is no doubt that, in everything they do, the Jews do better or worse than the Goyim, and there is no doubt that their influence today warrants very careful investigation, and it is not possible to envisage this influence without

---

[29] Such a thing is impossible in the year 2000: Jewish racist laws forbid any commentary, any truth that is unfavourable to them. We are in a coma.

[30] Let us recall once again this new unknown teaching: there are no races, only ethnic groups that are the result of hormonal adaptation to a fixed environment. The Jewish problem stems exclusively from circumcision on the 8th day, the only common denominator that accounts for a particularism that is constant in time and space.

serious alarm. We Jews have made a mistake, my friend, we have made a very serious mistake. Today there is nothing but falsehood and madness. A madness that will produce even greater misery and even deeper anarchy.

I confess it to you openly and sincerely, with the sorrow whose depth and pain only an ancient psalmist could measure in our burnt-out age. We posed as the saviours of the world, we who even boasted of having given you "the Saviour", today we are nothing but the world's seducers, its destroyers, its arsonists, its executioners. We promised to lead you to a new paradise, but in the end we have only led you to a new hell. There has been no progress, at least moral progress, and it is only our morality that has prevented any real progress and, what is worse, is blocking the way to any future and natural reconstruction in our ruined world. I look at this world and shudder at the sight of its horror, and I shudder all the more because I know the spiritual authors of all this horror.

But these authors themselves, unconscious in this as in everything they do, know nothing yet of this astonishing revelation. While Europe is in flames, while its victims groan, while its dogs howl at the conflagration, while its fumes descend in thicker and darker sheets over our continent, the Jews, or at least some of them, and not the least worthy, are trying to escape from the burning edifice, eager to pass from Europe to Asia, from the grim scene of our disaster, to the sunny corner of Palestine. Their eyes are closed to misery, their ears deaf to complaints, their hearts hardened to the anarchy of Europe. They no longer feel anything but their own sorrows, they no longer think of anything but their own fate, they no longer sigh under anything but their own burden."[31]

---

[31] The sickening climax of this psychology is the arithmetical-technical nonsense of the Holocaust, which serves as a lever for international extortion, when we know that Cyclon B is completely unsuitable for gassing 1,000 or 2,000 people at a time; and that the figure of six million (a country like Switzerland!) is contradicted by the American Jewish Year Book, which puts the number of Jews present in occupied Europe in 1941 at 3,300,000 (many left after that date!).

HERE IS AN ATROCIOUS DOCUMENT:

At a time when the Jews are fomenting world wars, this article is nauseating "*The Sentinel*", a Jewish weekly from Chicago, published the minutes of the Central Conference of American Rabbis on 24 September 1936. They have decided to ask the United States government to release from their military obligations Jews who, out of conscientious objection, are opposed to the war.

So it's good for them to start wars, but to have them waged by the Goyim.

The entire goyish elite will be decimated, as was the case in 1914-18.

BIG PROPERTY DESTROYS SMALL PROPERTY

In the "*Nouvelle Revue Internationale*" of January 1897, the great Jew Theodore Herzl told us: "*The agrarian question is only a question of machines. America must defeat Europe just as large-scale property destroys small-scale property. The peasant is a type destined to disappear.*

HISTORY'S TRUE GENOCIDES

Jews never talk about the cruel massacres of history. It is unheard of for people to talk incessantly about the "*Six Million*" (true or false) and never about the 80 million Goyim exterminated in the USSR by a regime that was quintessentially Jewish (200 million victims of Communist regimes worldwide).

In ancient times, under Ahasuerus, 70,000 Goyim were exterminated at the instigation of the Jews. They celebrate this feat with the festival of Purim. The day before the Jews left Egypt, all the first-born children of Egyptian families were massacred. When Christ was born, the Jews massacred the Holy Innocents throughout Palestine in the hope of killing the God-child. They forced Pontius Pilate to condemn Christ. They stoned Saint Stephen and had the apostles massacred. Nero's first advisor was the Jew Attilius and his favourite was the Jewess Poppaea: they encouraged him to massacre hundreds of thousands of Christians. The Jewish book *Sepher Juchasin* (Amsterdam 1919) reports that at the time of Pope Clement I (89-97), the Jews put to death in Rome and its environs "*a crowd of Christians as innumerable as the sands of the sea*".

Dion Cassius, the great historian of Antiquity, in his "*Roman History*" (translation by Anthoine de Bandole, 1660), writes: "*during this time, the Jews who lived along Cyrene, with a certain Andrew as their captain, killed all the Greeks and Romans, ate their flesh and entrails, bathed in their blood and clothed themselves in their skins.*

They killed some of them very cruelly, sawing them from the top of their heads right through the middle of their bodies. They threw them to the beasts and forced the others to fight against each other. They killed 220,000 of them. They exercised a similar cruelty in Egypt and in the island of Cyprus, having a certain Artemion as the leader and conductor of their cruelties. On the island of Cyprus, they slaughtered 240,000 people, for which reason it is no longer permitted for a Jew to go down there".

Edward Gibbon, in his famous historical study "*History of the Decline and Fall of the Roman Empire*" (1776) confirms: "*In Cyrene, they massacred 220,000 Greeks. They massacred 240,000 people on the island of Cyprus and a vast multitude in Egypt. Most of these unfortunate victims were sawn in two in accordance with the idea that David had authorised it by his conduct*".

The Jewish book *Sepher Hodoroth* tells us that Rabbenu Jehouda was favoured by the Emperor Antoninus the Pious. He pointed to the malice of the Nazarenes (Christians) as the cause of a pestilential disease and obtained the execution of all the Nazarenes in Rome in the year 3915 (155 AD). The same book tells us that it was through the influence of the Jews that Marcus Aurelius had all the Nazarenes he could slaughtered in the year 177. Among them were Saint Pothinus and forty-seven of his followers, including Saint Blandina and the Christians Macturus and Sanctus. It also tells us how the Jews had a field day under the monster Caracalla, "*the ferocious beast of Ansonia*". The book tells us that in 3974 (214 AD), the Jews killed 200,000 Christians in Rome and all the Christians in Cyprus.

The "*Sepher Juchasin*", a Jewish book, also tells us (page 108) that, "*at the request of the Jews, Diocletian killed a large number of Christians, including the popes Caius and Marcellinus, as well as Caius' brother and his sister Rosa*".

Mohammed was poisoned by a Jewish woman.

Jews assassinated Tsar Nicholas II and his entire family. Alexander of Yugoslavia and Louis Barthou were assassinated by the Jew Peter Kalmen, Huey Long by the Jew Weiss, Archduke Franz Joseph by the Jew Princip, Archduke Rudolf of Habsburg by a Jewess. There were numerous Judeo-Masonic assassinations: that of Tsar Alexander II, King Gustav III of Sweden, Louis XVI and his family, Pellegrino Rossi, minister to Pius IX, Garcia Moreno, President of Ecuador, King Carlos of Portugal, President Paul Doumer, the Marquis de Morès, Councillor Prince, President Felix Faure, President Abraham Lincoln, Prime Minister Stolypin, Count Tisza...

We mentioned the massacres of 30,000 Christians in three months by the Jews Bela Kuhn and Szamuely in 1918.

But the greatest political massacres in the history of the world took place in Bolshevik Russia: under the yoke of the Jews, who included Trostky, Sverdloff, Zinovieff, Kameneff, Litvinov, Yagoda, Joffe, Kaganovitch (Stalin's brother-in-law), Karakhan, Levine,

Rappaport, Parvus-Halphand, Radek-Sobelsohn, Garine and others.

One million nine hundred thousand bishops, priests, princes, nobles, army and police officers, middle-class people, teachers, engineers, workers and peasants were martyred in 18 months, often in atrocious conditions. Thirty million deaths from hunger and epidemics due to artificial famines since 1917 (Source: International Red Cross, Dr Fritjof Nansen).

Under the Jews Kurt Eisner and the Levine brothers, the Munich hostages in Bavaria were massacred.

In Spain, during the Civil War, a huge Jewish-Communist massacre took place: 400,000 Christians massacred behind the lines of fire, exclusively for their faith religious and national by the Jews Zamorra, Azana, Rosenberg.

In China, a huge Judeo-Communist massacre that claimed the lives of fifteen million Chinese over fifteen years in Communist-controlled provinces.

This is just a sample of the horrors. It is far from exhaustive.[32] The lives of the saints and the history of Antiquity, the Middle Ages and modern times are full of them. When the Jews were punished, they did not suffer a tenth of the evils they had inflicted on the peoples who had welcomed them.

In the objective history of the world, the Jews appear as a people of ferocious persecutors and not as a persecuted minority, even though their exactions in the host countries have systematically provoked

---

[32] I have extensive documentation on the victims of this Jewish war of 39-45, and after the war in Europe, not to mention the Negro slaves captured in Africa and killed by the millions, in a trade organised exclusively by the Jews (See also Professor Shahak on this subject).

pogroms and expulsions, in all the countries where they have lived and at all times, without exception. The Jews try to persuade us otherwise, but the facts are there, and very often confirmed by Jewish tradition and the Jewish books themselves.

INTERESTING DOCUMENT ON THE CONVERSION OF CHIEF RABBI NEOFIT

This great rabbi converted to Christianity and became a monk. In 1803, he published "*Christian Blood in the Israelite Rites of the Modern Synagogue*" in Moldavian. The book was translated into Greek in 1833. This is what it says on page 33:

"*This terrible secret is not known to all Jews, but only to the Chakams* (doctors in Israel) *and rabbis who bear the title of* "curators of the mystery of blood".

The fathers communicate it verbally to the fathers of the family, who in turn entrust the secret to whichever of their sons they deem most trustworthy, while adding dreadful threats against anyone who betrays the secret".

The converted rabbi then relates:

"*When I was thirteen years old, my father took me aside in a dark room and, after representing to me hatred against Christians as something pleasing to Jehovah, he told me that our God had ordered us to spill Christian blood and to reserve it for ritual use. My son,* " he said, *kissing me, "now that you have this secret, you have become my closest confidant, truly another me! Then he placed a crown on my head and explained the mystery of the blood revealed to the Hebrews by Jehovah. From now on, I would be the depositary of the most important secret of the Israelite religion. Terrible imprecations and threats were uttered against me if I ever revealed this secret to my mother, my brothers, my sisters or my future wife. I must reveal it only to the one of my sons who is best able to keep it. In this way, the secret would pass from father to son through the generations until the centuries to come".*

TWO INTERESTING QUOTES FROM ZINOVIEFF, A JEW

The first was published in *"The Gazette"*, a Bolshevik newspaper, and the second in *"The Commune of the North"* in Petrograd on 18 September 1918: *"We will make our hearts cruel, hard, merciless, so that clemency will not penetrate them and they will not tremble before an ocean of enemy blood. We will release the sluices of this bloody tide. Without pity, without mercy, we will kill our enemies by the thousands. We will drown them in their own blood. We will take all of the Russian population: 90 million are under the power of the Soviets; the rest we will exterminate.*

Note: The *"Black Book of Communism"* puts the number of victims of Russian communism at 80 million.

JEWISH GOLD, MASTER OF THE WORLD

The Jews control all the media: publishing, press, radio, television... They are therefore pseudo-democratic propaganda tools, because this is the only system that ensures their hegemony, which no traditional system would grant them.

So they control the masses and the politicians who are part of them (true elite would accept the diktat of the ballot paper or take part in competitions as stupid as the agrégation or ENA). They have complete control over the cinema: propaganda, violence, sex, distortion of all the fundamental values that are the essence of Man.

They control fashion: homosexuals are encouraged to pervert any sense of aesthetics, even at the most basic level of dress. Young people today are blue-jeaned, potato-like and colourful. Women are becoming dressier and more psychological.

The Jews control gold and its manipulation, which determines the price and value of national currencies. They include Rothschild, Bleichroeder, Kuhn, Loeb & Cie, Japhet, Seligmann, Lazard and others. During this century, the Sassoons controlled opium throughout the world. Today, Jewish high finance controls drugs.

➢ Alfred Mond (*Lord Melchett*) controls the nickel.
➢ Louis-Louis Dreyfus controls wheat.

The Jews control the three proletarian internationals founded by them. The Jews control the secret societies: Freemasonry, Bilderberger, CFR, Trilateral, in which all politicians are enslaved, most of them members. The Jews control the UN just as they controlled the League of Nations (see document at the end of the book). The Jews exert tremendous influence, directly or indirectly, on the governments of Western nations. (direct: England: Hore-Belisha, Sassoon, etc. France: Léon Blum, Jean Zay, Georges Mandel-Rothschild, Pierre Mendès-France, Michel Debré, Laurent Fabius, etc.).

➢ United States: Morgenthau, Perkins, Baruch, Colonel House, etc. In 1999, ten of the advisers to the President of the United States were Jewish.
➢ Belgium: Vandervelde, Hymans, etc.
➢ Russia: Kaganovitch and practically all those who made and administered the revolution, with its gulags and executions.

Indirect influence is ideological and financial.

The "*Jewish Encyclopedia*", written by a committee of Jews, gives us glaring details of the economic life of this century and their power. From the beginning of the industrial era, national loans and the loans of major companies, such as the railways, were financed by Jews. Since the beginning of the 19th century, they have dominated international finance.

We also learn here that the Sterns and Goldsmids financed Portugal almost exclusively. Baron Hirsh financed the railways in Turkey. The Rothschilds financed the railways in France. Strousberg financed the Romanian railways. Poliakov, Speyer & Cie financed the Russian railways. Kuhn Loeb & Cie, not forgetting a large part of the American railway network.

Perhaps the greatest contemporary enterprise financed by the Jews, says the Encyclopaedia, was the great Nile dam, financed by Sir Ernest Cassel.

As early as 1902, the Jews admitted that their tribe controlled the preponderance of the international market in the major countries. *"The activity of the Jews on the international market is directly linked to their work as brokers in foreign securities and to the worldwide movement of precious metals, which are for the most part in their hands"*.

Again in the Encyclopaedia: The Rothschilds control mercury, Barnato Frères and Werner, Bett & Cie control diamonds (after this period, we know that Oppenheimer controlled diamonds in South Africa).

Lewisohn and Guggenheim control copper and to a significant extent the silver market. The Graustein and Dreyfus interests also control the and paper market.

Here is how we can measure the power of a single Jewish financier, again taken from the Jewish Encyclopaedia: it is the example of Jacob-H. Schiff, who financed Lenin and Trotsky in 1917. Under Schiff's leadership, his firm financially rebuilt the Union Pacific Railroad around 1897. In 1901, he launched a battle against the Compagnie du Grand-Nord for ownership of the Northern Pacific Railway. This caused a panic on the Stock Exchange (9 May 1901) in which the firm of Loeb, Kuhn & Cie held the market at its mercy. Schiff's moderation and wisdom on this occasion prevented disaster and ensured that his firm became the most influential in the financial world of railways. It controlled more than 22000 miles of railway and $1,321,000,000 of railroad stock. It financed large issues of the Union Pacific, the Pennsylvania Railroad, the Baltimore & Ohio, the Norfolk & Western, the Western Union Telegraph and many others. It financed and partially underwrote Japan's three major war loans in 1904 and 1905.

All the capital of Canada's banks combined, representing the savings of millions of Canadians, was less than half the fortune of this Jewish bank, which represented the fortune of five people.

While the Jewish agitators demand the destruction of the national banks that hold the savings of Canadians, they never mention destroying the monstrous international banks that financed revolutions and communism.

The Encyclopédie juive also tells us that the house of Sasoon, the Rothschilds of the Orient, has a monopoly on the opium market throughout the world, and in Asia controls vast monopolies of textiles, spinning mills, dyeing factories, silk, cotton, etc., not to mention powerful banking, insurance, brokerage and trading organisations. Branches are located in Calcutta, Shanghai, Canton, Hong Kong, Yokohama, Nagasaki, Baghdad, etc.

According to the Encyclopédie juive, the Jewish Pereire family, from France, has branches in Spain and powerful interests in many countries. Here are just a few of the companies they founded, monopolise or hold stakes in: Crédit Foncier de France, Société Générale du Crédit Mobilier, Chemin de Fer du Midi, Chemin de Fer du Nord de l'Espagne, Gaz de Paris, Omnibus de Paris, Compagnie Générale Transatlantique, Éclairage de Paris, Assurances Union and Assurances Phénix d'Espagne, Chantiers navals de Saint-Nazaire, Crédit Mobilier d'Espagne, Banque de Tunis, Banque Transatlantique, Chemin de fer Paris-Argenteuil-Auteuil, Cie des Quais de Marseille, Gaz de Madrid, Banque

Ottomane Impériale, railway companies in Switzerland, Russia, Austria, Portugal, etc.

The Bischoffsheim family of Paris and Brussels owns: Société Générale, Banque des Pays Bas, Crédit Foncier colonial, Société du Prince Impérial, Banque Franco-Égyptienne, Union du Crédit (Brussels), Comptoir des prêts sur marchandises (Antwerp), Union du Crédit (Liège), Banque Nationale, etc.

The Strauss family of New York controlled several banks and financial institutions, R.H. Macy's shops, pottery and glassware (Source: Encyclopédie Juive). Seligman Brothers of New York, financial agent of the Secretary of State for the United States Navy since 1876, were involved in all American government loans. They headed the syndicate that distributed the Panama Canal bonds in America.

In 1879, the Rothschilds and Jesse Seligman alone absorbed the US government's loan of $150,000,000. They largely managed the finances of the American Civil War between North and South. In 1877, Judge Hilton refused to admit Seligman and his family on racial grounds to his Grand Union Hotel in Saratoga. It is believed that this incident caused the ruin of A.T. Stewart's store, then run by Hilton, which later became the property of John Wanamaker of Philadelphia. (Source: Encyclopédie juive)

This is true of every country, whether it's the fabulously wealthy Rothschilds, who are capable of destroying any British government that dares to defy them, or wealthy international bankers such as :

Camondo	Fould	Montagu	Stern
Bleichroede	Warschauer	Mendelssohn	Gunzbourg
Japhet	Lazard	etc.	

Compared to them, the Fords, the Mellons and the Carnegies are financial dwarfs. The Jewish press only tells us about the Christian financiers, but hides with the greatest care the names and the unheard-of power of these international blackmailers. Their power is out of all proportion to the Jewish population and Jewish production.

The tumble of a few small Jews in the French financial disaster of Panama, among other famous swindles, highlights the size of the biggest sharks:

- The Insull brothers (55 million)
- Staviski (450 million)
- Lévy (120 million)

The Jews are therefore the undisputed masters of world finance.[33] This enables them to consolidate their control over commodity prices, international organisations of all kinds, world propaganda and governments. It is immoral for one "race"[34] to hold so much power over all the ethnic groups on earth. Those days are gone. Either this colossal octopus will be wiped out or humanity will disappear with it. It feeds on all working peoples. The local controls of Jewry (alcohol, furs, meat, slaughterhouses, furniture, clothing, restaurants, gold, nickel, paper, etc.) represent only a tiny part of its power. The greatest power is the one that the masses do not see, but whose sad effectiveness bursts before our eyes every day, like the two world wars for which they are entirely responsible. (Treaty of Versailles, negotiated by the Warburg brothers who simultaneously

---

[33] I am planning a book on the Jewish financier Soros for 1999: "*An example of the effects of circumcision on the 8th day: the Jewish financier Soros*".

[34] For want of a better word. The word "sect" would be more appropriate. We know that the Jews are neither a race nor an ethnic group and that their particularity (financial here) comes exclusively from circumcision on the 8th day.

financed the belligerents and the Bolshevik revolution , declaration of war on Hitler in 1933 by American Jewry).

THE TSAR IN THE ROTHSCHILD CASTLE

The *Canadian Jewish Chronicle* of 7 September 1935 reported: "*The palatial residence of the Rothschilds has always been in such a state of Solomonic splendour that no Caliph could have sustained it without reducing his kingdom to poverty. In fact, at least half of the world's treasures are preserved in the Rothschild vaults. Rothschild wields his power over agencies inaccessible to other mortals. Kings fear him and the fortress of Sebastopol would never have fallen had he sided with Russia. This man controls the destiny of the nations: he is the Lord of Israel.*

"TAG

The New York Jewish newspaper of 9 April 1936 declared: "*The Jews of America, because of their numbers, their interests and their ability, constitute a great political force. It is theirs by right. They will use it as they see fit. What will you do about it?*"

"JEWS MUST LIVE

In his book *The Jews Must Live*, the Jew Samuel Roth does not hesitate to call the Jews a "race of vultures" that persecutes all other nations. The case of Samuel Roth is edifying. In 1934, this New York Jew, author and bookseller had a 320-page book illustrated by John Conrad published by Golden Hind Press. He had already published two books defending Jews against anti-Semites: "*Europe*" (Liveright, 1919) and "*Now and for Ever*" (Macbride, 1925). By studying the reasons why Jews had always and everywhere been unpopular, by examining them and suffering their blows, Roth changed his opinion 180° and sided entirely with the anti-Semites. As soon as his book appeared, the Jews attacked him ferociously and tried to pass him off as crazy. They did not succeed. Here are some important extracts from his book:

"Disraeli coined the phrase that the people get the Jews they deserve. It could also be said that the Jews have the enemies they deserve.

The history of the Jews has been tragic, tragic for the Jews themselves but no less tragic for the peoples who have suffered.

Our main vice today, as in the past, is parasitism.

We are a people of vultures living off the labour and good nature of the rest of the world. But despite our faults we would not have done so much harm to the world were it not for the genius for evil that drives our leaders. Our parasitism could have a good use, considered like that of certain parasitic germs essential to the regular flow of blood in the arteries. Israel's shame stems not from the fact that we are bankers and the world's dressers, but from the tremendous hypocrisy and cruelty imposed on us by our leaders and by us on the rest of the world.

The first of all Jewish laws is that Jews must live. It makes no difference how, for what purpose or by what means. They must live, and when they cannot conquer by force of arms, they return to their old methods of conquest by cheating, lying and seduction (pimping).[35]

It must therefore be reaffirmed that anti-Semitism is simply an elementary instinct of humanity. It is an important instinct by which a race seeks to defend itself against total destruction.[36] *Anti-Semitism is not, as the Jews would have us believe, an active prejudice.*

---

[35] This is a very harsh word, because in English *'a pimp'* is a mackerel.

[36] This is exactly the case for the whole of humanity in the year 2000, where we are now.

It's purely and simply the instinct for self-preservation that every human being is born with, like the instinct that makes you blink if something happens to your eye.

Anti-Semitism is just as automatic, just as sure an instinct. From time immemorial, Jews have been admitted freely and kindly, almost with pleasure, by the nations to which they have wished to be admitted. Never have Jews had to petition to enter a country the first time. You only have to study the history of Jewish penetration in Europe and America to be perfectly convinced of this. Everywhere, they were welcomed, helped to settle and to take part in community affairs. But soon the country's activities were closed to them because of their unjust practices. Then they were ignominiously expelled from the country. There is no exception in history. There is not a single case where the Jews have not fully deserved the bitter fruits of their persecutors' fury. We come to the nations pretending to want to escape persecution, we the deadliest persecutors in the annals of evil.

Judaism is like a moral venereal disease. The results for peoples who allow themselves to be infected by it are invariably treacherous and unhealthy. If you doubt this, just take a look at any European people in Jewish hands. If you want to be more convinced, take a look at what is happening in America today.

In Ustcha, in Austrian Poland, where I was born, the Jew Reb Sholom sent his wife to church every Sunday and on Christmas Day with the key to the church, and if the interest was not paid, she refused to open the iron door to the faithful. From my earliest childhood, I learned that the Jew's only reason for doing business was to get the most out of the Goy. When the Goyim had been plucked, then business was good. The greater the harm done to a Goy in a transaction, the deeper the pleasure seemed to the Jew I was listening to. The Jew's contempt for the Goyim was an integral part of Jewish psychology.

In the minds of the Jews, there was no question of their superiority over the Goyim. The matter was simple: they were Jews and the Goyim were only Goyim. Their superiority lay in the legal possession of things, and that was where it lay. What belonged to the Goyim was a temporary possession, which the stupid laws of the Goyim tried to make permanent. Since the beginning of time, hasn't God wanted all the good things on earth to belong to the Jews? It is the duty of the Jew to remember this at all times, and particularly in his dealings with the Goyim.

Jews do not convert others to their religion because they are particularly convinced that they will inherit all the riches of the earth and they want as few heirs as possible to share these riches.[37] We despise the Goy and hate his religion.

The Goy, according to the stories hummed in the ears of Jewish children, foolishly worships an ugly creature called Yoisel (Jesus), with dozens of other names too hideous to repeat. This Yoisel had once been a human being and a Jew. But one day he went mad and, in his pitiful insanity, announced that he was the Messiah himself (the rest of which can be read in the "Sepher Toldoth, Jeshou" or "Life of Jesus by the Jews" is too blasphemous to be reproduced). This extraordinary caricature of the founder of the Christian religion was one of the most incredible adventures of my life.

Since all the goods that the Jew sees have been created to enrich Israel, he must find a good way of wresting them from the coarse Goy who holds them. The Jew cannot overcome this dishonest feeling. It is a real instinct. This is how young Isaac was brought up, and what a little Jew has learned, he never forgets. To find out how a Jewish child is brought up, you have to live in a Jewish home.

---

[37] Note that all Jews, whether they follow their religion or not, still apply these religious commandments: circumcision on the 8th day, and taking as much interest as possible from the Goy by practising usury (which is forbidden between Jews). What's more, their religion has not changed one iota and is by definition fundamentalist. Whereas the Catholic religion has become grotesque through its modernist involution, which has practically drowned it in Marxism.

What is fundamental to the Jewish mentality is this: the preservation of Jewish culture and religion is above all a screen. What the Jew desires and hopes for through Jewish education is to cultivate in his child the living awareness that he is a Jew and that as such he must perpetuate the ancient war against the Goyim without ever assimilating. The Jew must always remember that he is a Jew and nothing else, and that his only allegiance is to the Jewish people. He can be a good American if it 'pays' to be one. He can even be a good Chinese. On the other hand, no obligation contracted with a Goy can be considered valid if it goes against the interests of his fundamental identity. The young Jew first learns that he is a Jew. Then he learns that being a Jew makes him different from all the peoples of the world. The young Jew is given the strong impression that he must be a professional.[38]

Being obliged to work, to do manual labour to earn a living, would be the worst state he could fall into. It would be a shameful and humiliating situation. The Jew's disdain for manual work is second nature, an innate feeling. The Jew does not regard the liberal profession in the same way as other peoples. There is no traditional deference to the profession. They see it (law, medicine) as a gangster sees a new racket: how much can they get for less work, which does not prevent them from being highly competent because of their analytical and memory skills. What happens to the young Jews who are unable to enter the liberal professions? If they don't have the means to buy a newspaper kiosk, or enough business acumen?

---

[38] We can't say that this training has been applied much in the twentieth century. Circumcision on the 8th day was enough to produce a Soros who was still unknown in the 90s and who, at the dawn of the year 2000, was investing in and destabilising national economies as far afield as Burma, and planning with governments helped by the Rothschilds and the Murdochs, the free sale of drugs in every country.

They become petty thieves, bandits, strike-breakers, dice players, narcotics peddlers and smugglers, agents of the white slave trade, kidnappers and racketeers *in every peaceful community in America.*

Other races also have their mischief-makers, but they become so through the hard necessity of life: the Jew sees a career in it. Nothing that Jew does is essential to the welfare of America.[39] On the contrary, it can be said that everything he does is contrary to the best interests of the nation. He does not contribute even manpower to the general welfare, except for that which he into his sweatshops and into the traps he sets himself... In literature, he contributes only through obscenity, journalism that delves into intimate affairs, and even blackmail. This is part of our national tradition. We are still a nation of lazy busybodies. In business, the Jew has only one code, that of knowing how to create something out of nothing, to enrich himself by haggling over things he has not made.

America is full of businesses with Christian names that are actually owned and operated by Jews. The Jew knows better than anyone how to dispossess the poor and the middle classes.[40] So we see the Jew as businessman, promoter, lender, salesman par excellence, the author and chief instigator of a credit system by which usury on a national scale rises like a monster with millions of hands on millions of throats to strangle the honour and freedom of movement of a hard-working people.

---

[39] We will see in the second part that Goyim like Benjamin Franklin were perfectly aware of this: "If you give citizenship to the Jews, your children will curse you".

[40] In this Jewish world, the middle classes have practically disappeared thanks to Jewish speculation and the fact that politicians of all parties, being bought off, have done nothing to prevent it, on the contrary. Treaties such as Maastricht, Amsterdam or Nice will finish the job of enslaving the entire world's Goyim to the Jews. All this in the total unconsciousness of the Goyim who have been radically zombified by the Jews, their secularism, their chemification, their Marxism, their Freudism, their pornography and their systemic laxity.

When the talented Jewish poet Henri Heine said "Judaism is not a religion but a misfortune", he may have been thinking only of his personal misfortune, but today we have to calculate the misfortune for the whole world.

No religion in the world offers such a contradictory, mischievous and unreasonable spectacle as the recitation of the Kol Nidre prayer in the synagogues on the evening of Yom Kippur. Whatever business he has undertaken with his neighbour, whether material or moral, the Jew makes it clear to God in advance that it will be on one explicit condition: the performance of it must be favourable to God, otherwise the Jew will consider it null and void, of no effect, entirely useless, as if it had never been mentioned, as if nothing about it had been negotiated. The specious argument that this prayer is exclusively religious in nature is obviously dishonest.

If the author had wanted to understand only obligations towards God, he would not have written

"Obligations and commitments of all kinds". *There is no more sense or sincerity in the other explanations. By reciting the Kol Nidre, the Jew denies responsibility for the crime even before committing it. Can there be any doubt about the terrible and evil influence this can have on his character as a citizen and as a human being?*

We live in a radically Jewish civilisation. The stamp of the Jewish spirit and temperament has deeply permeated our institutions. If Jews are ever expelled from America,[41] it will be because of the wicked practices of Jewish doctors and lawyers.

---

[41] They are unlikely to be, because financiers, lawyers and doctors have taken over all the power.

The author of these lines was optimistic a few decades ago. Today, racist so-called anti-racist laws forbid people from even uttering the word "Jew" (Fabius-Gayssot law).

The Jew is a nomad with a weakness for real estate. I mean real estate independently of land as soil to cultivate and bring to fruition. The Jew knows only one use for the possession of land, or of anything else: speculation. Civilised peoples attach a sort of sacred feeling to the possession of land, a 'sanctity' that the Jew will violate whenever he can. Herzl [the founder of Zionism] was certainly the first honest Jew for 2000 years. A Jew with no itch for money or real estate.

The presence of Jews in the theatre (and now the cinema, where they own everything) is an obstacle to its spiritual development. The history of the theatre and the arts proves that they were only able to flourish when the Jews were not involved. From the moment the Jew entered the theatre, a kind of impotence fell over the stage. In America, the Jew reigns over the theatre. For him, the theatre means only two things: an easy way to make money and a market for pretty women. The brothel gets its recruits from the impresario, and in 19 cases out of 20, the impresario is a Jew. The surplus of these charming creatures is shipped, along with our surplus cotton, potatoes and copper, to Japan, China, Panama, South America and all the ports in the dark regions of the Pacific. Cinema in Jewish hands has become a vulgar and obscene spectacle (the film industry is spreading violence and pornography on a massive scale at the end of the twentieth century, acting as an agent for the decomposition of all fundamental human values).

The Jew is physically unclean and makes a mess of any place he inhabits,[42] even temporarily. I say this without malice, because it is an observation from my own life among my fellow human beings. In the struggle for civilisation, there is always a struggle between the world and Judas: the world makes efforts to rise, but Judas pulls it down."

AN UNBRIDGEABLE CHASM

---

[42] It is remarkable that without bathrooms (rich Jews sometimes have five or ten in their homes), the Jew is not clean. This is easy to see.

In his book "*Vous les Goyim*" published in 1924, Maurice Samuels, a Jew and Zionist leader, wrote:

"*Between Goyim and Jews there is an unbridgeable chasm. Your life is one thing, ours is another. This first difference is radically irreconcilable: there is a gulf that separates. Wherever the Jew is, he is a problem. They are a source of misfortune for themselves and for those around them.*

Everywhere, Jews are, to the highest degree, foreigners. They are indisputably a foreign spirit in your academies. They do not accept your rules of right and wrong because they do not understand them. As far as the Jewish way of life is concerned, the Goyim have no morals. The two conceptions of life are essentially alien to each other: they are enemies. Our Jewishness is not a credo, it is a totality. A Jew is a Jew in all things. We cannot conceive of a duality, religion and life, the sacred and the profane. I could say: "We and God grew up together. In the heart of every pious Jew, God is a Jew. Only Jews can understand the universality of God in this way. To my knowledge, I know of no country with a history that has not been anti-Semitic at one time or another.

You might say: "Let's exist side by side and tolerate each other". But the two groups are not only different, they are opposed by a deadly enmity. In your world, a man must be loyal to his country, his province, his town. For the Jew, loyalty is incomprehensible.

We Jews don't attach much importance to the afterlife. We thank God for having made us different from you. The instinct of the Jew is to distrust the Goy. The instinct of the Goy is to distrust the Jew. Placed side by side with us, you are boasts, cowards, vulgar crowds. We are not among you of our own free will, but because of your actions. We are intruders among you because we are what we are, and we have more reason to hate you than you have to hate us. Liberal Jews, radical Jews, modernist Jews, agnostic Jews, are becoming the dominant element in Jewry. We have produced countless revolutionaries, the banner-bearers of the world's "Liberation" armies.

Repudiating the Jewish religion does nothing to change a Jew. We Jews, the destroyers, will always remain the destroyers. Nothing you do will satisfy our needs, our demands. We will always destroy because we want a world of our own.

THE JEWS ARE THE MOST RACIST OF ALL PEOPLES

The fact that they have persisted for eighty generations in maintaining their racial and spiritual identity is testament to a constant discipline of astonishing rigour and strength.

THE SOCIETY OF NATIONS, A JEWISH ORGANISATION

The Canadian government committed Canada to the arms race by saying that the country was obliged to do so because it had subscribed to the idea of *"collective security"* by joining the League of Nations. *"Collective security"* means *"collective war"* when the League of Nations deems that its interests so require. The world came to the brink of collective war at the time of the Italo-Ethiopian affair. If the war did not happen, it was because the British were not yet armed enough, as some statesmen said at the time.

What is the SDN? Where did it come from? What are its interests? Let the Jews say it for themselves.

DR KLEE, JEWISH

This Jewish lawyer from New York spoke publicly on this subject on 19 January 1936:

"The League of Nations was in no way the work of President Wilson. It is an essentially Jewish creation of which Jews can be proud. The idea goes back to the Sages of Israel. It is a pure product of Jewish culture".
(see previous pages, what a Jewish banker from New York had to say about the role of the League of Nations).

JESSE E. SAMPTER, JEWISH

In "*Guide to Zionism*", this Jew declares: "*The League of Nations is an old Jewish ideal*".

MAX NORDAU, JEWISH

This Zionist leader, quoted by the Jew Litman Rosenthal in his book "When prophets speak", had this to say about the League of Nations: "*Soon perhaps a sort of World Congress will have to be convened*". These words were spoken in 1903. At the same time Nordau said: "*Let me take you up the ladder that goes higher and higher: Herzl, the Zionist Congress, the English offer of Uganda, the coming world war, the Peace Conference where, with England's help, a free and Jewish Palestine will be created.*"

NAHUM SOKOLOV, JEWISH

This Zionist leader declared in Carlsbad on 22 August 1922: "*The League of Nations is a Jewish idea and Jerusalem will one day become the capital of world peace. What we Jews have achieved after a 25-year struggle, we owe to the genius of our immortal leader, Theodor Herzl.*"

LUCIEN WOLF, JEWISH

In his report to the American Jewish Congress on his work as Jewish plenipotentiary to the Peace Conference: "*If the League of Nations were to collapse, the whole edifice so laboriously constructed by the Jewish delegations from England and America in 1919 would crumble*".

LENNHORR, JEWISH

In the "*Wiener Freimaurer Zeitung*" No 6, 1927, this Jew declared: "*We are right to compare Freemasonry (a Jewish instrument) with the League of Nations. The League of Nations was born of Masonic ideas*".

"Judische Rundschau

This Jewish newspaper, in its No 83 published in 1921, declared: "*The exact seat of the League of Nations is neither Geneva nor The Hague. Ascher Ginsberg dreamed of a temple on Mount Zion where the representatives of all the nations would go to visit a temple of peace; eternal peace will only be a real fact when all the peoples of the earth have gone to this temple*".

Sir Max Waechter, Jewish

Speaking at the London Institute in 1909, he said: "*All the States will have to get together and draw up the Constitution of a federation of the countries of Europe on the basis of a single tariff, a single currency, a single language and a single frontier*".

Comment by the author: In 1999 we are already there, with the ruin of Europe and monstrous unemployment. They'll have trouble with "*one language*". What characterises the Jewish ideal is that it's either crazy or completely insane: everything that's currently happening in Europe is converging towards ruin and nothingness. A Europe of course, but not a Jewish Europe of banks and technocrats manipulated by a finance that will be accountable to no one and will no longer allow any national initiative. A Europe of Nations, retaining all its national characteristics, and not a people of cowherds in blue jeans, a shapeless mass of high finance.

Lenin, Jewish

In 1915 he wrote in "*Social Democrat*" No. 40, a Russian Jewish newspaper: "*The United States of the world, and not only of Europe, will be realised by Communism, which will bring about the disappearance of all States, even those which are purely democratic*".

Emil Ludwig, Jewish

In his book "*Genius and Character*", the Jewish writer declared: "*When the United States of Europe becomes a reality, Woodrow Wilson will be named its founder by the people (because he brought about the League of Nations)*".[43]

AT THE GRAND INTERNATIONAL MASONIC CONVENT

At this meeting, which took place on 28, 29 and 30 June 1917, even before anyone was officially thinking about the League of Nations, the Jews and Masons proposed the following: "We must build the happy city of tomorrow. It is to this truly Masonic work that we have been invited. What have we seen? This war has turned into a formidable quarrel between organised democracies and despotic military powers.

In this storm, the age-old power of the tsars of Greater Russia has already sunk. Other governments will also be swept away by the winds of freedom. It is therefore essential to create a supra-national authority. Freemasonry, the worker for peace, proposes to study this new organisation: the League of Nations".

AT THE GRAND ORIENT CONVENT

According to the official minutes published in 1932, page 3: "*Wasn't it within the Lodges that the spark ignited that led to the creation of the League of Nations, the International Labour Office and all the international bodies that make up the laborious but fertile outline of the United States of Europe and perhaps of the world*[44]

---

[43] It is interesting to note that this refined Jew did not survive the world that his fellow Jews were preparing for him, and that he expressed himself by committing suicide.

[44] In 1999, just look at the world's misery, the moral and biological collapse and the ecological damage these fine projects have caused! But we carry on: Jewish madness is suicidal.

At the American Jewish Committee Congress

According to the *Jewish Communal Register* of 1918 (Source: *Jewish Guardian* of 6 February 1920), at the 1909 Congress, the American Jewish Committee successfully opposed the requiring census questions to inquire into the race of the inhabitants of the United States.

The Peace Conference

This conference, at which the *Treaty of Versailles* (1919) was drawn up, was a triumph for Jewish rights thanks to the influential Anglo-Jewish delegation. The *Treaty of Berlin* (1818) was acclaimed for more than forty years as the Charter for the emancipation of the Jews in Eastern Europe, but its greatness is now cast into shadow by the splendid work of the recent Conference in favour of Jewish minorities in the States of the new Europe. The solemn meeting of the Nations in Paris offered a golden opportunity to resolve the old Jewish question in the East. The Jewish community was quick to grasp the magnitude of the opportunity before it and seized it with both hands. When you consider that these hands were those of Lucien Wolf, who spent almost an entire year pulling the strings in Paris, you will understand that the work of the Anglo-Jewish delegation to the Peace Conference was crowned with complete and resounding success.

Freemasonry, a Jewish Instrument

If a Jew is refused access anywhere, the cries of anti-Semitism are unleashed. On the other hand, in the name of anti-racism, the B'nai B'rith Masonic Lodge is open exclusively to Jews. It is the Masonic lodge with the largest membership. (5 to 600,000 in 1999).

The Jews present Masonry as an apolitical charitable institution. This soothing statement is all the more absurd in that many prominent Jews have made no secret of the fact that it is an organisation that they manipulate for purposes that they make no secret of either. As for their actions, anyone can see that they are political, and simplest and most spectacular demonstration of this was the public declaration by Masonry demanding that all parties refuse the slightest alliance with the Front National, even though this party is the only one presenting a programme against general decomposition and for the restoration of elementary values.

If Jewry controls all national currencies by controlling gold, if it controls the price of raw materials and foodstuffs through its major international trade bodies, if it controls world opinion through publishing, the press and the cinema, if it controls the proletariat through the socialist internationals, it also controls the crowd of politicians and businessmen of all countries through Masonry. It controls the industrial food supply, which degenerates the organism through the massive chemisation of products. The Popes have always called Freemasonry "*the synagogue of Satan*". It is no coincidence that the word "synagogue" is used in this way. The fundamental aim of Freemasonry is to de-Christianise and Judaize.

It imposes secular schools, which are in fact atheist,[15] wherever its members come to power. It preaches to its followers the cult of the "Great Architect of the Universe", an impersonal divinity fashioned by the rabbis, and ignores the Christian God of the Holy Trinity. The avowed aim of Freemasonry is "**the reconstruction of Solomon's Temple**", i.e. the Judaic world temple on the ruins of all other religions. Freemasonry helped the Jews to take Palestine

---

[45] It's absolutely clear that if a child, under the pretext of religious freedom, receives no moral or religious training (there is no morality without religion), he or she will automatically become a thug, a drug addict, an unemployed person, a disco music fan, and so on. You only have to open your eyes for ¼ of a second to see this. Look at the herds of cowboys in blue jeans leaving school, listening to pathogenic music, lacking ideals and ending up on drugs or committing suicide. As for the illiterate, their numbers increase every year, as does unemployment, which is a corollary of socialism in all its forms.

from the Arabs. It is forcing the English government to use force of arms to secure Jewish power there; it has undertaken to force England to make it an autonomous dominion for the Jews. It will soon help to rebuild Solomon's Temple on the debris of the New Testament, if it can. She almost succeeded in 1999.

BENJAMIN DISRAELI, JEWISH

In his novel "*The Life of Sir George Bentinck*", Benjamin Disraeli, the empire-builder who was Prime Minister to Queen Victoria (she owed her title of Empress of India to him), confirms: "*At the head of all these secret societies which form provisional governments are Jews*".

"THE ISRAELITE TRUTH

This Jewish newspaper published an interesting view of Freemasonry in 1861 (Volume V, page 74): "*The spirit of Freemasonry is the spirit of Judaism in its most fundamental beliefs. These are its ideas, its language, almost its organisation. The hope that enlightens and strengthens Freemasonry is the hope that enlightens and strengthens Israel. Its crowning glory will be this marvellous house of prayer for all peoples, of which Jerusalem will be the centre and the triumphant symbol*".

BERNARD SHILLMANN, JEWISH

In "*Hebraic influences on masonic symbols*", published in 1929, and quoted by "*The Masonic News*" of London, Bernard Shillmann says the following: "*Although I have by no means dealt with the Hebraic influences on the whole symbolism of Freemasonry, I hope to have sufficiently proved that Freemasonry as a symbolism, rests entirely on a formation which is essentially Jewish*".

BERNARD LAZARE, JEWISH

In "*L'antisémitisme et ses causes*", page 340, he states: "*The Martinezist lodges* [lodges founded by the Portuguese Jew Martinez de Pasqually] *were mystical, while the other orders of Freemasonry were rather rationalist, which may allow us to say that the secret societies presented the two sides of the Jewish spirit: practical rationalism and pantheism. These tendencies led to the same result: the weakening of Catholicism*".

LUDWIG BLAU, JEWISH

This rabbi, a doctor of philosophy and professor at the Talmudic College in Budapest (Hungary), declared: "*Jewish Gnosticism preceded Christianity. It is a fact worthy of note that the heads of the Gnostic schools and the founders of Gnostic systems* (from which Freemasonry originated) *are referred to as Jews by the Fathers of the Church*".

ISAAC WISE, JEWISH

This rabbi declared, in "*The Israelite of America*" of August 3, 1866: "*Freemasonry is a Jewish institution whose history, degrees, charges, watchwords and explanations are Jewish from beginning to end*".

BERNARD LAZARE, JEWISH

"*It is certain that there were Jews at the cradle of Freemasonry. Certain rites prove that they were cabalist Jews*".

"THE JEWISH HISTORICAL SOCIETY

According to this Jewish historical society (Source: *Transactions* of Vol 2, page 156): "*The crest of the Grand Lodge of England is composed entirely of Jewish symbols*".

"THE FREE MASON GUIDE

In this work, published in New York in 1901, we learn that: "*Freemasons are erecting a building in which the God of Israel will live forever*".

"ENCYCLOPEDIA OF FREEMASONRY

In this work, published in Philadelphia in 1908, we learn that: "*Each lodge is, and must be, a symbol of the Jewish temple; each master in his chair, a representative of the Jewish king; each Freemason, a representative of the Jewish worker*".

RUDOLPH KLEIN, JEWISH

Writing in "*Latomia*", a Masonic publication, on 7 August 1928, Rudolph Klein declared: "*Our rite is Jewish from beginning to end: the public should conclude from this that we have direct links with Jewry*".

REV. S. MAC GOWAN

In "*The Free-Mason*" of London, published on 2 April 1930, this clergyman declared: "*Freemasonry is founded on the ancient law of Israel. Israel gave birth to the moral beauty that forms the basis of Freemasonry*".

"SYMBOLISM

Extract from this Masonic journal (Paris, July 1928): "*The most important task of the Freemason is to glorify the Jewish race. You can count on the Jewish race to dissolve all frontiers.*

"THE TEXT BOOK OF FREE-MASONRY

In this lexicon published in London, we find the following definition on page 7: "*The initiate of the Master's rite is called a humble representative of King Solomon*".

"ALPINA

The magazine, which is the official organ of Swiss Freemasonry, states: *"Go to the Galerie des Glaces in Versailles, where you can read the immortal Declaration of the Rights of Man* (Treaty of Versailles). *It is our work: Masonic symbols decorate the header of the document.*

"THE ANDERSON CONSTITUTIONS

In the founding text of modern Freemasonry, *"That which was lost. A treatise of Free-Masonry and the English mystery"* by James Anderson in 1723, on page 5, we find the following explanation: *"It is easy now but also unfair to criticise the founders for having introduced Judaic traditions into Freemasonry. They had taken a great step in suppressing the New Testament for the advantage of harmony between Christians and Jews."*

SAMUEL UNTERMEYER, JEW AND FREEMASON

At a meeting reported in *The Jewish Chronicle* on 14 December 1934, Samuel Untermeyer had the following resolution approved: *"The Jewish boycott of Germany must continue until the German government has restored to the Lodges the status and property from which they have been deprived."*

FINDEL, JEW AND FREEMASON

Quote from the book *"Die Juden als Freimaurer"* (The Jew as Freemason), written by the Jew and Freemason Findel: *"It is less a struggle for the interests of humanity than a struggle for the interests and domination of Judaism. And in this struggle, Judaism reveals itself as the dominant power to which Freemasonry must submit. This should come as no surprise, for in a hidden and carefully disguised way Judaism is already the dominant power in many of the great lodges of Europe.*

As far as Germany is concerned, we must not forget that Judaism is master of the financial and commercial markets, master of the press at and master of the political and Masonic faith, and that millions of Germans are financially its debtors".

"THE JEWISH TRIBUNE

Journal published in New York. From the October 28, 1927 issue, Vol. 97, No. 18: "*Freemasonry is based on Judaism. Eliminate Jewish teachings from Masonic ritual and what is left?*"

"THE JEWISH ENCYCLOPAEDIA

1903 edition, Vol. 5, page 503: "*The technical language, symbolism and rites of Freemasonry are full of Jewish ideas and terms... In the Scottish Rite, the dates of official documents are designated according to the calendar and months of the Jewish era and the ancient Hebrew alphabet is used. The influence of the Jewish Sanhedrin is greater than ever in Freemasonry today*". (Reprinted in O. B Good, M. A. "*The Hidden* Hand *of Judah*", 1936.

"B'NAI B'RITH MAGAZINE

Quoting the rabbi and mason Magnin (Vol. 43, page 8): "*The B'nai B'rith are no more than a stopgap. Wherever masonry can safely admit that it is Jewish in nature and purpose, the ordinary Lodges will suffice.*

Note: the B'nai B'rith, it should be remembered, are Lodges forbidden to Goyim and therefore only Jews can be admitted. In 1874, Albert Pike (for the Scottish Rite) signed an alliance with Armand Lévy (for the B'nai B'rith), and by this secret treaty, the B'nai B'rith committed themselves to contributing 10% of their income to universal Freemasonry.

WHY CAN'T JEWS EVER BE THE NATIONALS OF ANY COUNTRY?

UNLIMITED PROOF OF THIS

DR CHAÏM WEIZMAN, JEWISH

In his pamphlet "*Great Britain, Palestine and Jews*", the great Zionist leader declared: "*We are Jews and nothing else: a nation among nations*".

LUDWIG LEWINSOHN, JEWISH

In his book *Israel*, published in 1926, this Jew declared: "*The Jew remains a Jew. Assimilation is impossible because the Jew cannot change his national character. Whatever he does, he is a Jew and remains a Jew. The majority discovered this fact as it was bound to discover it sooner or later. Jews and non-Jews alike have realised that there is no way out. Both believed in a way out: there is none, none.*

"ISRAEL MESSENGER

In the 7 February 1930 edition of this Shanghai Jewish newspaper: "*Judaism and Jewish nationalism walk hand in hand. The Jews have always been a nation, even when driven and dispersed from their ancestral homeland. The Jewish race is a pure race.*[46]

---

[46] Let's remember once again that this is a myth in the most pejorative sense of the term: Jewish particularism comes exclusively from circumcision on the 8th day and nothing else. Moreover, apart from their often caricatured features and their speculative and amoral spirit, their somatic appearance varies according to the

Jewish tradition is an unbroken tradition. Jews have always considered themselves to be members of the Jewish nationality. This is where the invincibility and solidarity of the Jewish people in the Diaspora lie".

JESSE E. SEMPTER, JEWISH

"Judaism, the name of the national religion of the Jews, is derived from their national designation. An irreligious Jew remains a Jew".

"JEWISH ENCYCLOPEDIA

Dr Cyrus Adler, a Jew, says that Jews, whatever their religious allegiance, are all part of the Jewish race.

"NEW YORK TRIBUNE

Rabbi Wise declared on March 2, 1920: "*When the Jew pledges allegiance to another faith, he is lying.*

MAX NORDAU, JEWISH

In his book "*The Jewish People"*, Max Nordau declared: "*The Jews are a people, a single people. Herzl understood the failure of assimilation*".

"JEWISH CHRONICLE

Rabbi M. Schindler declared in the April 28, 1911 edition: "*For fifty years I have been a firm believer in the assimilation of the Jews.*

---

nations where they have been for a long time. There is therefore no Jewish ethnic group. As for races, we know that they do not exist. The Great White, Yellow, Red and Black Races are the result of hormonal adaptation to a fixed environment. The same applies to ethnic groups, entities that Jews cannot claim to be.

But the American melting pot will never produce the fusion of a single Jew."[47]

"ISRAELITE ARCHIVES

Extract from this Paris publication dated 24 March 1864: "...*this unique miracle in the life of the world of an entire people dispersed for 1800 years in all parts of the universe, without blending or mixing in any way with the populations in whose midst they* live...".

LÉVY-BING, JEWISH

"*The whole Jewish religion is founded on the national idea.*"

BERNARD LAZARE, JEWISH

Speaking to the Alliance of Russian Israelites on 7 March 1897: "What is the bond that unites us, we who come from the most diverse regions? It is our status as Jews: we therefore form a nation".

"PRO-ISRAEL

For this Paris Zionist Association: "*Israel is a nationality, like France. The true Jew does not assimilate.*"

MAX NORDAU, JEWISH

"We are not Germans, nor English, nor French. We are Jews! Your Christian mentality is not ours".

---

[47] This is certain if they do not radically abolish circumcision. Otherwise, they will be assimilated within one or two generations, because the recovery of the interstitial potential they lack is almost immediate.

On the other hand, in a thousand years all the Negroes will be white (in the USA).

NAHUM SOLOLOW, JEWISH

This Zionist leader declared in "*Zionism in the Bible*", pages 7 and 8: "*The fundamental thought of Moses is the future of the Jewish nation and the eternal possession of the promised land. No sophistry can suppress this fact... It is strange and sadly comical to see Jews who are partisans of monotheism claiming to be Germans, Hungarians, etc. being of the opinion of Moses, if not a blasphemy, then a mockery. It makes no difference whether the Jews call themselves a religion or a nation: the Jewish religion cannot be separated from Jewish nationalism.*

S. ROKHOMOVSKY, JEWISH

Declared in "*Le Peuple Juif*" of 21 April 1919: "*We have the right to be what we are: Jews. Today more than ever, we want to say it loud and clear. We are a nation.*

"THE ISRAELITE WORLD

In its issue of 15 May 1918, this Paris magazine quoted the Bulletins du Comité Central de la Ligue des Droits de l'Homme et du Citoyen, Comité des Questions Juives. According to this Committee: "*Judaism is a national and not a religious bond. It therefore claims the right of peoples to self-determination.*[48] *The national feeling of a Russian Jew or a Romanian Jew is neither Russian nor Romanian, but Jewish*".

"ISRAELITE ARCHIVES

---

[48] Let us note in passing that no nation will ever have the right of self-determination to choose a monarchical regime, for example. Nations only have the right to self-determination if they are incapable of taking responsibility for themselves. In that case they have the right to their "nationalism". The others, on the other hand, are dictatorially forced into democracy, i.e. Jewish dictatorship.

This Paris magazine published the following text in 1864: "*Israel is a nationality. The child of Israelite parents is a Jew. By birth, all Jewish duties are incumbent upon him. It is not through circumcision that we receive the quality of Jew. We are not Jews because we are circumcised, but we have our children circumcised because we are Jews. We acquire the Jewish character by our birth and we cannot lose that character or discard it. A Jew who renounces the Israelite religion, even if he is baptised, does not cease to be a Jew. All Jewish duties are incumbent upon him.*

"JEWISH CHRONICLE

Issue of 8 December 1911, page 38: "*Jewish patriotism is only a cloak with which it covers itself to please the English. Jews who pride themselves on being both patriotic Englishmen and good Jews are simply living lies.*"

WODISLAWSKI, JEWISH

Article published in the "*Jewish World*" on 1 January 1909: "*Let's take off the musk, let's play the Judas lion for a change. Let us tear off our false patriotism. A Jew can only recognise one homeland: Palestine*".

"SUNDAY CHRONICLE

This Manchester newspaper published the following text on 26 September 1915, page 4: "*Whether we are naturalised in this country or not, we are not British at all. We are nationals, Jews, by race and faith, and not Britons.*"

"JEWISH WORLD

Extract from his edition of 15 January 1919, page 6: "*Jewish nationalism is a Jewish question which must be governed by Jewish principles and must not be subordinated to the convenience or demands of any government, however important. As a people, Jews have not fought wars among themselves. English Jews against German Jews or French Jews against Austrian Jews; to divide Jewry into allegiances to international differences seems to us to be to abandon the whole principle of Jewish nationalism."*

THEODORE HERZL, JEWISH

The great Zionist leader declared in his book *The Jewish State*: "*The Jewish Question is no more social than it is religious. It is a national question that can only be resolved by making it a question of world politics.*"

LÉON. LÉVY, JEWISH

In his "*Memorial*" published by B'nai B'rith in 1900, the President of B'nai B'rith made the following comments: "*The Jewish Question cannot be resolved by tolerance. There are right-thinking people who pride themselves on displaying a spirit of tolerance towards the Jews. It is certain that the race and religion of the Jews are so fused that one does not know where one begins and the other ends.*

There is no greater mistake than to claim that the word Jew has a religious meaning and not that of a race. It is not true that Jews are Jews only because of their religion. An Eskimo or an American Indian could adopt the Jewish religion: that would not make them Jews. The dispersion of the Jews did not destroy in them the national idea of race. Who can say that the Jews no longer form a race?[49]

Blood is the basis and substratum of the idea of race, and no people on the face of the earth can claim greater purity and unity of blood than the Jews. Religion does not constitute race. A Jew who abjures his religion remains a Jew. Jews are not assimilated: they have infused their

---

[49] They have never formed a race: as we will never stop repeating, they owe their particularity exclusively to circumcision on the 8th day, the 1st day of the first puberty, which lasts 21 days.

blood into other races, but they have taken very little foreign blood into their own race."

"JEWISH WORLD

Extract from its edition of 22 September 1915: "*No one would dare to claim that the child of a Japanese or an Indian is an Englishman on the pretext that he was born in England, and the same reasoning applies to the Jews.*

"JEWISH WORLD

Extract from its edition of 14 December 1922: "*A Jew remains a Jew even when he changes religion. A Christian who adopts the Jewish religion does not thereby become a Jew. Because being a Jew is not a question of religion, but of race, and a Jew who is a free thinker or an atheist remains as much a Jew as any rabbi.*

RABBI MORRIS JOSEPH

Extract from his book "*Israel as a Nation*": "*To deny Jewish nationality you would have to deny the existence of the Jews*".

ARTHUR D. LAWIS, JEWISH

Text published by the "*West London Zionist Association*": "*To regard the Jews as a religious sect similar to that of the Catholics or Protestants is an inaccuracy. If a Jew is baptised, there are scarcely any who will believe that he is no longer a Jew. His blood, his character, his temperament, his intellectual characteristics are in no way altered.*"

LÉON SIMON, JEWISH

"The idea that Jewry is a religious sect comparable to Catholics or Protestants is nonsense."

Moses Hess, Jewish

Extract from his book "*Rome and Jerusalem*": "*The Jewish religion is, above all, Jewish patriotism. Every Jew, whether he likes it or not, is united with the entire Jewish nation.*

"Jewish Chronicle

Extract from its edition of 11 May 1923: "*The first and most imperative duty of a nation, as of an individual, is the duty of self-preservation. The Jewish nation must above all look after itself.*

"Jewish Courrier

Extract from the January 17, 1924 edition: "*The Jews may adopt the language and clothing of the countries where they live, but they will never become an integral part of the indigenous population.*

G. B Stern, Jewish

Extract from his book "*Debatable Ground*": "*The Jews are a nation. If there were only a theological difference, would it have caused such marked distinctions in features and temperament? Does going to synagogue instead of church change the curve of your nose? Of course, we are a nation, a scattered nation, but through our race, the most united nation in the world*".

S. Gerald Soman, Jewish

Speech by an MP, quoted in "*The World Jewry*", to the seventeen Jewish MPs in the House of Commons: "*You cannot be English Jews. We belong to a distinct race. Our mentality is Jewish and it is absolutely different from that of the English. Enough subterfuge! Let us state openly that we are international Jews.*

As everyone can see, without even needing all these declarations, the Jews do not assimilate in the countries that welcome them. They refuse to associate with national interests, with national capital, except to exploit in their favour. They really only know the Jewish interest.

Their religion is a national and racial matter. They cannot be truly French, English, Canadian, etc., they always remain exclusively and fanatically Jewish. They constitute a state within a state, and the tragedy is that their state is international and tends to unify from below all the nations subject to their hegemony.

Why can't the Jew be an ordinary man? Why are they so intensely particular?[50]

Christians have a detailed code of religious and moral practices, the Catechism. Jews have a corresponding code called the Talmud. It consists of several volumes divided into two main parts: the Mishna and the Gemara. Both were codified into a simpler book: the Schulchan Arouk, by the famous rabbi Josef Caro. Encyclopaedias, newspapers and Jewish leaders categorically affirm that the Talmud is the law for all Jews today or tomorrow as it was yesterday.

At the turn of the century, Abbé Auguste Rohling, a doctor and Hebraic scholar, translated many passages from the Talmud. He offered ten thousand francs to anyone who could prove to him that a single word in his translation was inaccurate. The translation was revised by another learned doctor, Abbé Lamarque. It was reproduced in many books and newspapers in Europe and in many languages. No one ever disputed its translation. Here are a few passages from this "catechism" reproduced in a book by Abbé Charles, Doctor of Theology, former Professor of Philosophy,

---

[50] We've said it again and again: the cause is circumcision on the 8th day. But we are now going to see how the effects of circumcision are reinforced by psychology. Although this reinforcement is not causal, it is not negligible, as we shall see.

parish priest of Saint Augustin in France, entitled "*Juste solution de la Question juive*".

➢ The Bible is water, but the Mishna is wine and the Gemarra is aromatic wine (*Masech Sopharim*, 13 b).
➢ Anyone who despises the words of the rabbis is worthy of death.
➢ The words of the rabbis are sweeter than those of the prophets. (*Midras Misle*, fol 1)
➢ The words of the rabbis are the words of the living God (*Bochai ad Pent* fol 201, cab. 4).
➢ The fear of the rabbi is the fear of God (*Yadchaz hileh, Talmud, Torah*, Perq. 5-1).
➢ The rabbis have sovereignty over God (Tr. 6 *Madkatan* 16).
➢ Everything the rabbis say on earth is a law for God (Tr. *Rosh-Hasha*)
➢ Those who study the law of the rabbis are free from everything in the world (*Sahra* 1, 132 a).
➢ He who studies the Talmud will never fall into need, but he will draw from it the art of deception (Tr. 19 *Sota* 216).
➢ If the Jew switches from the sentences and doctrines of the Talmud to the Bible, he will no longer be happy. (Tr. chag. Fol.10b)
➢ If the Jews follow the Talmud, they will eat while the Goys work. Otherwise they will work themselves (Tr. *Beras chor* 351-b).
➢ Anyone who reads the Bible without the Mischna and without the Gemara (*Talmud*) is like someone who has no God (*Sepher, Safare Zedeq*, Fol.9).
➢ This is what Israel thinks of itself: first God weeps every day for the fault he committed in sending his people into exile (Tr. *Berachot*, ol.3a.).
➢ The souls of the Jews are parts of God, of the substance of God, just as a son is of the substance of his father (Tr. *Sela* 262a).

➢ A Jewish soul is therefore dearer and more pleasing to God than all the souls of the other peoples of the earth (*Sela I.C.* and *Sefa* Fol 4).

➢ The souls of other peoples are descended from the devil and resemble those of animals. The goy is the seed of cattle. (Treatise *Jebammoth. Sefa and Sela id. Sepher Hannechamma.* Fol 221. Col. 4. *Jalqût.* Fol 154b)

➢ All Goyim go to hell (*T. Sepher Zerov Ha-mor.* Fol 27b and Bachai 34. *Masmia Jesua.* Fol 19.Col.4)

➢ The Jews will have temporal empire over the whole world. (*Perus Hea-misma. Ad Tr. Sab. Ic*)

➢ All Christians will be exterminated (*Sepher Zerov Ha-Mor.* Fol. 125 b)

➢ All the treasures of the peoples will pass into Jewish hands (*Sanhedrin*, Fol. 110 b)

➢ For all peoples will serve them and all kingdoms will be subject to them. (*Sanhedrin*, Fol. 88b and *Kethuboth*, Fol. 111b)

➢ God measured the earth and delivered the Goyim to the Jews (*Baba Quamma*, Fol. 37b).

➢ The Goyim were created to serve the Jew day and night. God created them in the form of man in honour of the Jew, for it cannot be fitting for a prince (and every compatriot of Judah the Hanged is a prince) to be served by an animal in the form of a quadruped. (*Sepher Nedrash Talpoth*, Warsaw edition, 1875, page 225)

➢ The goods of the Goyim are things without masters: they belong to the first Jew who passes (*Pfefferkorn*, Dissert. Philos. Page 11).

➢ A Goy who steals from a Jew even less than a liard must be put to death (*Jebammoth*, Fol. 47b).

➢ But it is permitted for a Jew to rob a Goy. (*Babattez*, Fol. 54b)

➢ For the property of a Goy is equivalent to an abandoned thing. The true owner is the Jew who takes it first (*Baba Bathra*, Fol. 54b).

➤ If a Jew has a lawsuit against a Goy (says the *Talmud* to the Jewish magistrate), you will win your brother's case, and you will say to the foreigner: "This is the way our law wants it".

➤ If the Jewish colony has been able to impose some of these laws,[51] you will still win your brother's case and you will say to the foreigner: this is how our law wants it. But if Israel is not powerful in the country or if the judge is not Jewish, you will have to torment the foreigner with intrigues until the Jew has won his case. (*Tr. Baba Gamma*, Fol. 113a)

➤ Whoever returns to a Goy the object he has lost will not find favour with God because he strengthens the power of the Goyim. (*Sanhedrin*, Fol. 76b)

➤ God has ordered us to practice usury towards the Goyim, because we must harm them even when they are useful to us. If a Goy needs money, a Jew will know how to deceive him like a master. He will add usurious interest until the sum is so high that the Goy can no longer pay it without selling his property, or the Jew starts a lawsuit and obtains from the judges the right to take possession of the Goy's property. (*Sepher, Mizv.* Fol. 73-4)[52]

➤ You have to kill the most honest of the Goys.[53]

---

[51] These include divorce, schools without religion (secularism) and the theft of congregations' property.

But the worst of all is the global credit system, which is widespread usury, the cause of all our ills, of all our physical, moral, intellectual and ecological pollution...

[52] This generalised usury is called credit. It is the cause of all our ills. It is, for example, the reason why, in 50 years, French farmers, who used to make up 50% of the population, have shrunk to 5%.

A rich country is an agricultural country, not an industrial one. An agricultural country feeds its population, an industrial country pollutes it. Credit is also the cause of galloping demographics and pollution.

[53] It's worth noting that people with sound, traditional ideas are now officially branded as "bastards".

> Anyone who spills the blood of Goyim is offering a sacrifice to God
> (*Nidderas Bamidebar rabba*, p.21)
> Three Jews together are enough to release their compatriots from any oath
> (*Rosch-Haschana*)
> The famous Jew Frank says that in Kabbalah, it is impossible to explain the many texts of the Mischna and the Talmud in general. Kabbalah teaches the following: The Jew is therefore the living God. God incarnate; he is heavenly man. Other men are earthly, of inferior race. They exist only to serve the Jew. They are the offspring of animals (*Ad Pent*, Fol. 97-3).

THE KOL NIDRE PRAYER

Here is the wording of this very special prayer, which frees Jews from their obligations, quoted in the *Jewish Encyclopaedia*, Vol. 7, and in the prayer books in use. The following text is recited three times by Jews on the evening of the festival of great forgiveness, Yom Kippur.

"Of all the vows, obligations, oaths or anathemas, commitments of all kinds, which we have vowed, sworn, sworn by oath or to which we have committed ourselves, from this day of forgiveness until the same day next year, we repent in advance of all of them. They will be considered as absolved, forgiven, without force, null and void, and of no effect. They will no longer bind us or have any force. Vows will no longer be recognised as vows, obligations will no longer be binding, and oaths will no longer be considered as oaths".

This prayer is justified by the fact that it concerns commitments made to God. So why isn't the prayer amended? On the other hand, if we can behave in this way towards God, then what can we do towards the Goyim, *"that vile seed of cattle"*?

CONSEQUENCES OF THIS PSYCHOPATHOLOGY

What is striking about all the texts prior to this page is their serious psychopathological nature. Paranoia, megalomania, bestial and racist egoism. If all this stems from circumcision, as we have said and as is dealt with in other of my books, it is quite clear that this pathological mentality also acts to reinforce this atrocious particularism. The effects of circumcision are accentuated by the psychopathy it confers: a huge vicious circle.

Here are some of the symptoms highlighted by the following statements, which are unfortunately not exhaustive:

KLATSKIN, JEWISH

Extract from this Zionist leader's book, *Der Jude* (The Jew), published in 1916: "*Only the Jewish code regulates our life. Whenever other laws are imposed on us, we regard them as harsh oppression and avoid them. We form within ourselves a closed legal and economic corporation. A thick wall built by us separates us from the peoples among whom we live, and behind this wall is the Jewish State.*"

JACOB BRAFFMANN, JEWISH

In his two books, "*Les Fraternités juives*" (Vilna, 1868) and "*Livre du Kahal*" (Vilna, 1969), this former rabbi reminds us that Jews must obey the instructions of the Kahal and the Beth-Din, even if they are contrary to the laws of the land.

MARCUS ÉLI RAVAGE, JEWISH

Extract from "*The Century Magazine*", January 1928: "*We are intruders, we are troublemakers. We are subversives. We have sown discord and confusion in your personal and public lives.*

JAMES DARMESTETER, JEWISH

This historian of the East, author of the book "*The Prophets of Israel*", published in 1892, wrote the following: "*The Jew is the doctor of the unbeliever; all the rebels of the spirit come to him in the shadows or under the open sky. He is at work in the immense workshop of blasphemy of the great Emperor Frederick and the princes of Swabia and Aragon. It was he who forged the whole murderous arsenal of reasoning and irony that he bequeathed to the sceptics of the Renaissance and the Libertines of the great century, and Voltaire's sarcasm is but the last echo of a word whispered ten centuries earlier in the shadow of the ghetto and even earlier, at the time of Celsus and Origen, at the very cradle of the religion of Christ.*"

KURT MUNZER, JEWISH

Extract from his book, "*The Ways of Zion*", published in 1910: "*Let them hate us, let them drive us out, let our enemies triumph over our bodily debility. It will be impossible to get rid of us. We have corroded the hearts of peoples, and we have infected and dishonoured races, broken their vigour, putrefied everything, decomposed everything by our mouldy civilisation. There's no way of eradicating our spirit.*"

OTTO WEININGER, JEWISH

Extract from his book "*Sexe et caractère*": "*What distinguishes the Jew in the French Revolution is that he is an element of decomposition*".[54]

BERNARD LAZARE, JEWISH

Extract from his book "*L'antisémitisme et ses causes*": "*The Jew not only dechristianises, he Judaises. He destroys the Catholic and Protestant faith. He provokes indifference. He imposes his idea of the world, of morality and of life on those whose faith he ruins. He is

---

[54] Otto Weininger, a Doctor of Philosophy, was so ashamed of being a Jew, after studying the Jewish Question in all its breadth, that he committed suicide at a very young age.

working on his age-old project: the annihilation of the religion of Christ".[55]

RENÉ GROOS, JEWISH

Quote from "*Le Nouveau Mercure*", May 1937: "*It is a fact that there is a Jewish conspiracy against all nations*".

MR J OLGIN, JEWISH

Extract from an article published in a German-language Jewish newspaper in New York, "*Freiheit*", on 10 January 1937: "*According to the Jewish religion, the Pope is an enemy of the Jewish people simply because he is the head of the Catholic Church. The Jewish religion, it should be remembered, is opposed to Christianity in general and to the Catholic Church in particular.*"

MEDINA IVRIT, JEWISH

Extract from "*The Jewish State*", Prague, No. 33, 27 September 1935: "*In our hearts there is only one feeling: revenge. We command our hearts to banish all other emotions and to allow ourselves to be guided only by this one feeling: revenge. Our people, to whom the world owes the highest concepts, today have only one desire: to ravage, destroy and boycott.*

KOPPEN, JEWISH

Extract from the Jewish Marxist review "*La Révolution surréaliste*", published on 15 December 1920:

"(...) *every time you come across a servant of the p...* (a vile term for the Blessed Virgin) *in the street, in a tone that leaves no doubt as to*

---

[55] At the dawn of the year 2000, they succeeded. Just look at the "repentance" of Monseigneur de Béranger, a communist bishop! (cf. my "*Repentance of repentance*")

the quality of your disgust. But insulting priests has no other purpose, apart from the moral satisfaction it gives you at the time, than to keep you in that state of mind which will enable you, the day you are free, to playfully slaughter two or three tons of these dangerous malefactors every day."

BARUCH LÉVI, JEWISH

Letter to Karl Marx, reproduced in "*La Revue de Paris*" of 1 June 1928, page 574:

"In the new organisation of humanity, the children of Israel will spread over the whole surface of the globe and will become everywhere without opposition the leading element, especially if they succeed in imposing on the working masses the firm control of a few of them. The governments of the nations forming the universal republic will pass effortlessly into the hands of the Jews under cover of the victory of the proletariat. Private property will then be abolished by the rulers of the Jewish race, who will control public funds everywhere. Thus will be fulfilled the promise of the Talmud that, when the time of the Messiah arrives, the Jews will possess the property of all the peoples of the Earth."

DR EHRENPREIS, CHIEF RABBI

Commentary by the Chief Rabbi of Sweden published in "*Judisk Tidskrift*", No. 6, August-September 1929: "*Theodor Herzl foresaw 20 years in advance, before we had experienced it, the revolutions brought about by the Great War and he prepared us for what was to come.*

The Jews are indeed well informed. The premonitory "*Protocols of the Elders of Zion*", which some say is a forgery and others say was written by the Tsar's police, or by Herzl, has in any case an essential reality that makes a mockery of the details of authorship: it foretold 20 years in advance the events that took place and that have since been accentuated by an ocean of horrors that far surpass this "forgery" or "truth").

THE COLLAPSE OF RUSSIA

"BRITISH ISRAEL TRUTH

Commentary written in 1906 by the Jews Dinnis Hanau and Aldersmith (the date of this document is frightfully remarkable).
"*The complete, definitive and triumphant return of the Jews will take place after the collapse of Russia. We can expect considerable changes from the coming great war which hangs over the nations of Europe. According to our interpretation of the prophecies, the Turkish Empire will be dismembered and a great power like England cannot allow another power to occupy Palestine.*"

IS TOTALITARIAN JUDEOPATHY TOLERABLE?

The Jews themselves admit to us what everyone knows, namely that they control world finance, big business and international politics, the great instruments of propaganda, the arts and letters, and that they want to dominate all the countries of the world. Through trade and clothing, they control the female labour market. This last detail is important with regard to the blood of the race which certain Jews have boasted of contaminating.[56]

---

[56] It's all done. The Goys are rotten, the women are now transformed into clones of enjuivated humanoids. Motherless children (divorced or working outside the home) are given over to delinquency, pathogenic music, drugs, suicide and unemployment. Young people are nothing more than blue-jeaned cowherds, bewildered, without ideals, biotypological residues, physico-chemical amalgams governed by the profit and loss account of totalitarian Jewish pseudo-democracies.

How are the Jews mentally qualified to exercise such hegemony?[57]

Let's take a look at their answer:

"JEWISH ENCYCLOPEDIA

Under the heading "*Nervous Diseases*", Volume 9, it is stated that Jews are more prone to nervous diseases than the other races and peoples among whom they live. Hysteria and neurasthenia are the most common diseases.

Some doctors who had treated Jews claimed that the majority of them presented a syndrome of neurasthenia or hysteria. Tobler claims that all the Jewish women in Palestine are hysterical.

And Raymond says that in Warsaw, Poland, hysteria is common in both men and women. The population of this city alone is the inexhaustible source of male hysterics for all the clinics in Europe.

With regard to Austria and Germany, the same condition of neurosis among Jews was denounced by Kraft Ebing, who said that nervous diseases, and particularly neurasthenia, affected Jews with exceptional severity.

Biswanger, Erb, Joly, Mmobius, Lowenfeld, Oppenheim, Ferré, Charcot, Bouveret and almost all the other specialists in nervous diseases say the same thing in their studies on neurasthenia and hysteria, and stress the fact that hysteria, so rare in males of other races, is very common in Jews.

---

[57] Intellectual probity dictates that I step aside before what is said here, but we know the cause: the disappearance of providential elites, traditional regimes and the enormous Jewish speculative power due to ritual circumcision on the 8th day, automatically gives them all the power. This is the only reality.

The Encyclopédie juive adds that the study of Talmudic theology at an early age has something to do with the aetiology of this pathology.

BERNARD LAZARE, JEWISH

As quoted by Maingnial in "*La Question Juive*", 1903: "*As the world became kinder to them, the Jews - at least the mass of them - withdrew into themselves, they shrank their prison, they formed closer bonds. Their decrepitude was unheard of, their intellectual collapse was equalled only by their moral abasement*".

DR HUGO GANZ, JEWISH

This Jewish doctor from Romania wrote in "*Reiseskizzen aus Roumanaeniens*", Berlin 1903, page 138: "*It is to the over-exclusive study of theology that these unfortunate people owe their narrow chests and spindly, weak limbs. It is the pursuit of endless affairs that gives them their characteristic cunning and provides anti-Semitism with its raison d'être. It is also possible that they suffer from an "excess of head"*.

Author's note: Clearly this doctor was unaware of the effects of circumcision, which alone is responsible for these "cerebral-somatic" hormonal imbalances.

THÉODORE REINACH, JEWISH

Author of the article "Juif" (Jew) in the *Grande Encyclopédie*, page 273, volume 21: "*The long specialisation of the Jews in the money trade explains their hereditary superiority in this branch and in all the occupations connected with it, as well as the frequency of the defects that it engenders: harshness, an inordinate taste for lucre, finesse degenerating into duplicity, a tendency to believe that everything is for sale and that it is legitimate to buy everything*.

The sudden intellectual and religious emancipation produced other unbalanced effects: by breaking the ties that bound him to traditional Judaism, the Jew no longer found in his emptied conscience any brake or moral guide to stop him. Like an escaped horse, he gave himself over to the full effervescence of his imagination and logic, to all the excesses of thought and action. Since the end of the last century, Berlin society has offered remarkable examples of this radicalism, or rather moral nihilism.

Dr Rudolf Wasserman, Jewish

Extract from his treatise "*Étude sur la criminalité juive*": "*For the Jews, it is the intelligence, for the Goyim, it is the hand, the instrument of crime. The Christian achieves his criminal success through direct physical activity: robbery, theft, assault on property or people. The Jew, on the other hand, commits his crime indirectly by psychically inducing another person, by means of deception and trickery, to grant him an illegal advantage*".

Cerfbeer from Medelsheim, Jewish

Extract from his book "*L'Église et la Synagogue*", published in 1847, page 230: "*Let the Israelites of France beware; they are undoubtedly heading for a disastrous reaction, the effects of which we would like to prevent with our advice and warnings. They do not realise how relaxed and abandoned morality is among them. How sordid ideas and the lust for easy lucre lead them astray by dazzling them. A simple comparison of statistical calculations will make it easy to understand the truth and scope of our thinking.*"[58]

Usury gave the Jews half of Alsace

---

[58] This is the work I'm trying to do by shouting at them to stop circumcising on the 8th day, which explains their fundamental particularism over the centuries and in every country.

In his book "*Les Juifs*" Paris, published in 1857, page 39, this author tells us: "*This is the great plague of our time. Usury is committed in our countryside with as much impudence as impunity. Smallholdings are devoured by this canker that eats away at everything. It would take a volume to enumerate the shameful and perfidious means employed by the Jews to attract to themselves all the parcels of land that excite their lust, and we do not know whether there will be in the spirit of our modern laws any provisions strong enough to halt the progress of this evil, when we are obliged to refer the matter to the legislature. It is no longer the Jews who cover themselves with the sackcloth of sorrow, it is the peasants of our countryside who mourn the iniquities of Israel*".[59]

OSCAR FRANK, JEWISH

Extract from his book "*Les Juifs*", Leipzig, 1905 page 84: "*Jewish usury has always been stigmatised by poets. In the 16th century, the Jewish usurer was a well-known character. In the Carnival games, the Jew, usurer and swindler, was the role that was especially popular with the public. In this case, writers had no difficulty in lending him traits taken from life (page 98): a man who, in general, deceives the Christian environment in which he finds himself and is inspired by a desire to enrich himself. For this reason, the opinion prevails almost everywhere that the Jew is the exploiter of the Christian people*".

GRAETZ, JEWISH

The great historian of the Jewish people, quoted by the philosemite Bonsirven in his book "*Sur les ruines du temple*", page 324, put it this way: "*The defects in the method of Talmudic teaching, subtlety, quibbling, finesse, penetrated practical life and degenerated into duplicity, deviousness and disloyalty. It was difficult for the Jews to

---

[59] I can't count the number of farmers in my short lifetime who have been ruined by Crédit Agricole, for example. The bank as a whole is the executioner of farmers, their exterminator. In 50 years, as we have said, they have gone from representing 50% of the French population to 5%!

deceive one another because they had received more or less the same education and could therefore use the same weapons. But they often used cunning and disloyal means against the Goyim".

DR RUDOLF WASSERMAN, JEWISH

Extract from "*Zeitschrift für Sozialwissenschaft*", 12th year, 1909, page 663: "*We have copious material and figures showing that Jews in particular are prone to cerebral diseases* (statistics), *and specialists unanimously acknowledge this (case citations). In the Jew, the nervous system is the 'locus minoris resistentiae'* (place of least resistance)."

DR M. J. GUTTMANN, JEWISH

Extract from "*Zeitschrift für Demographie*", 3rd year, H 4 - 6, page 112: "*Dementia praecox is a mental disorder which, among Jews, is of quite extraordinary frequency*".

KREPPEL, JEWISH

Extract from his book "*Les Juifs et le Judaïsme d'aujourd'hui*", Edition Amalthéa, 1925, page 387: "*As far as insanity is concerned, it has been established that in public and private insane asylums, the percentage of Jews exceeds that of Christians by three times*".

The pathological development of the Jewish personality as a result of ritual circumcision is absolutely clear.

Didn't Nietzsche say: "*It was the sick who invented wickedness*".

Jewish speculative-parasitic disease will cease immediately with the abolition of circumcision on the 8th day.

THE FRENCH FLAG AS SEEN BY THE JEW JEAN ZAY

Jean Zay, a member of the "*L'Indépendance*" Lodge in Orléans and a minister in the Sarrault and Léon Blum cabinet, wrote the following article in a Paris newspaper on 6 March 1924, in which, alas, he forgot two small details:[60]

The flag

> Fifteen hundred thousand of them died for this shit. Fifteen hundred in my country, fifteen million in all countries. Fifteen hundred thousand dead men, My God!
>
> Fifteen hundred thousand dead men, each of whom had a mother, a lover, children, a home, a life, a hope, a heart.
>
> What's this rag they died for?
>
> Fifteen hundred thousand dead, My God, fifteen hundred thousand dead for this filth, fifteen hundred thousand gutted, torn apart, annihilated in the muck of a battlefield , fifteen hundred thousand that we will never hear from again, that their loves will never see again.
>
> Terrible piece of cloth, nailed to your flagpole, I hate you fiercely.
>
> Yes, I hate you in my soul, I hate you for all the misery you represent, for the fresh blood, the pungent-smelling human blood that spurts from beneath your folds, I hate you in the name of skeletons.

---

[60] Jean Zay's cries would be worthwhile if he were to mention that this war is of Jewish origin, financed by Jews, like the Bolshevik Revolution, and if he were to mention the tens of millions of corpses of Russian communism, where there is hardly any question of a flag.

There were fifteen hundred thousand of them.

I hate you for all the people who salute you, I hate you for all the asswipes and whores who drag their hats through the mud in front of your shadow.

I hate in you all the old secular oppression, the bestial god, the challenge to the men we don't know how to be.

I hate your dirty colours, the red of their blood,[61] the blue you stole from the sky, the white livid of your remorse.

Let me, ignoble symbol, weep alone, weep loudly for the fifteen hundred thousand young men who died, and do not forget, despite your generals, your iron and your victories, that you are for me the vile race of torche-culs.

(**The red torch of Marxism killed 200 million people**) Who benefited from Bolshevism?

The Bolshevik revolution was entirely Jewish: ideologists (Marx, Lassalle), financiers (Warburg, Loeb, etc.), politicians (Lenin, Trotsky, Kerensky, etc.), prison and concentration camp executioners (Kaganovitch, Frenkel, Yagoda, etc.).

---

[61] The French flag is white with a fleur-de-lys in the centre. The red of the flag, which was to cover it entirely when the Bolsheviks came to power, is Jewish. Like the Revolution of 89, like the financial origins of the Great War (14-18).

When the flag was white, only aristocrats were killed in wars that were more justified than strictly economic wars for the benefit of high finance. The unfortunate thing is that the people, not understanding this, may be susceptible to the pathos of such a text, which leads them towards nothingness...

The official directory of Jewry (the government of Israel), published in the United States, proudly gives the following list of Jews in power in Russia in the year 5678 of the Hebrew era:

Aaronson, manager in Witebsk;
Apfelbaum, known as Zinovief, leader in Petrograd;
Bernstam, magistrate in Petrograd;

Bloch, Ministry of Justice ;

Bothner, Head of the Moscow Police ;
Braunstein, known as Trotsky, dictator to the army;
Cohen, judge in Lodz ;

Dickstein, prosecutor in Petrograd ;

Eiger, Commissioner for Polish Affairs ;
Friedman, Mayor of Odessa;

Geilman, Commissioner of the Bank ;
Greenherg, Chief of the Moscow Police;
Grodski, judge in Petrograd;

Gunzburg, Supply Commissioner ;
Gurevitch, Deputy Commissioner for the Interior;
Halperin, Secretary General of the Government ;
Hefez, Deputy Commissioner for Justice;
Hurgin, Deputy Commissioner for Jewish Affairs;
Kachnin, Labour Commissioner in Kherson ;
Kalmanovitch, prosecutor in Minsk ;
Kantorovitch, deputy in Petrograd ;

Alter, manager in Kamenetz ;
Bekerman, magistrate in Radom ;
Bernstein, Commissioner for Coal ;
Boff, known as Kamgoff, leader in Petrograd;
Bramson (Abrahamson), manager in Petrograd ;
Brodsky, judge in Petrograd;

Davidowitch, judge in Petrograd;
Dalbrowsky, Petrograd Commissioner for Jewish Affairs;
Fisher, municipal judge in Petrograd ;
Friedman, Commissioner for Justice in Petrograd;
Ginzburg, head of Kolomensky ;
Greenberg, curator of the Petrograd district;
Grusenberg, investigator of naval affairs under the old regime, commissioner of the new navy ;
Guitnik, Trade Commissioner in Odessa ;
Gutterman, Commissar for Supplies in Saratov ;
Halpern, Deputy Mayor of Kolomensky;
Hillsberg, judge in Lublin ;

Isaacson, Commissioner for the Navy;
Kahan, judge in Petrokov ;

Kaminetski, judge in Petrograd;

Kempner judges in Lodz;

Kerensky, MP ;
Lichtenfeld, judge in Warsaw ;
Luria, Banking Commissioner ;
Mandzin, prosecutor ;

Minor, Chairman of the Moscow City Council ;
Per, judge in Warsaw ;
Perlmutter, member of the Polish Council of State;
Podghayetz, Mayor of Moghilev ;

Rabinowitz, Labour Commissioner in Tavrida ;
Ratner, administrator of the city of Nachichevanskz ;
Rundstein, Judge at the Court of Cassation;
Sacks, Deputy Commissioner for Education ;
Schreider, Mayor of Petrograd ;

Stechen, Senator ;
Sterling, judge in Warsaw ;
Unschlicht, Commissioner in Petrograd;
Weinstein, director of Minsk ;

Yonstein, Mayor of Oriel ;

Zitzerman, prosecutor in Irkutsk.

Lazarowitch mayor of Odessa;
Lublinsky, judge in Petrograd;
Maldelbert, Mayor of Zitomir ;
Meyerowitch, Commissioner for the Armed Forces ;
Nathanson, member of the Polish Council of State;
Prelman, judge in Saratov ;
Pfeffer, member of the Polish Council of State;
Poznarsky, Judge at the Court of Cassation;
Rafes, Deputy Commissioner for Local Affairs in Ukraine;
Rosenfeld, known as Kameneff, Member of Parliament ;
Phineas Rutenberg, second-in-command of the Petrograd militia;
Schreiber, prosecutor in Irkutsk ;

Silvergarb, Commissioner for Jewish Affairs in Ukraine;
Steinberg, Commissioner for Justice ;
Trachtenberg, judge in Petrograd;
Vinaver, MP ;

Warshavsky, Trade Commissioner in Petrograd;
Wegmeister, member of the Polish Council of State;

SYMBOLISM OF THE CLOSED FIST AND RAISED ARM, OPEN HAND

When the Jews celebrate their feast of revenge, Purim, which recalls the massacre of 70,000 Goyim, they all join in the closed fist salute, which would become the Bolshevik salute. This sign is religious and racist. It is the antithesis of the religious sign of the cross and the salute of friendship between the Latin and Saxon races. The arm outstretched and raised, hand open, means: "*I come as a friend, frankly, hiding no weapons*".

To the Socialist-Communist Internationals founded by the Jews, and from which they hope, very logically alas, because of the mental inadequacy of the majority of human beings, for world hegemony, they have imposed this closed fist salute which is a natural manifestation of their psychopathic mentality. It is the salvation of vengeance, the salvation of the enemy of civilisation, and of the white race which has come to accept such a salvation: that of Jewish vengeance and domination.

I remember as a child how they used to make fun of the "stupid Goyim".

They must be laughing to see so many de-Christianised Goyim serving their cause and marching towards their own suicide, arms raised and fists clenched...

DANGER!

Schlom Ash informed us that the slightest shake in the Soviet regime would mean the death of the Jews. In "*Jewish World*" of 19 June 1922 from London, he tells us: "*Not only in revolutionary circles but even in the Red Army, anti-Judaism is so strong that only the iron discipline imposed by the Bolsheviks and the fear of capital punishment keep soldiers and women from starting pogroms everywhere. In Russia, peasants, soldiers, women, city dwellers, everyone hates the Jews. All the Jews in Russia are unanimous in thinking that the fall of the Soviets and the passing of power into other hands would be the greatest possible calamity for the Jews. The flame of anti-Semitism burns brighter than ever in Russia today.*[62]

---

[62] In November 1998, a Communist general publicly called for pogroms. The Duma initially refused to pass a law opposing such demonstrations (the law was subsequently passed). (The law was subsequently passed).

Remember that in this Jewish Soviet regime, Stalin had planned a national pogrom which his death prevented (Historical programme on Channel V, 1998).

Neville Chamberlain revealed that the United States and world Jewry had forced England into war.

James Vincent Forrestal, Wall Street banker, former US Ambassador to England between 1937 and 1940, Under Secretary of the Navy under Roosevelt, then Secretary of Defense under Truman, refers in the following extract to a conversation he had with Joseph Kennedy (the father of the future President of the United States). Forrestal knew too much and committed suicide after the war by falling from the window of the military hospital where he was hospitalised.

"Playing golf with Joseph Kennedy, Roosevelt's ambassador to Britain in the years leading up to the Second World War, I asked him about the conversations he had had with Roosevelt and Neville Chamberlain since 1938. He told me that Chamberlain's view was that Britain was not ready to fight, and could not go to war with Hitler. Kennedy's view was that Hitler would have fought Russia without coming into conflict with Britain had it not been for Bullit, the American ambassador to France, who was pressuring Roosevelt to confront the Germans over the Polish question.

Neither the French nor the British would have made Poland a cause of war had it not been for Washington's constant intrigues. Bullitt repeated to Roosevelt that the Germans would not dare to fight. Kennedy said they would fight and take Europe.

Neville Chamberlain declared that America and world Jewry had forced Britain into the war".

Source: "*James Forrestal Diaries*", edited by Malter Millis, with the collaboration of U. S. Duffield, New York. The Viking Press, MCMLI, October 1951. Published the same day in Canada by Mac Millan Cie of Canada Limited.

COMMUNISM AND JEWISHNESS IN CANADA

Fred Rose, whose real name was Rosenberg, was accused spying for the Soviets and sentenced after the war to six years in prison. Released, he continued his work in Czechoslovakia.

➢ The Communist leader in Canada in 1966 was the Jew W. Kashtan.
➢ The Communist leader in Quebec is the Jew Samuel Walsh.

A VITAL INTEREST

In his book *Integrales Judentum*, Berlin 1922, Alfred Nossig, a Jew, wrote: "*The modern socialist movement is for the most part the work of the Jews, who put their own stamp on it. It was also the Jews who played a fundamental part in the leadership of the first socialist republics. However, most Jewish socialist leaders were far removed from Judaism.*

Despite this, the role they played did not depend on them alone. In them the old eugenic principle of Mosaicism operated unconsciously, the blood of the old apostolic people lived in their brains and in their social temperament. Today's world socialism is the first stage in the fulfilment of Mosaicism, the beginning of the realisation of the future world foretold by our prophets.

Only when there is a League of Nations, only when the Allied armies are effectively employed in the protection of all the weak, can we hope that the Jews will be able to develop their national State in Palestine without hindrance, and, likewise, only a League of Nations imbued with the socialist spirit will make it possible for us to enjoy our international as well as our national necessities.

That is why all Jewish groups, whether Zionists or Diaspora adherents, have a vital interest in the victory of socialism. They must demand it not only because of its identity with Mosaism, but also as a tactical principle."

Karl Marx, Founder of Communism

Bernard Lazare, again in his remarkable book "*L'antisémitisme et ses causes*", tells us about Marx: "*He was a descendant of a line of rabbis and doctors who inherited all the logical force of his ancestors. He was a lucid and clear Talmudist, unencumbered by the trivialities of practice. He was a Talmudist who studied sociology and applied his native exegetical skills to the criticism of political economy.*

He was animated by that old Hebraic materialism that perpetually dreamt of a paradise denied on earth and always rejected the distant and problematic hope of an Eden after death. But he was not only a logician, he was also a rebel, an agitator, a bitter polemicist, and he took his gift for sarcasm and invective where Henri Heine had taken it: from Jewish sources.

Systematic boycott of all works are not pro-Jewish, as far back as 1895

Saulus, a Jew, in the Mainz newspaper "*Wucherpille*" of January 1895, inaugurated a practice that continues today in a totalitarian manner: the impossibility of saying anything about the Jews that is unfavourable to them without being punished by fines and imprisonment (Fabius-Gayssot Law: a Jew and a Communist): "*If a book appears that is hostile to us, we don't buy it and the edition will soon be scrapped. The publicist is nothing: all we have to do is organise a conspiracy of silence against him*".

(Today, no publicist would publish a book, even a brilliant one, unfavourable to the Jew: Jewish censorship is radical and absolute. It masquerades as anti-racism, while they are building the "Lebanisation" of every country everywhere).

Russia's fate was decided in 1913

In October 1913, in issue 274, the Jewish newspaper "*Hammer*" published the following comments on the ritual murder trial in Kiev: "*The Russian government has decided to wage a decisive battle against the Jewish people in Kiev. On the outcome of this titanic struggle depends the fate, not of the Jewish people, for the Jewish people are invincible, but of the Russian state. "To be or not to be", that is the question for Russia. The victory of the Russian government is the beginning of its end. There is no way out, get that into your heads. We are going to demonstrate in Kiev, before the whole world, that the Jews will not allow us to make a mockery of them. If the Jews have hitherto, for tactical considerations, concealed the fact that they are leading the Revolution in Russia, now, after the attitude of the Russian Government at the Kiev trial, our tactics must be abandoned. Whatever the outcome of this case, there is no salvation for the Russian Government. This is the Jewish decision and it will be fulfilled.*"

(note that Jewish-American funding of the Bolshevik revolution began before the end of the 19th century)

ABOUT THE BIBLE

Rabbi Léonard Lévy gave an interesting sermon on 7 November 1909 about this holy book full of massacres, crimes, bloodshed, deceptions and lies: "*In the past, people believed that every word in the Bible was the absolute truth. This is no longer the case. The work of scholars has established that the Bible is a product of human intelligence, from beginning to end, containing certain errors, certain inaccurate views, due to the fallibility of its authors, who were men. This is a most valuable result*".

ABOUT JAPAN

In his book "Asiaten", the Austrian Jew Landberger writes: "*We cast our net over the whole of Japan. We have a decisive influence on all the instruments of love in that country. They will all play the tunes we give them. Think of a country as a gigantic body. He who regulates the abdominal functions of this body holds it in his power. Do you see what I want? The struggle for universal domination between America and Japan must be conducted in such a way that Japan is absorbed. America not only trusts love, it takes the country by its most developed instinct. In a country where the carnal act is a natural function of the body, similar to all the others, we only have to be skilful to provoke the necessary impulse and unleashed sexuality will be extinguished in an intoxication whose duration we will determine. By constantly renewing the processes of seductive excitement, we can make this intoxication permanent and make this country the most possessed country in the world".*

This is certainly an example of Jewish culture as I have observed it in my life the twentieth century. However, it should be noted that when this Jewish author says "*We Americans*", this is a usurpation, because in America there are on the one hand the American people, and on the other the Jewish government. These ideas are Jewish and not American. Similarly, Freud's psychoanalytical farce belongs only to Freudian pathology and not to Austria.[63]

What the corrupting Jewish spirit threatens to do in Japan, still a relatively healthy country, it has done in Western countries with immense success among all those who have lost their faith. We have seen in the preceding pages how "*the Jews are dumbfounded by the stupidity of the Goyim*". When the Jews debase and demoralise a people through the white slave trade, pornography, cinema, subversive fashion, theatre and rotten art, they do so by calculation, executing a deliberate plan. They can only defeat the people if the latter, weakened, have lost all their values. As Nietzsche said: "*The Jews can do nothing against a people in good physical and moral health*".

---

[63] See *Freud a menti*, by Dr J. Gautier, who has demystified Freudism in order to demystify those who take such an imposture seriously (Editions de la Vie Claire).

WHAT THEY HAVE DONE FOR HUMANITY

LATZIS, JEWISH

This instigator of the Red Terror in Russia based it on class hatred: *"We will exterminate not only individuals, but the bourgeoisie as a class. It is useless for us to ask for proof of the criminal actions of the accused. Their fate is decided by the class to which they belong and the education they have received.*

DR. FROMER, JEWISH

Extract from his book "*Das Wesen des Judentum*", Berlin, 1905, page 35: "*The anarchic situation demonstrates that the Jewish religion applied with consequence is essentially incompatible with the maintenance of an ordered State, that it cannot live in lasting peace with the representatives of another conception of life. And this conclusion applies with equal force to religion, remaining on the strictly orthodox basis, and to religion in so far as it seeks to adapt itself as well as possible to the spirit of our day.*"

Same author: "*Reading the accusations of the rhetors against whom Josephus defends himself, one is astonished that a common life of three centuries and the most intense participation in the civilisation of the fellow-citizens in Egypt, could not establish a basis for compromise and friendly understanding, that in their way of thinking, of being and of feeling, the Jews remained so entirely foreign and antipathetic to their fellow-citizens*".[64]

---

[64] In Egypt, they were called "*the Immondes*" and caricatured with donkey heads. They were expelled, along with all their belongings and those stolen from the Egyptians. Moses, condemned for murder and banished (he could not be executed

Same author: "*Since that time [of the transmission of Aristotle's writings] the Jews have done nothing for humanity, nor have they tried to do anything. Where is the sense of the Jewish mission being accomplished if modern Jews ruin every new movement by participating in it with their words and their activity?*

SOME SIGNIFICANT STATEMENTS BY JEWS

"*On the stock market, there comes a time when, to win, you have to know how to speak Hebrew*" (Rothschild).

Question: Why, being so rich, are you still working to become richer? "*Oh, you don't know what it's like to feel a bunch of Christians under your feet*" (Saint Victor, at the end of a dinner party).

The Jew Mires in 1860: "*If you Catholics haven't hanged us in fifty years, you won't have a rope left to hang yourselves with*[65]

"*Le Peuple Juif*", 20 Tamouz, 1936: "*The infiltration of Jewish immigrants, attracted by the apparent security, and the ascendant social movement of the native Jews, act powerfully together and push towards a cataclysm*".

In *The Jewish State,* Theodor Herzl wrote: "*The longer anti-Semitism waits, the more furiously it must erupt*". (This is exactly what I have

---

as he had the rank of prince), was recalled from exile to lead these people elsewhere and rid Egypt, which could no longer bear their presence.

[65] This is perfectly stated but completely incomplete: in reality, the rejection of the laws of life and nature by usury and communism will lead to multiform cancers (galloping demography of coloured ethnic groups, moral extinction, aesthetics, multiple criminality, increasing madness in geometric progression, homosexuality and paedophilia, disappearance of species and water, etc.). In reality, without the immediate and radical abolition of circumcision on the 8th day, the Jews will reign over an empire of ruins, or worse still, over nothingness, as Adolphe Hitler predicted. Today, in the year 2000, everyone can understand this, because Jewish domination is no longer occult.

been shouting to the deaf Jewish community for years, with the categorical imperative of abolishing their circumcision).

Catholic fantasists who for decades have been tampering with rites and traditions to the point of derision should ponder this statement by a rabbi: "*If I were a Catholic, I would be a fundamentalist, because being a Jew, I am certainly a fundamentalist*". We should also ponder this statement by Dr. Mayer Abner of B'nai B'rith, Bukovina's deputy to the Romanian Chamber, reproduced in the "*Ostjüdische Zeitung*" (organ of Bukovina's Jews) on 14 July 1929 (No. 1235): "*For all Jews without exception, the Torah, the Talmud and its systematic recapitulation, the Schulchan Aruch, are the indisputable and recognised source of Jewish religious life. There can be no dogmatic differences among us Jews. Our strength lies in the rigid maintenance of the three-thousand-year-old tradition.*

FUNDAMENTAL CORRUPTION

Today, a new social programme is practically complete. It was drawn up by the "*World League for Sexual Reform*", whose president was the Jewish doctor Imianitoff from Belgium.

Let's look at the ten points of this programme which, in the year 2000, are practically normative:

> ➤ Political, economic and sexual equality for men and women.
> ➤ Liberation of marriage, and particularly divorce, from the tyrannical rules of Church and State. (Note that from Naquet's divorce law to Simone Veil's pathogenic pill and free abortion, everything is Jewish).
> ➤ Control of conception so that procreation is consented to deliberately and with an accurate sense of responsibility.
> ➤ Race improvement through the application of eugenics and childcare methods. (Eugenics has become criminal and

forgotten: the birth of freaks is more profitable for Jewish hegemony).

➢ Protection of girl mothers and illegitimate children.

➢ Human and rational behaviour towards sexual abnormals, such as homosexuals, men and women, fetishists, exhibitionists, etc.

➢ Prevention of prostitution and venereal diseases.

➢ Incorporation of disorders due to the sexual drive into the class of pathological phenomena and no longer considered as crimes, vices or sins.

➢ Only sexual acts that transgress the freedom or infringe the rights of another person may be considered criminal. Mutually consensual sexual relations between responsible adults must be respected as private acts involving only their persons.

➢ Sex education with the greatest possible freedom and respect for oneself and others.

A quote from Léon Blum, a Jew who was Prime Minister of the Popular Front government in 1936, in his essay on morals entitled *"On Marriage"*: *"They will return from their lover's house as naturally as they return now from the classroom or from tea at a friend's house"* (...) *"Virginity, happily and early rejected, would no longer exert that singular constraint made up of modesty, dignity and a sort of fear".* (...) *"Virginity rejected cheerfully and early would no longer exert that singular constraint made up of modesty, dignity and a kind of fear."* (...) *"I have never discerned what it is about incest that is truly repulsive; I simply note that it is natural and common to love one's brother or sister with love."*

Quote from Kroupskaya, Lenin's widow, in the Soviet newspaper *"Outchi Gazetta"* of 10 October 1929: *"It is imperatively necessary for the State to resume its systematic anti-religious work among children. We must not only make our boys and non-religious, but actively and passionately anti-religious. The influence of religious parents in the home must be vigorously combated. Although the socialisation of women is not yet officially sanctioned in Soviet Russia, it must become a reality and penetrate the consciousness of the masses. Consequently, anyone who tries to defend a woman against an indecent assault shows a bourgeois nature and declares himself in favour of private property. To oppose rape is to oppose the October Revolution.*

Author's note: The whole thing is so psychopathic it's hard to believe it's real.

Quote from Karl Marx in "*Deutsch-Franzosiche Jahrbucher*", 1844: "*It is in vain to search in the labyrinth of the Jewish soul for a key to its religion. On the contrary, the mystery of its religion must be sought in the mystery of its nature. What is the basis of Judaism? A practical passion and lucre for profit. To what can we reduce its religious worship? Extortion. Who is their true God: cash.*"

Quote from Walter Ratheneau, a Jew, in his book *Der Kaiser* (Paris, 1930): "*In 100 years, the French Revolution has circled the globe and has been unrestricted; no State, no institution, no society, no dynasty has been spared by it. The oratory of the Russian Revolution is Humanity. Its secret desire, the provisional dictatorship of the proletariat and idealised anarchism.*

Its practical plan for the future, the suppression of European stratification in the political form of socialised republics. In a century's time, the East's plan will be as fully realised as the West's is today. After centuries of our planet building, gathering, conserving, preserving and accumulating material and intellectual treasures for the enjoyment of a few, here comes the century of demolition, destruction, dispersion and a return to barbarism. Ruins behind us and ruins in front of us. We are a transitional race? Destined for the unworthy dunghill of the harvest," I wrote at the beginning of the war. Yet not only must we travel the road we have embarked upon, we want to travel it.

A Jew, Paul Mayer, wrote the "*Joyous road song of the wandering Jew*". It cannot be said that he is insincere:

I have no home and no country,
I'm not going anywhere.
No more vain nostalgia
I don't care about the blues!
My soul has hardened.
From all your thresholds, like a thief,
Drive me away - I know I'm envied
And eagerly seek me out.
I drink from your springs of life
And I know your value.
Under the humble rag where my soul sleeps,
I hide the gold of the universe.
The virgin you want for a wife,
Turns an eye of flame
Towards the cursed son of the desert!
Smoking your tobacco without delight,
You chew over your heavy troubles,
But here I am, king of vices,
And I offer to your novice mouths
The fruit of new sins.
So I'm playing with the ball,
This subtle game, this fatal game,
Who amuses you and catches you
And the secret escapes you,
The game of oriental blood!

THE JEWISH CHRONICLE COMMENTS ON THE WORK OF AN IRISH THEOLOGIAN

On 23 October 1936, this London Jewish newspaper published the following article: "*The Mystical Body of Christ in Modern Times*" on the work of Father Denis Fahey, Professor of Philosophy and Church History at the Senior House of Studies, Blackrock University, Dublin.

"This priest is the author of several theological works and is seriously alarmed by the expansion of secularist tendencies in the modern world. Hence the publication of his new book, the main aim of which is to deal theologically and historically with the aspect of modern revolt against the divine plan for the organisation of human society.

So far, so good. But, unfortunately, Father Fahey is convinced that all the troubles in the world today are due to an extraordinary alliance between Jewish revolutionaries and Jewish financiers for the overthrow of the existing order of things and the establishment of Jewish world domination over its ruins.[66]

In support of this curious thesis, Father Fahey brings in all the usual anti-Semitic tripe. He gives documentary evidence that the Russian Revolution was financed by Jacob Schiff at a cost of $12,000,000. He reprints a list of notorious names to say that of 25 architects of Bolshevism, only Lenin was not a Jew."

THE JUDEO-COMMUNISTS OF THE SPANISH POPULAR FRONT AND 1837

The Judeo-Communists of the Spanish Popular Front named the group of 400 Canadian volunteers fighting in Spain after Joseph Papineau to extend the rule of Stalin, Litvinoff, Kaganovitch, Karakhan, Ioffe, Rosenberg, etc.

The Jews are very fond of Papineau, who fled abroad when his unfortunate companions were on the scaffold. They loved him very much because it was Papineau who, in our history, fought the hardest for the emancipation of the Jews, in other words for them to be on the same footing as genuine Canadians in 1832.

---

[66] We now know that this is not true: Lenin's mother was Jewish, so Lenin was a Jew according to Jewish law.

The "*Jewish Encyclopedia*", under the word "David", tells us that it was the two sons of the Jew David of rue Notre-Dame who commanded the cavalry against our heroes of Saint-Eustache and Saint-Denis in 1837.

A book published by the Jews of Canada in 1926, "*Jews in Canada*", tells us that it was the Jew Benjamin Hart who, after spying on our heroes of 1837, signed the arrest warrants for those who were imprisoned.

The same book tells us that, at that time, the Jews, and particularly the Franck family, controlled the trading posts between Montreal and New York along the Richelieu. Many people believe that it was these Jews who enabled Papineau, by leading him from post to post, to flee to the United States under the disguise of a woman, while the lowly and unworthy were put on trial. This would have been the Jews' reward to Papineau for their emancipation in 1832.

The Judeo-Communists like to tell Canadians about the revolt of 1837, but they don't say that the victims of that movement were arrested because of the treachery of a Jew, and that the Jews of Montreal commanded fire against our patriots. The dirtiest work of 1837 was done by a Jew, Benjamin Hart. No doubt because no white, English, French, Scottish or Irish Canadian would have wanted to do it in those cruel circumstances.

UNANIMOUS TESTIMONY FROM JEWS AND GOYIM ALIKE

Everything admitted in this book by the Jews has long been admitted by superior minds in Christendom and elsewhere. Has Christendom done what is necessary to prevent the triumph of worldwide Jewish Judeopathy? This is doubtful, and the words of Julian the Apostate take on their full value in the year 2000:

"If Christianity triumphs, in two thousand years the whole world will be dominated by the Jews".

Was this prophecy or simple logic? Whatever the case, saints, general and local councils of the Church, popes, emperors, kings, princes of every country, famous statesmen, Protestant reformers like Luther, Muslim clerics, bishops, pastors of every religious denomination, writers of every school, as we shall see in the second part of this book, illustrious historians, scholars, diplomats, socialist, liberal and conservative leaders, official statistics and archives from many countries, ALL have said the same thing about Jewish financial and ideological perversity ;

But since all these thinkers are not part of the chosen race, the Jews accuse them of :

- Fanaticism,
- Persecution,
- Obscurantism,
- Narrow-mindedness,
- Intolerance,
- Hate,
- Jealousy

That's why, in the first part of this book, it was essential to include the words of leading Jewish figures:

- Karl Marx
- Benjamin Disraeli,
- Adolphe Crémieux,
- Bernard Lazare,
- Alfred Nossig,
- Max Nordau,
- Emil Ludwig,
- Otto Weininger,
- Kurt Munzer
- Léon Blum
- Oscar Lévy,

- Nahum Sokolov
- Walther Ratheneau,
- Theodor Herzl,
- and myself R. D. Polacco de Ménasce

It is therefore grotesque to speak of anti-Semitism if we want to denounce the great modern miseries, their revolutions, their wars, their crimes, the crises of demoralisation, the polluting and destructive consequences of their capitalism, the collapse of everything by Rothschildo-Marxism.

To conclude this first part, here is a very explicit, very clear statement by the Jew Bernard Lazare in his book "*L'antisémitisme et ses causes*", which has already been quoted several times:

"It seemed to me that an opinion as universal as anti-Semitism, having flourished in all places and at all times, before the Christian era and after, in Alexandria, in Rome, in Antioch, in Arabia and in Persia, in medieval Europe and in modern Europe, in a word, in every part of the world where there have been and still are Jews, it seemed to me that such an opinion could not be the result of a whim or a perpetual caprice, and that there must be deep and serious reasons for its emergence and permanence.

What virtues or vices earned the Jews this universal enmity? Why were they alternately and equally mistreated and hated by the Alexandrians and the Romans, by the Persians and the Arabs, by the Turks and the Christian nations?

Because everywhere, and right up to the present day, the Jew has been an associable being".

In the year 2000, the parameters of anti-Semitism have never been so concentrated at any time in history; Jewish hysteria, their laws, like the Fabius-Gayssot law, are veritable cannons pointed at themselves. The banning and sentencing of revisionists is the most enormous publicity they have ever received free of charge.

The Jews themselves should take stock of the Holocaust and correct the arithmetical and technical ineptitude of the official version. And finally, to cure everything: radically abolish this ritual circumcision, the source of uncontrollable anarchic financial and revolutionary speculation.

TRAGIC CONCLUSION

It is certain that the facts are there and that we no longer have any questions to ask ourselves, but a problem to solve: that of the "*Jewish Question*". The only solution to the mental inadequacy of the majority of human beings is the radical abolition of circumcision on the 8th day.

Jewish liberalism, like Jewish Marxism, will destroy the planet just as Hitler predicted.

We are witnessing a general liquefaction under the Jewish grip, assisted by all the politicians of all parties who are their stipendiary henchmen.

Two world wars, millions of deaths, reigning finance, tentacular Marxism, untreatable and non-neutralisable atomic waste, systematic vaccination which destroys the immune systems and degenerates the race with the help of chemotherapy and food, horribly pathogenic music, (brooded over by a Jew in gatherings of unfortunate young people for "techno" music), drugs, delinquency, rampant homosexuality and paedophilia, youth unemployment, abortion, pathogenic pills inducing ovarian blockages, growth disorders, frigidity, etc. in teenage girls, and imbalances in adults. and in adults, hormonal imbalances, cancers, obesity, cardiovascular diseases, etc. disappearance of forests, animal and plant species, children deprived of all spiritual and moral reference points due to a lack of religious education.

We're in a bottomless pit, practically in a coma...

WHAT DID THE JEWS SAY IN THIS FIRST PART OF THE BOOK?

They confirmed that they want to dominate the world, which they are now doing, that they control the economic and financial life of the world, that they have the power to provoke crises and unemployment, in order to ruin individuals and States, to prepare the Revolution, that they are born revolutionaries, and provide the direction and execution of all the great revolutions , that they are the creators, directors, propagators and financiers of Marxism (socialism, communism, bolshevism), that they absolutely want to make nationalities and religions disappear in order to bring about the Universal Republic, i.e. their absolute world dictatorship, through their stranglehold on the media, the press, television, radio, publishing, cinema and press agencies.

They work to kill national, social and religious sentiment in order to bring down a civilisation created by White geniuses; they control the secret societies that are the real governments, which turn all political and social upheavals to their advantage; they are never nationals, but remain unassimilable Jews who cannot think like the citizens of the countries that welcome them; they are at the root of all the troubles, disturbances, conflicts and revolts in the modern world, and they Judaize the others.

That they want to practically destroy all peoples into an infra-ethnic mush for the benefit of their own interests, that they corrupt, rot, degrade and demean peoples and nations. It is they themselves who say this: No goyish criticism is as profound and lucid as that made by the Jews themselves.

After studying the statements of some famous Jews, particularly in modern times, we will look at the statements of famous Goyim.

R. Dommergue Polacco de Ménasce, author of this book: *"International financial and Marxist Jewry is the leprosy of humanity. The fascinating folly of Israel! It has been bubbling away for 5,000 years and today beats the record for all downfalls. Either it will be a banker or an idealist against the banker: Rothschild against Marx, Marx against Rothschild, the brilliant dialectic of brother enemies that produces the movements of History.*

Through money, masters of governments; through revolution, masters of the masses. I confess to being radically stunned by Israel's double and grandiose madness, which is leading mankind, the planet and itself to annihilation. The political pseudo-right would rather commit suicide than disobey the whipping father of B'nai B'rith by joining the Front National, the ultimate therapy for a comatose France. Never have the parameters of anti-Semitism been so concentrated as at the end of the twentieth century. But the zombification of the Goyim and their pseudo-elites in politics and the judiciary is the guarantee of Jewish "bigbrotherism".

The following analysis of National Socialism complements very well that at the beginning of this book by another eminent Jew, on the question of the Jews in Germany and the advent of Hitler.

Finkielkraut told us on FR3: "*Nazism sinned because it was too good*". A remarkable sentence, although inaccurate, because Nazism merely restored basic traditional orthodox values. "*Hitler was the most constructive spirit of his time*", said Baron Pierre de Coubertin. We know what Neville Chamberlain said about the responsibility of the Jews for the declaration of war in 1939, which he repeated in a letter to his sister.

Abba Ahimeir, head of the Betar, said: "*Hitler saved Germany, without him it would have perished in less than four years. It was neither nor Kerensky, nor Weimar who could fight Bolshevism, but Fascism*".

When the Faurisson affair broke out in 1979, I wondered why a clarification of the claimed figure of six million Jews as supposed victims of Nazism caused such a stir in the '*Marx-merdia*' and the '*atheist-levy-sion*'... This simple reaction, unique in history as regards the number of victims of this or that war, already exuded imposture. Then the thought started to occur: Six million, in seven camps in one year of the Holocaust 1943-44, the official duration, (advanced crematoria installed at the end of 43!), a country like Switzerland! Where would we have put these six million in seven concentration camps, including Dachau, which exceptionally held 60,000 prisoners? In seven camps, that would mean a maximum of 420,000 prisoners, and the figure is impossible! No traces of hydrocyanic acid in ashes that cannot be found. And the American Jewish Year Book puts the number of Jews in occupied Europe in 1941 at 3,300,000!

This figure is moreover inaccurate, since many Jews have since left for Israel, Soviet Russia, England and the United States, as have all the members of the Polacco de Ménasce family and myself. I then followed the Faurisson trial in France and the Zündel trial in Canada. The arithmetical-technical nonsense flashed into my mind. Most German towns with more than 100,000 inhabitants were 95% destroyed: how could the camp inmates have been supplied and not become the skeletons you see in "*Night and Fog*", for example? On the eve of the year 2000, Faurisson estimated the number of Auschwitz victims at 150,000, all ethnic groups combined, and J.-C. Pressac, an exterminationist sponsored by the Klarsfelds, puts the figure at 700,000!

The arithmetical-technical nonsense began to scream and is still screaming. Why was this revision forbidden? Wasn't Gorbachev the most important revisionist when he exposed the Nuremberg lie attributing the murder of the entire Polish elite at Katyn to the Germans, even though this unheard-of crime was Soviet? Why should anyone, apart from Gorbachev, have the right to question the judgement of a court of victors judging the vanquished and therefore having no moral credibility whatsoever? On the other hand, it is certain that many fellow creatures were killed between Germany and Russia, particularly in Belarus. But these were tragic facts of war. Didn't the Jews declare war on Hitler in 1933? Wasn't the Bolshevik regime quintessentially Jewish? Were Jews not unconditional supporters of Soviet soldiers and partisans?

So if my colleagues lied about the pseudo-Holocaust, why wouldn't they have lied about Hitler and everything to do with him? So we had to dig into the subject, from his participation in the 14-18 war to his suicide in the bunker at the end of the 1939-45 war.

We dug deeper: every day we were pestered about Hitler's responsibility for the war and the so-called '*Holocaust*'. My search went from stupefaction to bewilderment. Everything was wrong. Even "*the situation of the prisoners was no more terrible, far from it, than that of the Gulags*", as Bloch-Dassault himself revealed. Some camps had music rooms and swimming pools (Red Cross Inspections)! The emaciated skeletons we see in propaganda films are those of prisoners who were dying of hunger as a result of the supplies made impossible by the Allied bombardments, which razed entire towns to the ground, including women and children (sometimes, as in Dresden and Hamburg, 200,000 dead in a single bombardment), even though Hitler, well before the war, had submitted a memorandum of understanding to the nations so that, in the event of war, civilian populations would be spared. This agreement was refused by the West, which was subject to finance (denounced by Karl Marx himself: "*suppress trafficking, you suppress the Jew*"!!!) and Jewish Marxism... It is understandable that Rudolf Hess was never received in England, despite his heroic flight, and that "*this criminal of peace*", as Alain Decaux calls him, was murdered at the age of 90 to avoid exploding uncomfortable truths! Why doesn't everyone inform themselves like I do? Why don't they? Are the Goyim so stupid that domination by, and zombification by, my congeners (with Gayssot and Maastricht) are inevitable for them? Even Abbé Pierre cannot defend the integrity and constitutional freedom of expression of his friend Garaudy!

Hitler, born in Austria, which he always considered part of the Germanic nation, was a sensitive young man with a vocation and a talent for painting. His mind was vast, his conscience acute and his love for his country infinite. He was mobilised during the 14-18 war, and was a courageous soldier, loved by his comrades, but fell victim to combat gases and was temporarily blinded. The years that followed the war saw him miserable, both materially and morally, a relentless observer of his country's misfortunes and very knowledgeable about the aetiology of the serious diseases that were eating away at it. The iniquity of the Treaties of Versailles and Trianon ("*Treaties of Rapine*" as Lloyd George put it, "*paving the way for a second world war*"), negotiated by the Warburg brothers who simultaneously financed the Allies, Germany and the Bolshevik Revolution (small detail), tortured him. He lived through the horror of the Weimar Republic and its six million unemployed. He was perfectly aware of the major and frightening role played by my fellow members of high finance and Marxism. The people were starving. The blockade had strangled Germany. The middle class had nothing. 300,000 officers were unemployed. Jewish mercantilists were ruining shopkeepers and workers. Now, at the end of the 20th century, fifty years on, the Jews are claiming huge sums of money, masterpieces and collections of objets d'art. The question arises: who were the speculators and usurers of the Weimar Republic? A band of Galician Jews, Kutisker, Barmatt and Skalarek, had rushed into the dying Germany. After being expelled, they continued their practices in Holland (which were to be found in the case of Joanovici, a collaborator and later benefactor of Resistance networks). One postage stamp bore the figure of 12 billion Marks! For Hitler, the crushing of his country was unbearable pain.

He put all his energy into coming to power to get his country out of the hell of the Treaty of Versailles and the Weimar Republic. When he was imprisoned in Landsberg, where he wrote Mein

Kampf, a judge asked him: "What do you want, Mr Hitler, a ministerial post?" and he replied: "I would be very contemptible, Mr. Judge, if I only wanted a ministerial post". The prison governor described him as "an affable man, discreet, always ready to help, generous and of an exceptional nature".

So he decided to come to power democratically, because the people had sensed in him sincerity, farsightedness and energy. In six years, he got six million unemployed people back to work. He eliminated the S.A. and Röhm, who would have prevented synergistic action to restore his country, which rivalries would have consigned to perpetual ruin. He created the "Labour Front", which ignored the class struggle, an aberrant concept invented by Jewish ideologists. The Front had 25 million members and was the largest socialist organisation in the world. It formed a truly popular community of producers. Professor Goldhagen tells us (ARTE, 30 September 1996): "*I don't agree that there was no freedom in Nazi society. The more we learn about the Third Reich, the more we see that there was a certain amount of freedom.*"

Everyone had their rightful place in the life of the nation, and such an organisation was incompatible with war. He created a concept of the dignity of work. Factories had libraries, swimming pools and paid holidays. The workers had a little house where their wives could devote themselves to the care of their children, who would not become like ours, customers of music that kills, drug addicts, delinquents, suicides, the unemployed. He restored the cult of honour, country and ideals to young people. The little Volkswagen Beetle became a popular car. He created a special code to protect animals: harming them would have been severely punished. He advocated vegetarianism, banned vivisection, regulated hunting and organised a remarkable and effective ecological and zoological campaign. Natural medicine was made official in 1939, whereas in France, only chemical medicine, which is pathogenic and teratogenic, has the force of law. Luc Ferry (*Le Nouvel Ordre écologique*) recognises a Nazi project "of unparalleled scope, a monument to modern ecology, the education of the people in the love and understanding of nature and its creatures" (...) "the Nazi regime makes us witness a veritable eulogy of difference, a rehabilitation of diversity"...

Employers and workers worked together as equals to build the nation. "*Social honour*" meant conscientious performance of duty and was rewarded with dignity and esteem. The number of workers entitled to paid holidays was double that of other countries. War was necessarily excluded from the system, as Germany traded goods and commodities fairly with neighbouring countries. War was declared on Hitler by my fellow Americans in 1933. Hitler's hegemonic aims are a joke.

All he ever wanted was to reunite German-speaking and German-ethnic countries. Austria had wanted to join the Reich long before Hitler came to power and Czechoslovakia had three million Germans in the Sudetenland. Hitler took the country under his protectorate because the Czechs were exercising a dictatorship that was resented by the Slovaks and Ruthenians. Hitler did not exercise world hegemony like the United States, nor did he have an empire like Britain, over which the sun never set. In 1918, the rapacious capitalist powers had robbed Germany of Togo, Cameroon and South West Africa, which represented only 5% of the British and French colonies...

Perfectly unselfish, Hitler never owned anything but his dog and his house. There has never been any mention of a personal fortune acquired by Hitler as Reich Chancellor. As for his unshakeable desire to preserve the Germanic ethnic group, today we can understand it in the face of the globalist hysteria of institutionalised miscegenation, while my congeners are the most racist in the world.

The sixteen proposals concerning Danzig presented to the head of the Polish government, Colonel Beck, were the most reasonable in the world. Beck had accepted them, but England, under the influence of the financier Baruch, persuaded him to refuse. Hitler, with the help of Mussolini and the French minister Yvon Delbos, made every human effort to avoid war (England admitted at the Nuremberg trials that at that moment in history peace could have been saved!) while in Posnania (Poland) the Germans were persecuted and sometimes massacred. Hitler was forced into war, and France declared war on him unconstitutionally, following in England's servile footsteps, since the two chambers were not convened.

Today's world is riddled with all the moral, physical and ecological pollutants of Judaeo-Cartesianism, with the Mafia as the investor of choice. Seventy départements are invested in paedophilia. 70% of babies in the United States have no father.[67] Communism, created entirely by my fellow human beings (ideologists, financiers, politicians, administrators, prison and concentration camp executioners), has two hundred million corpses behind it and is still alive and kicking. It is true that in today's arithmetic, six million - even real - Jews are greater than two hundred million Goyim. The Zohar confirms this: "*The Goyim, that vile seed of cattle*"! We can understand Goebbels' words when he committed suicide with his wife and children, at the same time as his Führer: "*We are not going to let our children live in the hell that the Jews are going to prepare for them*". He certainly didn't imagine the absolute horror of the hell he would have left them in. There was indeed a holocaust: sixty million victims in a war declared against Hitler in 1933, who wanted to shake off the yoke of the dollar and the high finance of my fellow human beings. Then the holocaust of a hundred and fifty capitalist-Marxist wars that followed what was derisorily called '*Liberation*'.

All in all, a holocaust of two hundred million corpses in a regime that is essentially Jewish. Is this the truth? No, that's anti-Semitism!

---

[67] *The march of the century* on 28 May 1997.

Claiming the truth, no matter how vivid, is always "*filthy anti-Semitism*"; it is stupid abjection and can only be met with contempt.

Let's stop circumcision on the 8th day, which, through its hormonal and psychological repercussions, is the cause of our mentality and of the anti-Semitism that has resulted from it for 5000 years, during which we have spoken too much, "*words of death for ourselves and for others*" (George Steiner).

"*The Third Reich was the only force capable of overcoming absolute Communist horror*" (Solzhenitsyn).

The following document, a letter from Hitler to Daladier, President of the Council from 1938 to 1940, shows Hitler's pacifist mentality and his desire to do everything possible to avoid war: it received no reply, which is something to ponder, as is the fact that Rudolf Hess was never received in England, even though he had come to talk about peace, and that in the end he was murdered at the age of 90 in his prison!

"*May I take the liberty, Monsieur Daladier, of asking you how you would act, you French, if at the unfortunate end of a courageous struggle, one of your provinces were separated by a corridor occupied by a foreign power. If a large city, say Marseilles, were made unable to proclaim itself French, and if the French people residing in that territory were currently being pursued, beaten, ill-treated and even bestially murdered? You are French, Monsieur Daladier, I know how you would act.*

I am a German, do not doubt my sense of honour and my awareness of my duty to act in exactly this way. If you had this misfortune which is ours, would you understand, Monsieur Daladier, that Germany wanted to intervene without any reason so that the corridor remained through France? So that the return of Marseilles to France would be forbidden? Under no circumstances can it occur to me, Monsieur

Daladier, that Germany would enter into battle against you for this reason.

The Chancellor ended his letter by pointing out how pointless this bloody war undertaken by the Allies for Poland would be, for it is a certain fact that whatever the outcome of a war born of this problem, the Polish state would be lost in any case.

Poor Poland, reduced to what we know. Its entire elite massacred by the Bolsheviks in the Katyn forest and ships deliberately sunk in the Antarctic! Don't the Jews demand reparations for themselves?! This country is bankrupt, unable to meet its debts, and in a no-win situation. It is true that in the year 2000, Poland is not the only country to find itself in this sorry state!

While the Jews are on the subject of racism, let's talk to my colleague and fellow Jew Israel Shahak about their 'megaracism'.

In his *"Political Testament"* (which Robert Faurisson believes to be a forgery, but which corresponds perfectly to Hitler's psychology), Hitler says: "*It is normal for everyone to feel the pride of his race and this does not imply any contempt for others. I have never thought that a Chinese or a Japanese would be inferior to us. They belong to ancient civilisations and I even accept that their past is superior to ours. They have reason to be proud, just as we are proud of the civilisation to which we belong. I even think that the more the Chinese and Japanese remain proud of their race, the easier it will be for me to get along with them.* These words are full of basic common sense. When Professor Israel Shakak introduces us to the true nature of traditional Jewish writings, the essence of which he can penetrate because he knows Hebrew, nowhere do we find a single sentence that comes remotely close to this human and reasonable view.

So why should we be surprised that the Israelis massacred 254 men, women and children at Deir Yassin? These acts have been no exception for forty years, but no one has ever dared to officially accuse Israel of "Nazism". Not only was the Oradour-sur-Glane affair exceptional, as were the reprisals that followed the assassination of Heydrich, or that of a hundred soldiers killed in an attack in Italy, but for more than twenty years I have known that it took place in a way that was completely different from the version imposed by the official propaganda (the German captain Kämpfe had his eyes gouged out and his tongue ripped out by the Resistance, between Limoges and Oradour...). The church at Oradour was not burnt down, but an unexplained explosion occurred in the bell tower... (explosives stored by the Resistance).

In Israel, poor peasants were driven off their land and had no choice but to flee or die. This was blatant and cruel colonialism. As for those who denounced the horror, they were murdered, like Count Bernadotte and Lord Moyne. The methods used to dispossess the Palestinians amount to ruthless colonialism, blatant and inescapable racism.

The land from which the Palestinians are dispossessed cannot be sold to a non-Jew, rented to a non-Jew or worked by a non-Jew. Israel's agrarian policy results in the methodical, systematic plundering of the Arab peasantry. This is total racism. Laws of systematic and implacable spoliation did not exist in Nazi Germany. For example, the law on land acquisition of 12 March 1953 and all the measures taken legalise theft by forcing Arabs to leave their land to build Jewish colonies. The mass exodus of Arab populations under terror, as in Deir Yassin and Karf Kassem, liberated vast territories that were emptied of their rightful owners and Arab workers and given to the Jewish occupiers.

In 1975, Professor Israel Shahak gave a list of 385 Arab villages destroyed and bulldozed out of the 475 that existed in 1948. To convince people that Palestine was a desert before Israel, hundreds of villages were bulldozed, along with their houses, fences, cemeteries and tombs. Between June 1967 and November 1969, more than 20,000 Arab houses were dynamited in Israel and the

West Bank. Article 49 of the Geneva Convention of 12 August 1949 stipulates that "*The Occupying Power shall not transfer parts of its own civilian population into the territory it occupies*". Hitler himself- never broke this international law. 1116 Palestinians have been killed since the start of the intifada, including 233 children. The UN estimates that 80,000 Palestinians have been injured by bullets. 15,000 Palestinians are held in Israeli prisons. 20,000 are tortured every year, and this torture has been legal since 1996. All this is part and parcel of despoilment, discrimination, apartheid and racism.

The unfortunate Hitler, who wanted to preserve his ethnic group from the institutionalised miscegenation we know today, did not invent racism. Who came up with the idea of enslaving "*inferior races*"? A representative of the Chosen People who will be punished if he takes a pagan woman as his wife, who will choose his slaves from among the Goyim without mixing with them. "*For a thousand years*" said Hitler, "*for eternity*" say the Jews.

One law, one race, one destiny until the end of time. "*And Joshua burnt Ai to the ground, leaving nothing but a heap of ashes; and he employed the vanquished to chop wood and draw water for the community*. Men, women, children and slaves all under the yoke of Israel. But more often than not, there was no one left to enslave: "*And they destroyed everything in the city: men, women, children, young and old, oxen, sheep, mules, by the edge of the sword*".

The smell of blood is on every page of the Bible. The doctrine says that a people must be chosen for their destiny to be fulfilled. No other people can have the same glory. A true nation is a mystery, a unique body willed by God. To conquer its promised land, to slaughter or enslave those who stand in its way, to proclaim itself eternal: "*Let the trumpets sound in Zion, let the cherubim of the Almighty bring down fire and pestilence on our enemies. They razed the city to the ground and everything in it.*

In Samaria, because the Samaritans did not read the scriptures as they did, and because they had built their own sanctuaries; in Terebinth: instead of 6 cubits, they had used 5 or 7 or God knows what. Every man, woman, child and livestock was put to the sword. Massacres of cities for an idea or a matter of words. Joshua, the Lord's anointed, exterminated tens of thousands of men and then danced in front of the Ark. Where did Hitler learn to choose a race, preserve it pure and spotless, offer it a promised land? Woe betide the Amorites, the Jebusites and the Kenites, who do not deserve the name of man! Hitler's racism is a miniature of Jewish racism.

A THOUSAND YEARS! NEXT TO THE ETERNAL ZION!

How charming those pagan gods were, hidden under foliage, rocks and consecrated springs: they would have protected nature against the monstrous pollution of atheistic materialism. The Jewish God is the God of vengeance up to the thirtieth generation. It is a God of contracts, of derisory bargains, of credits, of bribes, of derisory tips. *"And the Lord gave Job twice as much as he had before, a thousand mules"*. Who knows the enormous role played by the Jews in the slave trade until 1870? (article by Professor Shahak published in 1967, before the Six-Day War).

All we know about traditional Jewish religious texts is what has been translated into Western languages. We don't know the reality of the texts because that requires a knowledge of Hebrew. Professor Shahak, who has a perfect knowledge of Hebrew, introduces us to these texts, whose racism is beyond imagination (*Jewish History, Jewish Religion, the Weight of 3000 Years*). Any Jew passing a cemetery must say a blessing if it is a Jewish cemetery. On the other hand, if it is a Goyim cemetery, he must curse the mother of the dead. Gratuitous hostility towards any human being.

Let's look at the anti-black racism of Maimonides, the famous Jewish philosopher: "*Some of the Turks* (i.e. the Mongols) *and the nomads of the North, the Blacks and the nomads of the South, and those who resemble them in our climes; their nature is similar to that of dumb animals and in my opinion they do not attain the rank of human beings. Among existing things they are inferior to man but superior to apes, for they possess to a greater extent than apes the image and likeness of man".* As for the United States, if the Jews support Martin Luther King and the Black American cause, it is to obtain tactical support in the name of Jewish interests. The aim was to win the support of the black community for the Jewish community and Israel's policies. Institutionalized miscegenation everywhere (except in Israel, where no Black or North African will enter) has two aims: to rule over a world of undifferentiated zombies, and to have entire communities, even homosexual ones, vote for the puppets of all the parties whose strings they pull. In Israel, Hasidism, an avatar of Jewish mysticism, is a living movement with hundreds of thousands of followers who have enormous political influence. But what does the Hatanya, the movement's bible, say? Non-Jews are creatures of Satan in whom there is absolutely nothing good. The qualitative difference between Jews and non-Jews exists from the embryonic stage. The life of a non-Jew is something inessential because the world was created only for the benefit of the Jews. The rabbi of Lubavitch and other Hasidic leaders are constantly issuing the most violent declarations and bloodthirsty exhortations against all Arabs. The influence of the philosopher Martin Buber is very important in the rise of Israeli chauvinism and hatred of non-Jews. Many people have died of their wounds because Israeli military medics, under the influence of Hasidism, refused to treat them. Yehezkiel Kaufman, sociologist, advocated genocide along the lines of the Book of Joshua.

Hugo Shmnel Bergman advocated the expulsion of all Palestinians in Iraq. The apology of inhumanity is preached not only by rabbis, but by people who pass for the greatest thinkers in Judaism. The most horrifying acts committed in the West Bank are inspired by Jewish religious fanaticism. Jewish racism and fanaticism are obvious: a friend of Marx, Moses Hess, well known and respected as one of Germany's first socialists, displayed extreme Jewish racism and his ideas about "the pure Jewish race" are no match for "the pure Aryan race".

"It is forbidden to save the life of a gentile because he is not your companion". Not only have some 400 villages been razed to the ground, as we have said, but hundreds of Muslim cemeteries have been destroyed by Israel (Book of Shahak, page 84).

As for the Talmud, it does not mince its words: *"It is a religious duty to extract as much interest as possible when lending to a Goyim"*. This speculative-parasitic mentality has been the major cause of anti-Semitism in all times and places. Neither the Church nor Nazism has exclusive rights to anti-Semitism. It existed everywhere, as it did in Persia five centuries BC.

The Church has often protected Jews throughout history. It has to be said that the nobility and the crown used the Jews to keep the peasants oppressed. This is perfectly despicable on the part of the Goyim, but the Jews took advantage of the situation to put pressure on the peasants for their own benefit. In eastern Poland, for example, during the rule of the magnates, the Jews were the immediate exploiters of the peasantry and virtually the only urban dwellers. In "*The rise of Christian Europe*", Trevor Roper (page 173-74), establishes that the Jews were the main slave traders between medieval Europe and the Muslim world. This is what Dr Prinz wrote: "*A state founded on the principle of purity of nation and race can only be honoured and respected by the Jew who declares that he belongs to his own people*". As we can see, institutionalised miscegenation is good for the Goyim, *"that vile seed of cattle"* (*Zohar*). This is what Maimonides says about murder: "*The Jew who deliberately kills a gentile is guilty only of a sin against the law of heaven; he is not punishable by a court of law*".

"*The indirect cause of a gentile's death is not a sin at all*". "*The best of the Goyim, kill him*" (Commentary on the *Shulhan Arukh*). Here is an extract from the treatise "*The Purity of Weapons in the Light of*

Halakhah": *"When, in the course of a war or during an armed pursuit or raid, our forces come up against civilians who we cannot be sure will not harm us, these civilians, according to the Halakhah, may and even must be killed.... Under no circumstances can an Arab be trusted, even if he looks civilised... In war, when our troops engage in a final assault, they are permitted and ordered by Halakhah to kill even good civilians, i.e. civilians who present themselves as such".* The Talmud says that it is forbidden to desecrate the Sabbath in order to save the life of a seriously ill Goyim, nor to give birth to a non-Jew on the Sabbath.

This is what you have to read to believe it in the Encyclopaedia Talmudica: *"He who has carnal relations with the wife of a Goyim is not liable to the death penalty, for it is written: "Just as the precept "a man shall cleave his wife",* which *is addressed to the Goyim, does not apply to a Jew, so there is no sacred marriage for a pagan; the married wife of a Goyim is forbidden to other Goyim, but a Jew is in no way affected by this prohibition"...*

From this quotation we should not conclude that this authorises intimate relations between a Jew and a non-Jew, quite the contrary . But the main penalty is inflicted on the woman. She is the one who must be executed, *even if she has been raped.* If a Jew unites sexually with a non-Jew, whether she is a child of three years (sic) or an adult, whether she is married or nubile, and even if he himself is a minor of only nine years and one day, as he has committed voluntary coitus with her, *"she must be killed as a beast would be because because of her a Jew has put himself in a bad situation".* It should be added that women of all nations are considered prostitutes. *Indirect deception"* is permitted. Theft at the expense of a Goyim is permitted if he is under Jewish rule. These precepts are not followed *"if they harm the Jews".* We can understand the violent dispossession of the Palestinians by the Jews, who have an overwhelming superiority over them. If the Jews are powerful enough, their religious duty is to expel the Palestinians. Clearly, according to the genocidal exhortations of the Bible and the Talmud, all Palestinians must be exterminated. Talmudic literature vehemently repeats: "*you shall leave nothing alive*". The Palestinians of Gaza are like the Amalekites. The verses of the Bible exhorting the genocide of the Medianites were taken up by an Israeli rabbi to justify the massacre of Qubbiya. Halakhic laws inculcate contempt and hatred for the Goy. The devout Jew thanks God "*that he was not born a Goy*". "*May all Christians perish at once*". It has become customary to spit three times at the sight of a church or crucifix. "*The Jews are the best of humankind. They were created to recognise and worship their creator and are worthy of having slaves to serve them.* (See references in Shahak's book). *We must show mercy to the Jews but refrain from doing so to the rest of mankind*". (cf. Shahak). Shakak, who lives in Israel, tells us: "*Anyone who lives in Israel knows how widespread and deeply rooted attitudes of hatred and cruelty towards all Goyim are among the majority of Jews in the country. The inhuman precept that servitude is the natural role of the Goyim has been quoted publicly in Israel, even on television, by Jewish farmers exploiting Arab labour, especially children*". (page 198).

Human rights have never been anything other than the rights of the Jew, as can be seen spectacularly throughout the West. The United States and Canada unconditionally support Israeli policy. There is not a single reaction when it is in flagrant contradiction with fundamental human rights.

It is impossible to enter a Jewish club or a Masonic obedience such as the Bnai' B'rith: but if a Jew is refused access, the cries of anti-Semitism are heard. In other words, those who constantly claim to uphold human rights are the ones who are constantly violating them. And the slouching Goyim nod in agreement... Faurisson and Garaudy are not entitled to that elementary human right of freedom of speech. They are responded to with Stalinist-Orwellian laws and convictions for thoughtcrime.

400 villages razed to the ground, Sabra, Chatilla, Deir Yassin, the constant massacres of Muslims deprived of their homes and land, 50 Muslims at prayer shot dead with revolvers, the incessant

massacres and, now in the West, the panic of opening our mouths to utter any truth: these are the human rights imposed on us by the Jews. In his book *"Germany must perish"*, published just before the United States entered the Second World War, T. Kaufman, an American Jew, advocated the total extermination of the Germans.

"Small detail", as Le Pen would say. Judaism is a crushing racist totalitarianism.

Before going any further, let us recall a few thoughts from the Jewish religious tradition we have just been talking about:

Deuteronomy 4:10-11: "*When the Lord your God leads you into the land he is giving you, you will find there great and beautiful cities which you have not built, houses full of all kinds of riches which you have not stored up, wells which you have not dug, vineyards and olive groves which you have not planted...*".

If this psychology is not that of the courageous Israelis who have escaped the determinism of circumcision, which makes them ideal victims of anti-Semitism, then we have here, in a nutshell, the speculative-parasitic psychology that is the mother of anti-Semitism.

The Talmud: "A Jew who rapes or corrupts a non-Jewish woman and even kills her must be absolved in court, because he has only harmed a mare". (Nidderas bammidebar rabba).

Wilhelm Marr was a Jew who took part in the 1848 revolution in Germany. When it was over, he realised that it had benefited Israel alone. He was also an honest Jew, and in 1860 he published a book entitled *"The Mirror of Judaism"*. It undoubtedly aroused the indignation of German Jews (Jews can never stand the truth about themselves, hence the totalitarian and racist laws that forbid any examination of the facts).

Here are a few mind-boggling passages from this breathtakingly relevant book: "*I declare aloud, without the slightest intention of irony, the triumph of Judaism in world history. I am publishing the bulletin of the lost battle, of the victory of the enemy, with no quarter given to the defeated enemy. In this country of thinkers and philosophers, the emancipation of the Jews took place in 1848. That was the start of the thirty-year war that the Jews are now openly waging against us. In 1848, we Germans declared our official renunciation of Judaism. From the moment of their emancipation, Judaism became for us Germans an object which it is forbidden to touch. It is not appropriate to criticise the domestic policy of the Prince of Bismarck since 1866. I will content myself with noting one fact: since that time, His Serene Highness has been regarded by Judaism as the Emperor Constantine was by Christians*".

Outlining the victory of Judaism over the peoples of Europe, Wilhelm Marr concludes: "*The advent of Jewish Caesarism - I base this assertion on deep conviction - is now only a matter of time. World domination belongs to Judaism. The twilight of the Gods has already arrived for us. If I may address a prayer to my reader, it would be this: That he keep this book and pass it on to his children, asking them to bequeath it to their descendants too. I do not intend to consider myself a prophet, but I am deeply convinced of the opinion expressed here: within four generations there will no longer be any office in the State, not excepting the highest, which will not be in the possession of the Jews... The capitulation of Russia is only a matter of time. In this enormous empire, Judaism will find a lever that will enable it to tear the whole world of Western Europe from its hinges once and for all*".

Marcel Bernfeld (*Le Sionisme*, 1920): "*It matters little whether the Jews are a pure race or not. What is essential is that all Jews have a deep and intimate conviction of being of very ancient stock and of being able to trace their genealogy back to the ancient Hebrews. More than any other people, they have the idea of being a pure race, hence a feeling of superiority*".

Knut Hamsun, winner of the Nobel Prize for Literature in 1920: "*A great man indeed, this Roosevelt, stiff and stubborn, going his own way, Jew that he is, in the pay of the Jews, a leading spirit in America's war for Jewish gold and power*" (Oslo, 1942). (Oslo, 1942)

Simone Weil (*Gravity and Grace*): "*To speak of a God who educates these people is an atrocious joke.*" "*The lie of progress is Israel.*" "*The Jews, this handful of uprooted people, caused the uprooting of the entire globe.*"

That about sums it up.

End of the first part

PART TWO
WHAT THE GOYIM SAY ABOUT THE JEWS

It would be impossible to compile a huge book of what the Goyim said. But we could quote the following authors:

- Henri de Montherlant
- Léon Bloy
- Romain Rolland
- François Mauriac
- Roger Martin du Gard
- Alfred de Musset
- René de Chateaubriand
- Mme de Sévigné
- Racine
- Molière
- Shakespeare
- Dickens
- Walter Scott
- Daniel Defoe
- And so on.

WINSTON CHURCHILL

Extract from an article published in 1920 under the title "*Juif internationaux*", the full text of which can be found in my book "*Auschwitz, le silence de Heidegger, et la clef de la tragédie juive*"[68] : "*In violent opposition to this whole sphere of Jewish endeavour are the projects of the Jewish International. The members of this sinister confederation are, for the most part, drawn from the unfortunate*

---

[68] Published by Omnia Veritas Ltd -

populations of countries where Jews are persecuted because of their race. The majority, if not all, have abandoned the faith of their ancestors and removed from their minds any spiritual hope of another world.

This movement among Jews is not new. Since the time of Spartakus, from Weishaupt to Karl Marx, and then Trotsky (Russia), Bela Kuhn (Hungary), Rosa Luxembourg (Germany), and Emma Goldman (U.S.A.), this worldwide conspiracy for the overthrow of our civilisation and the reconstitution of society on the basis of arrested development, envious malfeasance, and impossible equality, has been constantly growing.

It played, as a modern writer, Mrs Webster, has shown, a definitively obvious role in the tragedy of the French Revolution. It was the mainspring of every subversive movement in the nineteenth century. Now this clique of extraordinary personalities from the underworld of the great cities of Europe and America has clutched the hair of the Russian people and has become virtually the undisputed mistress of this enormous empire.

There is no need to insist on the role played by these international Jews, for the most part atheists, in the current achievement of the Russian Bolshevik revolution. It is, without doubt, of the greatest importance. Their role here outweighs all others.

With the exception of Lenin, the majority of leading figures were Jewish. Moreover, both the driving force and the inspiration came from Jewish leaders. The influence of Russians like Bukharin or Lunacharsky could not be compared to the power of Trotsky or Zinovieff, the dictator of the Red Citadel (Petrograd) or Krassin or Radec, all of whom were Jews.

In the Soviet institution, the preponderance of Jews is even more astonishing. And the dominant, if not the main, part of the system of terrorism applied by the Extraordinary Commission for Counter-Revolutionary Combat was taken in hand by Jews, and in some remarkable cases, by Jewish women.

The same nefarious dominance was exercised by the Jews during the brief period of terror when Bela Kuhn ruled Hungary.

The same phenomenon occurred in Germany (particularly in Bavaria) for as long as this madness was allowed to descend upon the temporarily prostrate Germans. Although in all these countries there were many non-Jews every bit as bad as the worst of the Jewish revolutionaries, the role played by the latter, when one considers the insignificance of their numbers in relation to the population, is staggering."

MOHAMMED

"I don't understand why we haven't hunted down these evil beasts that breathe death long ago. Wouldn't we immediately kill beasts that would devour men, even if they were in human form? What are the Jews if not devourers of men?

ERASMUS

"What theft, what oppression are the poor victims of the Jews subjected to? God have mercy on them.

If it is good Christianity to hate the Jews, then we are all good Christians". (1487)

LUTHER

"How the Jews love the book of Esther, which fits in so well with their bloodthirsty appetite for vengeance and their murderous hopes! The sun has never shone on a more bloodthirsty, more vindictive people than this one, who think they are the chosen people, so that they have the right to murder and strangle the gentiles. There are no creatures under the sun more greedy than they are, have been or will be. You only have to watch them practising their cursed usury. They flatter themselves with the hope that when their messiah comes, he will gather up all the gold and silver in the world and share it with them."

Ronsard

"Son of Vespasian, great Titus, in destroying the city you were to destroy its race. (1560)

Voltaire

"The Jews are nothing but an ignorant and barbaric people who have long combined the most repugnant avarice and the most abominable superstition with an inextinguishable hatred for all the peoples who tolerate them and thanks to whom they enrich themselves. They are the most abominable people on earth". (*Philosophical Dictionary*, 1745)

Emmanuel Kant

"The Palestinians [Jews] who live among us have the very justified reputation of being swindlers... But a nation which is composed only of traders, that is to say, of non-productive members of society, cannot be anything else than that." (*Anthropology*, 1786)

Benjamin Franklin

"In every country where Jews have settled in large numbers, they have lowered its moral standards, debased its integrity and ridiculed its institutions. I warn you, gentlemen, if you grant citizenship to the Jews, your children will curse you in your graves. In every country where Jews have settled in large numbers, they have lowered moral standards, discredited commercial integrity, and gone their own way without ever assimilating with other citizens. They ridiculed the Christian religion and tried to undermine it. They built a state within a state, and when they were resisted, they tried to strangle the country financially.

If you do not exclude them from the United States in this Constitution, in less than 200 years they will swarm there in such vast numbers that they will dominate and devour our homeland and change the form of government. If you do not prohibit the Jews from entering this country, in less than 200 years your descendants will be working the land to supply the needs of intruders who will remain rubbing their hands behind their counters. I say to you again, gentlemen, if you do not exclude the Jews from our community forever, our children will curse us". (Speech to Congress in 1787, preliminary to the drafting of the Constitution)

All this has been achieved perfectly, just as Franklin predicted.

MALESHERBES

"There is in the hearts of most French people a very strong hatred of the Jewish nation, a hatred founded on the custom of Jews in all countries to engage in trades which Christians regard as their ruin.

FICHTE

"To protect ourselves against them, I see only one way: to conquer for them their promised land and send them all there". (*On the French Revolution* 1793)

NAPOLEON

"We must consider the Jews not only as a distinct race, but as a foreign people. It would be too great a humiliation for the French nation to be governed by the lowest race in the world. I cannot regard as French those Jews who suck the blood of true Frenchmen. If I did nothing, the result would be the spoliation of a multitude of families by rapacious and merciless usurers. They are caterpillars and locusts ravaging France". (*Address to the Council of State*, 6 April 1806)

CHARLES FOURIER

"Once these were well spread out in France, the country would be no more than a vast synagogue, for if the Jews held only a quarter of the

properties, they would have the greatest influence because of their secret and indissoluble league".

SCHOPENHAUER

The German philosopher calls them "*the great masters of lies*".

ALFRED DE VIGNY

"*The bourgeoisie is the mistress of France; it owns it lengthwise, breadthwise and depthwise: Man becomes a monkey again. The Jew paid for the July Revolution because he handles the bourgeois more easily than the nobleman.*" (1837)

HONORÉ DE BALZAC

"*The Jews have cornered the gold. They are more powerful than ever.*" (*Lost Illusions*, 1843)

ALPHONSE TOUSSENEL

"*But how do you find these poor children of Israel who continue to pose as victims? Doesn't this tearful attitude suit them? So in spite of all the false philanthropists and charlatans of Liberalism, I repeat that France must cruelly atone for the wrongs of its charity towards the Jews. A reckless charity, a deplorable charity, the perils of which all the great thinkers of all the centuries had warned her of in advance; for on this point Tacitus is in agreement with Bossuet, with the Encyclopaedists and with Fourier. Tacitus, the most illustrious historian of Antiquity, speaks out against the indomitable pride and deceitfulness of the Jewish people*". (*Les Juifs, rois de l'époque*, 1845)

PROUDHON

For the father of libertarian socialism, "*The Jew is the enemy of the human race. They are wicked, envious, bilious beings who hate us. We must send this race back to Asia*". (*Notebook*, 24 December 1847)

MICHELET

"*Patient, indestructible, they have won through time. They are now free. They are masters.*

From bellows to bellows, here they are on the throne of the world". (1853)

ERNEST RENAN

"*The Jew knows no duty except to himself. To pursue his revenge, to claim what he believes to be his right, is in his eyes a kind of obligation. On the other hand, to ask him to keep his word, to render justice unselfishly, is to ask the impossible of him.*" (1864)

BAKUNIN

"*Well, this whole Jewish world, which forms a single exploiting sect, is at present at the disposal of Marx on the one hand and the Rothschilds on the other.*" (*Letter to the Bologna Internationals*, 1871)

DOSTOYEVSKY

"*What is coming is materialism, the blind and rapacious thirst for material well-being, the thirst for the accumulation of money by all means. Then, at the head of them all, will be the Jew, for although he preaches socialism, he nevertheless remains, in his capacity as a Jew, with his brothers of race, outside socialism, and when all the wealth of Europe has been plundered, there will be nothing left but the Jewish bank.*" (*Diary of a Writer*, Passim, 1880)

VICTOR HUGO

About Waterloo, which made Rothschild's fortune, "*Old man, hats off, this passer-by made his fortune at the very moment when you were spilling your blood. He played downwards and upwards as our fall became deeper and more certain. Our dead needed a vulture, and he was one.* (The defeat at Waterloo was the source of Rothschild's fortune)

WAGNER

"*The most urgent thing is to emancipate ourselves from Jewish oppression. I consider the Jewish race to be the born enemy of humanity and of all that is noble. It is certain that the Germans in particular will perish because of it. Perhaps I am the last German who has been able to assert himself against Judaism, which already has everything under its thumb.* (Letter to Ludwig II of Bavaria, 1881)

ÉDOUARD DRUMONT

"*When the Jew rises, France falls; when the Jew falls, France rises. High Banking, Freemasonry, the Cosmopolitan Revolution, all three in Jewish hands, work towards the same end by different means. One always finds a Jew preaching socialism or communism, asking that the property of the former inhabitants be shared, while their co-religionists arrive barefoot, get rich and show no inclination to share anything. I have no intention of stirring up all the filth of Jewish journalism, of recalling all the insults, all the ignominy they have poured on Christians... Christian masterpieces are left in the shadows, but on the contrary they beat the drum for everything that bears the Jewish mark.*

The misfortune of the Jew is that he always crosses an almost imperceptible line that must not be crossed with the Goy. You can do anything to the Goy, but you mustn't annoy him. He will let himself be robbed of everything he owns, but will suddenly fly into a rage over a simple rose that someone wants to snatch from him. Then, suddenly awakened, he understands everything, picks up the sword that was lying in the corner, strikes like a deaf man and inflicts on the Jew who exploited and plundered him one of those punishments of which the other bears the mark for three centuries... He disappears, vanishes into a fog, buries himself in a hole where he ruminates on a new combination to start again...". (*La France juive*, 1886)

EDMOND DE GONCOURT

"To me, who for 20 years has been shouting aloud that if the Rothschild family is not dressed in yellow, we shall very soon be domesticated, iloticized, reduced to servitude...when we published Manette Salomon, the order was given in the Jewish press to keep silent forever about our books..." (*Diary*, April 1886).

GUY DE MAUPASSANT

"In Bou-Saada, you see them crouching in filthy dens, bloated with grease, squalid and watching for the Arab, like a spider watching for a fly. He calls him, tries to lend him a hundred pennies against a note that he will sign. The man senses the danger, hesitates, doesn't want to, but the desire to drink and other desires keep pulling at him. A hundred pennies means so many pleasures for him! He finally gives in, takes the silver coin and signs the greasy paper. At the end of six months he owes ten francs, at the end of a year twenty francs, at the end of three years a hundred francs. Then the Jew sells his land, his horse, his camel, his donkey, everything he owns. The caïd chiefs, aghas, or bachaghas, also fall into the clutches of these vultures who are the scourge, the bleeding sore of our colony, the great obstacle to civilisation and to the well-being of the Arab". (*Au soleil*, 1887)

JULES VERNE

"They practice the profession of moneylender with a harshness that is worrying for the future of the Romanian peasant. Little by little, the land will pass from the indigenous race to the foreign race. If the Promised Land is no longer in Judea, perhaps one day it will appear on the maps of Transylvania. (*The Carpathian Castle*, 1892)

Adolphe Hitler

"France is and remains the enemy we have most to fear. This people, which is sinking lower and lower to the level of the Negroes, by the support it lends to the Jews in the attainment of their goal of universal domination, is putting the very existence of the white race in Europe in danger". (*Mein Kampf*, 1924)

Georges Simenon

"Everything fits together, everything becomes clear. The Jews, in their rage for destruction and also in their thirst for gain, gave birth to Bolshevism. Thus the Jewish octopus extends its tentacles into all classes of society". (*Le Péril juif*, Gazette de Liège, 1921)

Jean Giraudoux

"The Jews are a constant threat to the spirit of precision, good faith and perfection that used to characterise French craftsmanship". (1940)

Lucien Rebatet

"I left my papers and books behind. I set off again through Paris. I found everywhere the most impudent signs of Jewish sovereignty. The Jews savoured all the delights: flesh, vengeance, pride, power. They slept with our most beautiful girls. They hung the most beautiful pictures by our greatest painters in their homes. They lounged in our most beautiful châteaux. They were petted, praised and stroked. The smallest lord of their tribe had ten plumitifs in his court to sing his praises. They held in their hands our banks, the titles of our bourgeoisie, the land and livestock of our peasants. Through their press and films, they agitated the brains of our people at will. Their newspapers were always the most widely read, and there was not a single cinema that did not belong to them.

They had their ministers at the pinnacle of the State. From the top to the bottom of the regime, in every undertaking, at every crossroads of French life, in the economic, political and spiritual spheres, they had an emissary of their race, posted, ready to withhold the tithe, to enjoin the vetoes and orders of Israel. The Church itself offered them its alliance and lent them its weapons. They were free to cover their enemies with mud and filth, to heap the most deadly suspicions on them. The Jews had acquired nothing but theft and corruption. The more they extended their power, the more the rot spread with them". (*Les Décombres*, 1942)

PAUL MORAND

"All I'm asking for is a place for our compatriots, a very small place in the national cinema. In defending the French, I am simply claiming for them the right of minorities". (*France la doulce*, 1934)

MARCEL AYMÉ

"We are in communion with integral Marxism, because it is the weapon of our nationalism. You might say that Marxism is the antithesis of capitalism, which is also sacred to us. It is precisely because they are poles apart that they give us the two poles of the planet and allow us to be its axis". (quoted in "*Genève contre la paix*", 1936, by the Count of Saint-Aulaire, French ambassador, who reports the words of a major Jewish banker in New York)

PIERRE-ANTOINE COUSTEAU

Captain Cousteau's brother wrote: "*And right away, we could see that the conquest of money by Jewish plutocrats did not go hand in hand with the conquest of the masses by Jewish agitators. Always the same dualism, whose most perfect expression today is the alliance between Wall Street and the Kremlin*". (*Jewish America*, 1942)

LOUIS FERDINAND CÉLINE

"Our French Republic is nothing more than an enormous undertaking to debase and negrify the French people under Jewish leadership. The white man seeks above all the artificial, the convoluted, the Afro-Asian contortion. All French, English and American films, i.e. Jewish films, are always infinitely biased. They exist and are propagated only for the greater glory of Israel. They do so under various masks: democracy, racial equality, hatred of "national prejudices", the march of progress, in short, the army of democratic hogwash. Their strict aim is to dumb down the Goy even more, to get him as quickly as possible to deny his traditions, his taboos, his religions, to make him abjure his past, his race, his rhythm in favour of the Jewish ideal.

The trick of the hunted Jew, the martyr, is still inevitably played on this cuckolded Goy. The pitiful little story of the persecuted Jew, the Jewish jeremiad, always makes him wet. Infallible! Only the Jew's misfortunes affect him. He swallows it all. When the Jewish plunderer cries for help, the goy pear immediately jumps. This is how the Jews possess all the wealth, all the gold in the world. The aggressor screams for his throat to be slit! The trick is as old as Moses.

Modern music is just a transitional tam tam. It's the Jew who tests us to see how degenerate and rotten we are, our Aryan sensibility negrified. So, having robotised us, they give us trade junk good enough for our filthy slave meat. Who cares? The world has lost its melody. It's still folklore, the last whispers of our folklore that lull us to sleep. Then it will be over, the night. And the tam tam nègre...". (*Bagatelle pour un massacre*, 1937)

I have reserved far less space for the Goyim than for the Jews to converge towards the same lucidity.

Indeed, in this age of zombism, what the Jews say is more convincing...

There is nothing more to add to all this: unless there is a miracle, unless primo-pubertal circumcision is radically abolished, we are heading for a cataclysm in which Jews and Goyim will be exterminated.

Let's leave a final word to Dostoyevsky, and see whether the involution we are experiencing was not foreseen by superior minds in the last century. This is what Dostoyevsky said about a century ago: "*Their kingdom is near, their kingdom complete. The triumph of ideas is coming, before which the feelings of humanity, the thirst for truth, Christian and national feelings, and even the feelings of popular pride of the peoples of Europe will no longer breathe a word. On the contrary, what is coming is materialism, the blind and rapacious thirst for personal material well-being, the thirst for the accumulation of money by all means, all that is considered as a supreme goal, as reason, as freedom, instead of the Christian ideal of salvation through the only means of the closest moral and fraternal union between men. We'll laugh about it...*

All these Bismarcks, Beaconsfield (Disraeli), the French Republic, Gambetta and others, all of them are only an appearance to me: their master, like that of all the rest and of all Europe, is the Jew and his bank. We shall again see the day when he pronounces his veto and Bismarck is ruthlessly swept away like a bundle of straw. Judaism and the bank now reign over everything,[69] *over Europe, over public education, over all civilisation and especially over socialism, for with its help Judaism will root out Christianity and Christian culture. And if nothing comes of this but anarchy, then at the head will still be the Jew, for although he preaches socialism, he will nevertheless remain, in his capacity as a Jew, with his brothers of race, outside socialism, and when*

---

[69] This is true, but there is more than one nuance: Dostoyevsky could still say it and publish it. The media were not yet entirely controlled by the Jews as they are today, nor was the judiciary. Today, the media, like the government and the judiciary, are entirely controlled by them. The fact that a Minister of Justice was Jewish in 1981 (Badinter) is a definitive symbol. There is no more freedom: in the name of racist laws disguised as "anti-racist", Dostoyevsky would be charged. If he were a Jew, like Wilhelm Marr, he would be subjected to psychiatric commissions: that is a fact.

all the assets of Europe are plundered, then only the Jewish bank will remain. The Jews will lead Russia to her doom."

This text was written in 1880. In other words, about 120 years ago.

THE SHERLOCKHOLMIZED HOLOCAUST

The Jews have suffered many painful pogroms. It was undoubtedly their fault, but the pain they suffered was gigantic. Why invent the lie of the Hitler Holocaust, a veritable arithmetical-technical nonsense? Incorrigibly, it is a fantastic swindle that makes it possible to extort as much money as possible from every possible nation by making everyone feel guilty (without ever mentioning the tens of millions of victims of the Jews by Bolshevism).

Let's put the finishing touches to this pseudo-holocaust by sherlockholmisating it:

Is there a single ethnic group in human history that would not rejoice to learn that in a war that ended fifty years ago, it had suffered infinitely fewer casualties than it thought? Would the person who discovered this not be celebrated, rewarded for such good news? Would huge fines be levied? Would attempts be made to assassinate him, just as attempts were made to assassinate Professor Faurisson? Wouldn't such a reaction be clearly psychopathic?

Do the living skeletons in films such as Alain Resnais's *Nuit et Brouillard* have anything to do with gassing? Were they not reduced to this state by the impossibility of supplying the camps as a result of the bombardments by the Anglo-American air force, which reduced to ashes German towns with more than a hundred thousand inhabitants and holocausted hundreds of thousands of women and children, who were never mentioned?

Where would the six million have been during the intensive Holocaust period of 1943-44, when a single camp could not hold more than sixty thousand prisoners, and when, officially, Claude

Lanzmann himself states that there was no gassing with Cyclon B anywhere other than Auschwitz. As for mass gassings with other gases, there has never been any question of this, and there is no proof of it.

What is the value of "*witnesses*" when everyone knows how testimony was obtained at the Nuremberg trials, such as that of Major Hoess, the absurdity of which is now legendary, when there are one hundred testimonies of gassings at Dachau, where it is official that there were never any gas chambers?

It takes 130 kg of coal to cremate a body. We were told that the Germans burned 1,300 a day. During the official duration of the Holocaust, the American air force took hundreds of photographs of Auschwitz. Why don't any of the photos show huge wisps of black smoke, or the gigantic piles of coal that were needed?

Why do radio, films, television and the press continue to inflict on us daily the myth of the "Six million - gas chambers", according to the Jewish technique of the jeremiad, pursuing fifty years later, nonagenarians who had tried to save Germany from the iniquity of the Treaty of Versailles, from the rot of the Weimar Republic, from the collapse of German youth, from an unemployment of six million people by giving bread to the 215,001 people who depended on them?

Why does the *American Jewish Year Book*, on page 666 of its 1943 issue, inform us that in 1941 there were 3,300,000 Jews in occupied Europe?

How could gas chambers have adjoined crematoria when cyclon B is a hyperinflammable gas?

Why are revisionist historians being persecuted for demonstrating that the Shoah was a sham, when a scientific dialogue on an essentially arithmetical and technical problem of a primary nature, which has been called for since 1980, would establish the truth once and for all, thereby shutting everyone's mouth, as was the case for Katyn thanks to the revisionist Gorbachev?

How could Cyclon B, hydrocyanic acid, be used to gas a thousand people at a time, when the American gas chamber, for a death row inmate (maximum 2), is incredibly complex and expensive? Why was it claimed at the DEGESH trial in 1949 that such gassings were impossible and unthinkable?

Why did the report by Fred Leuchter, an engineer responsible for maintaining the gas chambers in the United States, state in an expert report that there was no gassing at Auschwitz?

Why is the Rudolf Report, which confirms the findings of the Leuchter Report, banned? Why are those who divulge it condemned in court, with no regard for the quality or accuracy of the report?

Why was Henri Roques' thesis on the *Gerstein* Report, a document that was rejected at the Nuremberg trials, annulled (for the first time in history), when the famous historian and socialist minister Alain Decaux declared in his book ("*La guerre absolue*", 1998): "*I admired the perfection of the true chartist's work in which Mr Roques engaged*" *(in his doctoral thesis on the Gerstein Report)*. (In his doctoral thesis on the Gerstein Report).

Why did Raymond Aron and François Furet assert, at a conference at the Sorbonne to which no revisionists were invited (no doubt out of intellectual probity and democratic freedom), that there is not the slightest oral or written trace of an order to exterminate the Jews? Why is there no mention of the plan to exterminate the Germans, by general sterilisation, as planned in the book "*Germany must perish*" by the American Jew Kaufman? Surely this is just a small detail?

Why was Cyclon B used by the hygiene services in Germany from the 1920s onwards for anything other than delousing clothes to prevent typhus? Why were large quantities of Cyclon B found in camps where it is officially acknowledged that gassing never took place?

Why are we always told about the "Six million - gas chambers" and never about the 80 million goyim exterminated in the USSR under an entirely Jewish regime in which the prison and concentration camp executioners were called: Kaganovitch, Frenkel, Jagoda, Firine, Apetter, Jejoff, Abramovici, Rappaport, etc.? (around fifty Jews).

Why, at the Zündel trial in Canada, did the notorious Jewish exterminationists go so far as to make fools of themselves by speaking of "poetic licence" to justify blatant lies, and why did they fail to appear in court at subsequent summonses?

Why do we need the Fabius-Gayssot law? (Laurent Fabius, the Jew, the man responsible for contaminated blood, and Alain Gayssot, the Communist, who has two hundred million corpses to his name).

Is it not the supreme proof of the imposture, the proof by nine, necessary and sufficient? We don't need a Stalinist-Orwellian law, a law *"instituting the crime of opinion"* (the thought crime of *"1984"*), *"the crime of revisionism sets back the law and weakens history"* as Mr Toubon said, shortly before becoming Minister of Justice, an anti-democratic, anti-human rights, anti-constitutional law, to establish the truth. Facts, arguments and evidence are enough. Professor Faurisson ardently demands a public debate with an unlimited number of opponents and he has never obtained one. Abbé Pierre asked for it: we pretended to accept it, then we finally refused it. Such a forum took place during a programme broadcast by Ticino (Swiss) television, in Lugano. No one knows this because the media, which takes its orders from the Jewish lobby, only lift a finger if the globalist lobby authorises them to do so...

Why, when a teacher declares that "*the holocaust of six million Jews exterminated in cyclon B gas chambers*" is arithmetical-technical nonsense, is he immediately dismissed, thereby instituting for the first time in history the aberrant concept of a historical-religious dogma liable, in the event of perpetual non-adoration of the holocaust myth, to the wrath of the secular Inquisition?

Why, in its January 1995 issue, did L'*Express* claim that "*the gas chamber shown for decades in Auschwitz I was a post-war reconstruction in its original state and that everything about it was false?*

Conclusion: there was indeed a holocaust of 60 million people in a war declared by the Jews against Hitler in 1933. Hitler had lifted six million workers out of unemployment and given bread to the 21,500,000 people who depended on them. He had rejected the dictatorship of the dollar god, and Jewish totalitarianism, the polluter of mankind and the planet, called "democracy" by semantic mystification. There are now only two parties: globalism, the totalitarian Judeopathy that exterminates mankind and the planet, and the nationalism of the Goyim who have not yet been totally necroticised by the Jewish capitalist-Marxist influence.

In the weekly *Marianne,* Jean François Kahn attacks the bureaucrats of the World Jewish Congress. Commenting on the conference on the spoliation of Jewish property which ended in Washington on 2 December 1998, he wrote: "*They have reduced the Shoah to a financial market. Thus the typical victim of Nazi barbarism, the primary object of the most appalling genocide of our time*[70] *was neither*

---

[70] This Jewish journalist ignores or pretends to ignore the arithmetical and technical realities of this pseudo-holocaust, but what he says is no less courageous and exceptional.

the exploited worker in Krakow, nor the humble craftsman in Lodz, nor the junior civil servant in Kiev, nor the small shopkeeper in Rue des Rosiers, nor the unknown craftsman in Riga, but the cosmopolitan billionaire who collected Rembrandts and Rubens, slept on a pile of gold bullion, grew his immense fortune in Switzerland, took out comfortable insurance policies everywhere and sent his children to pursue careers in the United States. This powerful lobby of American oligarchs is not ashamed to reduce the Shoah to a matter of big money".

If Faurisson had dared to say that, he would have had one more lawsuit brought against him by a justice system subservient to these oligarchs...

I will give the last word in this section to the writer Paul Chevallet, author of the remarkable book "*Urnocratie*":

"The essence of devastating globalism is Jewish. The Jews are its inventors and profiteers, to the great detriment of the whole of humanity. Article 131 of the Treaty of Amsterdam states:

"The common commercial policy must contribute, in accordance with the common interest, to the harmonious development of world trade, to the gradual disappearance of restrictions on international trade and to the reduction of customs barriers.

It is obvious to anyone still thinking that Article 131 is fundamentally inspired by Soros-type stateless speculators. It is not about manufacturing or production, but exclusively about commercial development, the removal of restrictions on international trade and customs barriers!

It is perfectly clear that the world must favour not those who work, but those who profit from the work of others (CQFD)! All states today are oriented and directed in every sector by the Jews. The system is suicidal in the long term, on a human scale. The masters are so obsessed with gold that they don't realise that the most important thing is to preserve drinking water for the survival of everyone!

So we simply note these indisputable facts, but we are careful not to denounce them because, on the contrary, we feel a deep jubilation at the idea that the End Times announced by the Scriptures are approaching.

"For 5,000 years, we've been talking too much: words of death for ourselves and for others". (George Steiner, Jew).

ADDITIONAL INFORMATION ABOUT THE UN

Like the old League of Nations, the United Nations is radically Jewish. Here are the names of the world government's top bureaucracy in Flushing Meadows, New York. The bureaucrats are as Jewish as their shadowy directors.

What can be said without error is that the UN, which wants to act as a world super-government made up of Jews, Freemasons and leftists to govern the peoples who are not yet under the socialist-communist dictatorship.

We had learned from Jewish newspapers themselves that a third of all Jews in Communist-controlled countries, some four million, form the main leadership and bureaucracy of the countries imprisoned in Communist red hell. The same proportion controls the UN.

In short, both East and West are under the rule of the circumcised.

It is not possible to name all the Jews embedded in the political delegations of the various countries meeting at the UN; to do so would require printing an enormous directory. The same applies to the innumerable Jewish bureaucrats of minor importance: the aim here is merely to give a non-exhaustive idea of the important leaders of the UN's permanent body.

GENERAL SECRETARIAT

➢ Dr H. S Bloch, Head of the Armaments Section.
➢ Antoine Goldet, Director of the Economic Affairs Department.
➢ David Weinstraub, Director of the Economic Stability and Development Division.
➢ Karl Lachman, Head of Tax Division.
➢ Henri Langier, Assistant Secretary General in charge, Social Affairs Department.
➢ Dr Léon Steinig, Director, Narcotics Division.
➢ Dr E. Schwelb, Director, Human Rights Division.
➢ H.A.Wieschoff, Head of the Analysis and Research Section, Department of Trust for Non-Self-Governing Peoples.
➢ Benjamin Cohen, Assistant General Secretary in charge of the Public Information Department.
➢ J. Benoit-Lévy, Director, Film and Visual Information Division.
➢ Dr Ivan Kerna, assistant in charge of the legal department.
➢ Abraham H. Feller, General Adviser and Principal Director of the Legal Department.
➢ Marc Schreiber, Legal Adviser.
➢ G. Sandberg, Legal Counsel, Development and International Law Division.
➢ David Zablodowsky, Printing Division Manager.
➢ Georges Rabinovitch, Director of the Interpreting Division.
➢ Max Abramovitch, Deputy Director of the Planning Office.
➢ P. C. J. Kien, Head of the General Accounts Section.

- Mercedes Bergman, Executive Officer, Personnel Office.
- Paul Radzianka, Secretary of the Appeals Office.
- Dr A. Singer, medical officer in charge of the health clinic.

INFORMATION CENTRE

- Jarzy Shapiro, Director of the UN Information Centre in Geneva.
- B. Leitgeber, Director of the UN Information Centre in New Delhi, India.
- Henri Fast, Director of the UN Information Centre, Shanghai, China.
- Dr Julius Stawinski, Director of the UN Information Centre, Warsaw.

INTERNATIONAL LABOUR OFFICE (ILO).

- David.A. Marse (Moscovitch), Director-General of the ILO in Geneva.
- Of the four members who govern the ILO, three are Jewish: Altman (Poland), Finet, (Belgium), Zellerbach, (USA).
- V. Gabriel-Garces, delegate for Ecuador, attached to the ILO office.
- Jan Rosner, correspondent for Poland, attached to the ILO office.

FOOD AND AGRICULTURE ORGANISATION (FAO)

- André Mayer, First Vice-Chairman.
- A.P Jacobsen, representative of Denmark.
- E. de Vries, representing the Netherlands.
- M.M. Libman, Economist, Fertiliser Section.
- Gerda Kardos, Head of Fibre Section.
- B. Kardos, Economist, Miscellaneous Products Section.

- Mr Ezechiel, Head of the Economic Analysis Section.
- J.P. Kagan, Technical Officer, Timber and Equipment Section.
- M.A Huberman, Technical Officer, Law, Management and Organisation Section, Forestry and Forest Products Division.
- J. Meyer, Technical Officer, Nutrition Division.
- F. Weisel, Administrative Division.

EDUCATIONAL, SCIENTIFIC AND CULTURAL ORGANIZATION (UNESCO)

- Alf Sommerfelt and Paul Carneiro, Executive Board.
- Alf Sommerfelt, Chairman of the External Relations Committee.
- J. Eisenhardt, Director of the Temporary International Council for Educational Reconstruction.
- Miss Luffman, Head of the Tension Division.
- H. Kaplan, Head of the Public Information Office.
- H Weitz, Head of the Administrative Management and Budget Office.
- S.Samuel Selsky, Head of the Personnel Office.
- B.Abramski, Head of the Housing and Travel Division.
- B.Wermiel, Head of the Recruitment and Placement Division.
- Dr. A Welsky, Director of South Asia, Office for Cooperation in Applied Sciences.

WORLD BANK FOR RECONSTRUCTION AND DEVELOPMENT

- Léonard B. Rist, Chief Financial Officer.
- Leopold Scmela, member of the Board of Governors, representing Czechoslovakia.
- E. Polak, member of the Board of Governors, representative of Czechoslovakia.

➢ Mr De Jong, Board of Governors, representing the Netherlands.
➢ Pierre Mendès-France, member of the Board of Governors, representing France.
➢ Mr Bernales, member of the Board of Governors, representing Peru.
➢ Mr M. Mendels, Secretary.
➢ Abramovic, member of the Board of Governors, representing Yugoslavia.

INTERNATIONAL MONETARY FUND (IMF)

➢ Josef Goldman, Board of Governors, Czechoslovakia representative.
➢ Pierre Mendès-France, member of the Board of Governors, representing France.
➢ Camille Gutt, Chairman of the Executive Board and Managing Director of the IMF.
➢ Louis Rasminsky, Executive Director for Canada.
➢ W. Kaster, alternative director for the Netherlands.
➢ Louis Altman, assistant to the managing director.
➢ E.M. Bernstein, Director of the Research Department.
➢ Joseph Gold, Senior Advisor.
➢ Lee Levanthal, Senior Advisor.

WORLD REFUGEE ORGANIZATION

➢ Mayer Cahen, Managing Director, Welfare and Maintenance Department.
➢ Pierre Jacobsen, Managing Director, Repatriation and Resettlement Department.
➢ R.J. Youdin, Director of the Repatriation Division.

WORLD HEALTH ORGANIZATION (WHO)

It is chaired by Dr Chishlam, a former federal minister in Canada.

This doctor, speaking as an authority on mental health, told Canadian radio that children's brains are being derailed by teaching them notions of good and evil, by telling them Christian legends.

The UN has found the world's most qualified Jew for the physical and mental health of humanity.[71]

- Z. Deutschnobb, Head of the Technology Section.
- G. Mayer, Head of Translation Section.
- Dr. N. Goodman, General Manager of the Operations Department.
- Mr Siegel, Director of Finance Administration.
- A. Zorb, Director of the Legal Department.

WORLD TRADE ORGANISATION (WTO)

- Max Suetens, Chairman of the Interim Committee on International Trade.

INTERNATIONAL TELECOMMUNICATION UNION (ITU)

- P.-C de Wolfe, American member of the Board of Directors.
- Gerry C. Cross, Assistant General Secretary.
- H.B.Rantzen, Director of the UN Telecommunications Service.
- A.G. Berg, International Civil Aviation Organisation: Head of the Airworthiness Section. In addition, Colonel A.G. Katzin represented the UN during the Korean War.

---

[71] This is just one of a Niagara of examples of the eradication of the moral sense produced by circumcision on the 8th day, which has fed anti-Semitism down the centuries with speculative powers uncontrolled by the moral sense.

➢ Georges Movshon, UN Information Officer in Korea.
➢ Ernest A. Cross, US Deputy Representative to the UN.
➢ Isador Lubin is the US representative on the Economic and Employment Commission.
➢ Julius Katz-Sachy is Yugoslavia's permanent delegate to the UN.

It should be noted that the State of Israel does not tolerate any non-Jewish representatives on any of its delegations to the UN, nor does the American Jewish Committee, international Zionism, the World Jewish Congress and other parasitic organisations that give themselves the status of real States, a perfect illustration of Jewish non-racism (good for the others!).

End of the second part

PART THREE
AN OVERWHELMINGLY TRUE TEXT ATTRIBUTED TO A JEW

The following text, published in 1914 and again in 1934, has precise references and an author's name. The audacity and aggressiveness of this text are such that I doubt a Jew could have written them in this way. The first part is obvious, but at this level of direct action, so to speak, the Jews are rather discreet. Their discretion goes as far as changing their names on a massive scale. I will give all the references to this text with the necessary reserve, and if I give it, it is because its content is rigorously accurate. This text could belong to the category of the "*Protocols of the Elders of Zion*": a forgery that tells the truth.

Not only is everything in it true, but since 1934, the date of its final publication, everything has been surpassed in horror: world war, unemployment, moral, physical and intellectual disintegration, music that kills, drugs, pornography, ecological collapse, extinction of animal and plant species, violence, crime, etc. And finally the triumph of Rothschildo-Marxist globalism, signalling the death of the planet. And finally, the triumph of Rothschildo-Marxist globalism, signalling the death of the planet.

Here are the exact references for the text that follows, which I did not want to attribute to my fellow human beings or to the Goyim, but simply to the long-proven truth.

The author is said to be Isaac Blümchen, born in Krakow on 14 November 1887 (although it should be noted that this Scorpio nativity corresponds well with the text). He was the son of Jacob Haïm Blümchen, a casket maker, and Salomé Sticka Pfaff, his wife. His uncle Blümchen, who lived in Leipzig, was known throughout

Saxony and indeed the whole of Germany for his Blümchen-Kaffe. Isaac Blümchen came to Paris in 1904, invited by the Alliance Israélite, whose president was Maurice Leven and whose expenses were paid by the Société des Enfants de Cracovie, whose president was Henri Weinstein of Maisons-Alfort. He waited to become a naturalised French citizen until he reached the age of active military service. He played an important role in the 1914 election campaign when the war gave him other things to do.

The books, entitled *"Le Droit de la Race supérieure"* and *"A nous la France"*, were published in 1914 and again in 1934. The books were deposited with the Bibliothèque Nationale de France in 1913, reference No 8°Lb 57 18013 and Lb57 18012 A.

The extracts that follow are by no means exhaustive, as these two books are, as you might expect, impossible to find anywhere...

THE RIGHT OF THE SUPERIOR RACE

At last the Jewish people are masters of France. Governments and nations officially recognised the fact. Alfonso XIII, King of Spain of the House of Bourbon, came to France in November 1913. He went to see President Poincarré for a hunting trip to Rambouillet. But he also went to see our own Edouard de Rothschild to discuss Spain's affairs with France. His Catholic Majesty the King of Spain, host to a Jew. Charles V, Philip II and Henry IV never expected this.

When Carlos of Portugal hung the Grand Cordon of the Order of Christ around the neck of a Rothschild, he was only prostituting his God to the Jew, but Alfonso XIII prostituted himself. Ferdinand, the Bulgarian Tsar of the Houses of Orleans and Coburg, who came to France to deal with his country's affairs, did not even visit President Fallières: he went straight to the home of our own Joseph Reinach, where he found all the ministers of the Republic.[72]

Our conquest is now an accomplished event.

I have explained (see the rest of the text) *that we did not want to drive the French out of France, as some of our people who were exalted by the victory recklessly said. We only suppressed the French who rebelled against our domination, in other words a handful of energetic people. We need the docile, hard-working mass of natives, just as the Spartans needed the ilots in Laconia and the English needed the Hindus in Hindustan. All we need to do is control the country and exercise command. We can exercise it in broad daylight. For the first thirty years of the Republic, we concealed our power and our progress; with the twentieth century, the Jewish era began. We rule and we want the world to know it. We rule France by virtue of the same right that Europeans invoked to annihilate the Redskins, and to enslave the Cafres or the Congolese. The right of the superior race over an inferior race. It is a law of nature. The superiority of the Jewish race and its right to domination are established by the very fact of that domination. The vanquished bow to the evidence.*

The native Frenchman is not lacking in a certain intelligence. They are beginning to understand what they can gain by accepting the inevitable. They seek our teachings, our advice and our encouragement in all areas of political, economic, artistic, philosophical and literary activity.

It is at primary school, at the lycée, at the Sorbonne, in the great institutions of higher learning that all the classes of the nation are formed, that the plebs acquire the few notions on which they will live

---

[72] When the police of the Republic decided to search the home of Reinach, the bandit of the southern Panamanian railways and military beds, they found diplomatic files that the Ministry of Foreign Affairs had refused to disclose to the parliamentary committee on the grounds of "state secrecy".

Our secrets are well kept by the Reinachs of Frankfurt am Main (translator's note).

their whole lives, and that the bourgeoisie acquires the ideas that it then holds to be definitive. We had wisely taken control of public education at all levels before unmasking our political design. The University, its councils and its programmes are in our hands. The most modest primary school textbooks and the proudest university chairs are subject to our censorship. At the École Normale Supérieure and the Polytechnique, our men control everything and decide on everything. Many of the publishers of textbooks are Jewish and the native teachers who work for them must conform to our thinking. The entire Sorbonne is devoted to us, the Collège de France trembles before us. In the scandalous Curie affair, the pontiffs and masters of "French" culture united against the mother of the family to serve our sister Salomé Slodowska.

We have purged the history of France of its splendour. Thanks to our will, the indigenous French ignore or deny the centuries of their past that preceded our advent. They believe that France was plunged into barbarism, fanaticism, servitude and misery before the time when the emancipated Jews devoted themselves to emancipating it. The history of France is now no more than the history of the conquest of France by Israel, beginning with the intervention of the Masonic lodges at the end of the eighteenth century and ending in apotheosis in the twentieth century. Joseph Reinach said in 1895: "At the same time as we are erasing from the syllabus or eliminating from teaching these useless legends, these absurd revivals of the past, we are outlawing what the French naively called 'l'Histoire Sainte', i.e. the history of our tribulations, the picture of our superstitions, the account of our fury and the memory of our origins.

Ask the French conscripts who will soon make up the electorate when they arrive in the barracks: they will readily say that Louis XI was the father of Louis XII and the grandfather of Louis XIV, all imbecilic, lecherous and ferocious tyrants, or that Joan of Arc was one of Napoleon's generals. They will never tell you, because they don't know, that the Jews arrive from Palestine via the ghettos of Russia and Germany, because two hundred thousand closely supervised teachers teach them that a Jew is a Norman, a Provençal, a Lorrain of a particular religion as good and true a Frenchman as the natives.

We have opened a School of Advanced Social Studies in Paris to teach bourgeois youth morality, philosophy, pedagogy, sociology, journalism and everything else relating to public life. The directors, including a general with the predestined name of Bazaine, are Théodore Reinach and Bernard, and the board of directors includes our Jews, Eugène Sée, Felix Alcan, Dick May (Jewish, secretary general), Diehl, Durkheim, Joseph Reinach and Felix Michel.

The Professors for the year 1913-14 (with a few natives whose blind submission is guaranteed) are: Théodore Reinach, Léon Friedel, Cruppi-Crémieux, Dwelshauvers, Hadamard, Brunschwig, Milhaud, Meyerson, Blaringhem, Rosenthal, Lévy-Wogue, Gaston Raphaël, G. Bloch, Hauser, Mantoux, Moch, Worms, Yakchtich, Weyll-Raynal, Lévy-Schneider, Bergmann, Zimmermann, Rouff, Léon Cahen, Caspar, Georges-Cahen, Bash, Mandach, Boas-Boasson, Mortier, Bluysen, Elie May, Edmond Bloch, etc.

All of them hold important positions, positions of command, in higher education or in central government. We've had enough of the names of our ghettos thrown in our faces in the past! Well, we have turned the Sorbonne into a ghetto, the University into a ghetto, and the French grandes écoles into as many ghettos. It is in the ghetto of the Hautes Études Sociales that young French people from the well-to-do or wealthy classes come to learn to think, to learn to live public life, to model their thinking on Jewish thinking, to abolish their hereditary instincts in the face of the Jewish will, to practise the only role that we allow them to aspire to: that of zealous servants, perfect servants of Israel!

But our young Jews always take precedence. When Lévy-Brühl, presiding over the philosophy juris, awarded the diplomas at the Sorbonne, he named the students Abraham, Durkheim, Flilgenheimer, Gintzberg, Lambrecht, Kaploum, Lipmann, Guttmann and Spaler first, and then the natives.

Our Joseph Reinach was vice-president of the army commission, of the commission in charge of excavating the archives of the Revolution, of the commission in charge of exploring the diplomatic documents of the Second Empire, and of shedding light on the causes of the Franco-Prussian war. All the military secrets and historical files were at Joseph Reinach's mercy.

When Joseph Reinach stepped down from the parliamentary gallery where he had just settled the organisation of the French army, Théodore Reinach took over (11 November 1913) *to defend the old churches of France against the vandalism of the natives.*

At the education congress, it was Théodore Reinach who proposed civic and political disqualification and infamous penalties for native fathers who did not hand over their children to an approved Israeli teacher.[73] It was Théodore Reinach who took the trouble to write little grammar treatises to teach the French their own language. And Joseph Reinach revealed to the readers of Le Matin (between Blum, Porto-Rich, Weyll and Saüerschwein) that Corneille was the author of Phèdre. We could have used more of our own in these various roles.

We have Herr at the Ecole Normale, Carvalho at Polytechnique, Bloch, Cahen and Lévy in all the higher chairs. But we thought it necessary to repeat everywhere the name of Reinach, who suffered so many outrages at various times. The more insolence the French natives showed at the time, the more important it is to humiliate them, to prostrate them before the Jewish family they had dared to sully. When Jewish scholars have taught French to the natives of France, they will then teach them Hebrew and Yiddish, for the vanquished must speak the language of the victors. L'Univers Israélite and l'Écho Sioniste made this proposal

---

[73] Secularism and (pseudo) democracy are the two necessary means of total enjuvement. They are the radical means of dumbing down and zombifying the masses, of which politicians of all parties, left and right, are the tip of the iceberg. We therefore need to impose these two impostures by every means possible, starting at nursery school.

with great reason in October 1912 . "Hebrew is a classical language in the same way as Greek and the Republic should create a Hebrew-Latin baccalaureate where candidates could choose Isaiah and Proverbs as texts. This teaching would provide remunerative work for our provincial rabbis".

On the other hand, it makes sense to teach our language to the French, just as the French teach their language to the Annamites and Madagascans. It is even essential, since Hebrew and Yiddish are becoming the language of public meetings (salle Wagram, Jaurès presidency), professional meetings (Bourse du Travail, special invitations for l'Humanité) and election campaigns (municipal elections in Paris, 4th arrondissement, Socialist candidacy, with posters in Hebrew characters). The achievement of our aims would be delayed if the Jews imported from Germany, Russia, Romania and the Levant were obliged to learn French. We need them to be immediately safe from expulsion, and immediately electable, eligible, and eligible for the highest offices in the land.[74] *This is why we have appointed our Grümbach, carefully chosen by the Alliance Israélite, as head of the department of declarations of residence, residence permits, home admissions and naturalisations at the Sûreté Générale.*

This is why we have also imposed a special procedure for Jewish immigrants on the Public Prosecutor's Office and the Tribunal de la Seine. For Jews, and for Jews only, the Court and the Public Prosecutor's Office accept as sufficient proof of identity, replacing any civil status, an act of notoriety drawn up by any rabbi and certified by seven of our brothers. So when our Jews arrive, they take the names they like, hiding their past, their convictions and the reasons why they are

---

[74] During my Jewish childhood, I witnessed the naturalisation of many Jews who barely spoke French. But this disadvantage was quickly rectified because Jews have a gift for languages and it didn't take them long to speak perfectly. I once knew a Jewish philosophy major at the Sorbonne who, despite speaking perfect French, had an appalling accent, so that in a sentence like this, the comic effect was staggering: "I was accused of having sartré Heidegger and of having Heidegerrisé Jean Paul Sartre"...

seeking refuge in France. The Public Prosecutor's Office goes so far as to exempt Jews, and Jews alone, from any legalization for the documents they are willing to produce. The signature of a rabbi, who does not even have to prove that he is a rabbi, is a talisman before which everything bows. This is how we have been able to install in Paris an army of fifty thousand Jews, who do not know French, but who are French citizens.

Almost entire electoral districts speak only our language, in Algeria for example, and in Paris in the 3rd, 4th and 18th arrondissements. Several thousand names on the Constantine electoral roll are Zaouch, Zemmour, Zammit, Zerbola, Kalfa son of Simon, Kalfa of Judas, Kalfa of Abraham, Marchodée of Abraham, Samuel of Aaron, Salomon of Isaac, Chloumou of Simon, Chloumou of Moses, Elie of Isaac, etc. And our brothers who give France its legislators and ministers (Etienne, Thomson) do not only know French. So the French must know Yiddish.

We want Hebrew to be the official language of France for the next generation, at least on the same footing as the indigenous dialect. In a thesis approved by the Sorbonne and prefaced by Professor Andler, of the Paris Faculty of Letters, our doctor Pines has sufficiently established that Yiddish is a literary language illustrated by our writers 'who have transformed into diamonds the stones of the road of exile' and well worthy of taking its place alongside French jargon. The Sorbonne awarded our Pines a doctorate in literature to back up his claim.

There are no Jewish teachers in state primary schools because the pay is too low. But the staff of primary schools is made up of our men. In Paris high schools such as Janson de Sailly and Condorcet, our Jews are in charge of everything. We would never allow a Frenchman to teach in a Jewish school, to teach the history of Israel and to comment on our holy books in front of Jewish children. French children, on the other hand, are taught by our Jews and are shaped by Jewish thought.

Note this feature which sums up the situation of two races: in no French family will you find Jewish servants, Jewish maids. All our Jewish families are served by French servants: the superior race served by the inferior race.[75] *Stop in front of the Rothschild bank on rue Laffite or the Rothschild hotel on rue de Rivoli and rue Saint-Florentin: you will see uniformed police officers watching over our leaders, over the masters of France. Not a crime, not a catastrophe would divert them for a moment from their duty. It is the symbol of France dedicated to the service of Israel.*

Here is a congress of the Young Republicans. On the platform, as guest of honour, our Reinach, Strauss, Roubinovitch. The chairmen, secretaries and speakers are our Jews Hirsh, Stora, Lévy, Cahen, etc. The young natives listen and obey. The young natives listen and obey. Here is an association of young republican girls: on the committee, Mlles Klein, Halbwachs.

At the Annales conferences, at the work of the Women's Secretariat, in the leagues for women's rights, for women's suffrage, at the head of philanthropic and educational works, at the Ecole Normale de Sèvres, de Fontenay, at all feminist or women's meetings in Paris and the provinces, who presides, inspires, directs?

Our Jewish women, our modern Judiths, our devoted Esthers : Mme Cruppi-Crémieux, Mme Moll-Weiss, Mme Dick-Meyer, Mme Léon Braunschweig, Mme Boas, Mme Marguerite Aron... And the French women, the young French girls, docile, aware of the inferiority of their race and their personal inferiority, stand modestly before the Jewish president, the Jewish lecturer, the Jewish director,[76] *like the little*

---

[75] I've seen this happen hundreds of times, particularly in my own family.

[76] The symbol of this frightening goyish mental inferiority and of zombism's capacity for global uniformity is the hideous wearing of blue jeans by Levis, a frightening manifestation of the disappearance of even elementary aesthetic judgement, of all personality. No one can believe that the mental distortion is such that it is often not only out of gregarious conformity that this garment is worn, but also out of coquetry! !

Annamites and the little Madagascans around a European teacher. Superior race, inferior race!

Thirty-eight million French natives read only magazines and newspapers written by our Jews or Goyim in our pay. They study their history only in textbooks produced under our control and their classic authors only in annotated editions commented on by our scribes. Morality, psychology, politics, journalism, art or finance, they know nothing except from us.

And when they think they're drinking beer from a "Pousset" brewery, they're actually drinking Jewish beer from a "Lévy" brewery (the Lévy, Jacob and Reiss family). If they think they're arming their boats with French artillery, they're actually buying their cannons from a Lévy factory (Commentry).

Unable to produce and sell the objects necessary for their material life or the works necessary for their intellectual life, how could the French govern themselves? How could they exploit the admirable country that Jehovah had destined for us since the destruction of the Temple?

We took power into our own hands. In the 1910 elections, thirty Jews stood for election. A dozen were elected. This means that in a dozen or so constituencies, the indigenous French have already understood that they will not find among their brothers representatives like our Jews. The superiority of the Jew is obvious to the people. In 1914, we will have twice as many candidates and we will occupy twice as many seats.

The President of the Republic is under our close dependence.[77] *The ministries are occupied by Jews or Goyim married to Jewish women.*

---

[77] Our witty and considerable Henri Amshell (at the Henri de Rothschild theatre), who uses the words of an author, familiarly calls M. Poincarré "le sire concis". Our great critics Blum, Weyl and Porto-Rico dit Porto Riche find this word exquisite. We had already seen it applied to Pepin the Short in *La vie de Bohême*. But Henri

When an unmarried politician shows ambitions like the young Besnard or Renoult, we force him to marry a Jewess if he wants a portfolio. If a politician is married to a French woman, we force him to divorce and marry a Jewess.

Such as Baudin, "Le grand dépendeur d'andouilles", whom we had pushed into the Navy. He repudiated his French wife to marry our sister Ochs, who accompanied him on fleet inspections (April 1913). When he arrived in the Rue Royale, his first move was to appoint our brother Schmoll as the Ministry's lawyer. The Paris bar did not flinch. We have to admit that he lacks heroism: all he has is a cult of success. It had harshly rejected Aristide Briand, a beggar with a bad reputation. During the Dreyfus affair, when the victory of the Nationalists seemed likely, the lawyers insulted the Dreyfusards at the Palais de Justice, beat them up and wanted to throw them into the Seine. Since the Jewish victory, the Bar Association has been subject to the Jews. Our Jewish lawyers seize the good cases, monopolise the fruitful publicity, intimidate the uncircumcised magistrates.

I attended a hearing of the ninth chamber, where our Lévy-Oulmann, defending some Jews from the underworld, fresh from a Russian ghetto, confidently proclaimed: "My clients are good Frenchmen, they are as good Frenchmen, better Frenchmen than anyone else in this courtroom". *The indigenous lawyers, as well as the deputy and the three judges, remained mute under the insult. That's how you have to treat the French. The time for caution has passed. Boldness brothers, insolence: the defeated bow their noses.*

This trait of the Paris bar is symmetrical to the trait of the Société des Gens de Lettres choosing to represent French writers in Russia, our Jew Kohan, from Odessa, known as Séménoff, who boasted of getting troublesome Frenchmen out of France. The Société des Gens de Lettres was warned and told to spare its members this outrage, but it persisted.

Amschel's joke is more delicious because it targets both the stature of the President and his zeal for Israel.

Because it is afraid of us: Who are the paper daubers that we do not hold by some sportula? "Oignez vilain, il vous poindra, poignez le Français, il vous oindra". *This is why our sister Ochs forced her husband Baudin to hand over the naval files to our Schmoll. If the husband does not plead against the suppliers Lévy and Paraf, the case is heard: Baudin, the minister, has fallen, Schmoll remains.*

To attack the Minister of War, Etienne, the Socialist opposition repeated that this businessman was at the same time a supplier to the army: President of the wire-drawing works in Le Havre, which supplied the material for cartridge cases. But the socialists never pointed out that the Board of Directors included, along with the chairman Etienne, our Jews Weiller, Hauser, A. Cahen, E. Cahen, Einhorn (vice-chairman), etc. The proportion of Jews is the same in all major supply companies, especially for the war and the navy. We need confidential information and we want big profits. Our Lazarel-Weiler has the luxury of giving a few rolls of gold coins to military aviators: it's money well invested. Our Cornélius Herz and our Reinach of military beds knew this. Our Lévy, Salmon, Caïn, Hanen and Wertheimer who sent "La charogne à soldats" *to the frontier garrisons also knew this. But we don't like to talk about it.*

In the Chamber, whether the President's name is Brisson or Deschanel, it is never permitted to utter the name of Rothschild any more than it is to incriminate a Jew. The Socialist Party is ours because we maintain its newspapers, its organisations and its tribunes. The radical and radical-socialist party is ours: its general secretary is a Cahen. Its members solicit and receive subsidies for their elections from the Rothschild and Dreyfus banks.

The Mascuraud committee, which is the richest and perhaps the most influential electoral agency of the Republic, is 80% Jewish: five Bernheims, nine Blochs, six Blums, nine Cohens, four Cahens, ten Kahns, seven Dreyfuss, five Goldschmidts, four Hirshs, twenty-nine Levys, etc. The Mascuraud committee is the richest and perhaps the most influential electoral agency of the Republic.

From the socialist Jaurès to the radical Clémenceau, there isn't a fat or skinny politician who isn't in our pay. We keep an eye on them through their Jewish secretaries and their Jewish mistresses, theatrical or gambling girls, baronesses of adventure or grooming merchants. When their rivalries give rise to quarrels that would interfere with our policy, we force them to keep the peace. It was we who reconciled these two mortal enemies, Clémenceau and Rouvier, on the sinister night when one Reinach perished.

It was we who reconciled the two perfidious rivals, Deschanel and Poincaré, at Astruc, before our Merzbach, Sulzbach and Blumenthal. To support the synagogue and the Committee of the Alliance Israélite, we have founded Masonic Lodges in Paris where our brothers deliberate alone, sheltered from secularists. All the Masonic Lodges are populated by our Jews, but no one can penetrate our Jewish Lodges, such as the Goethe Lodge founded in 1906 by our brothers Dubsky, Fisher and Bouchholtz. Only German and Yiddish are spoken there.

From there, the orders will go out that will throw our fifty thousand immigrants into the streets, browning in fist, for the great Passover to the sound of German cannons. Our brother Jost van Vollenhoven, a good Jew from Rotterdam, has been appointed viceroy of French Indochina by the Republic. His good fortune is even better than that of Gruenbaum-Ballin, a good Jew from Frankfurt, President of the Seine Prefecture Council, or that of Isaac Weiss, Secretary General of the Municipal Council. As soon as he was naturalised, Vollenhoven joined the colonial administration as a two-thousand-franc scribe. Ten years later, he reigned over an immense empire sprinkled with French blood and gold. Never had a Frenchman made such a career. The Annamites saw with their own eyes the distance between the Jew and the Frenchman: they now knew their true master.

A country where, out of twelve million inhabitants, there is not a man capable of administering its largest colony, which is reduced to bringing a little Jew from Rotterdam to govern Paris, and from all the German, Russian, Rumanian and Levantine ghettos, Jews to govern its provinces, its finances, its offices, its armies, is a finished country, a vacant country, a country to be taken: Well, we'll take it!

Morocco would suffer the same fate as Indochina. Commercially, everything that escaped the Germans fell into the hands of companies founded by our own Cahen, Nathan, Schwab and Blum. French officers speak with naive emotion of the Jewish children who greeted them in Moroccan towns with a compliment in French: As if it were not natural to see our brothers oppressed by the Moroccans receive the French as liberators. In a few years, thanks to the French, the Jews of Morocco will find themselves masters of the country where they were groaning in filth, masters of the defeated Moroccans, masters also of the French army, "the sword and shield of Israel".

Algeria is a case in point. The Arabs and Kabyles who once treated us like dogs are today, thanks to France, less than dogs before us. Their land, their herds, the fruits of their industry are ours. If they move, French soldiers will defend us.

In Crimea, in Italy, in Mexico, in Madagascar, in Tonkin, on the battlefields of 1870, Arabs and Kabyles shed their blood for France. But France continues to hold them in the dust of our sandals. France has made us citizens, voters and sovereigns. It is we who appoint the Etienne and the Thomson, managers of our affairs, arbiters of French destinies.

In the Journal Officiel of 16 December 1912, we find this impudent petition signed by several thousand signatures (Algeria, Madagascar, Tebessa etc.):

Mr. Chairman,

We take the liberty of pointing out to you the truly deplorable situation in which we find ourselves compared to that of Israelites and foreigners domiciled in Algeria. As we, like them, are subject to blood tax, we are their equals from the point of view of duty, but from the point of view *of law, this will not be the case and we find our children in a situation that is clearly inferior to theirs.*

As soon as they leave the regiment, the Israelites enjoy all the rights of French citizens, whereas we do not. Allow me to give you two examples:

1/ Today, a family of any nationality arrives in Algeria, most of them neither speaking nor understanding a word of French. The family has a son who wants to join the army and his father simply signs a declaration to have him drafted and the son does two years' military service. When he left the regiment, he was French and enjoyed all the rights and prerogatives of a French citizen. Can we draw a parallel with our children who, from their earliest childhood, have loved France? Well, this foreigner who, in spite of his military service, does not speak French, and when he returns home resumes his language of origin, is French and our children remain foreigners.

2/ A retired former Spahis or Tirailleurs officer, almost always decorated with the Legion of Honour, returns to civilian life. He remains an absolute foreigner. He has no rights as a French citizen, even though for thirty years he has laid down his life on the battlefields, whereas a foreigner who has only done two years' military service has French nationality!

If we have duties to fulfil, we would like to have the same rights as the Israelites... Look at that! The same rights as the Israelites!

The MPs did not honour this insane request with a response.

The Arab is the subject of the Frenchman, who is the subject of the Jew.

Our conquest of France has been facilitated by a series of fortunate circumstances. Jehovah fights so openly on our behalf that he turns even the resistance to our efforts to our advantage. We find unexpected allies at every step. And our enemies unwittingly serve us.

For the last twenty years we have had before us the nationalist party, the Catholic party, the neo-royalist party: the nationalists capitulated immediately, the Roman Church does not risk returning blow for blow, the neo-royalist party is our best safeguard. The nationalist party, made up of the debris of the Boulangiste party, was ours without a fight. Déroulède, subsidised by Rothschild (200,000 francs),[78] close friend of Arthur Meyer, former acolyte of Alfred Naquet; Messrs Galli and Dausset, future associates of our Isaac Weiss from Budapest at the Hôtel de Ville. Barrès, the ornament of Willy Blumenthal's salons; and the nineteen Jews of Le Gaulois, the twenty Jews of Le Figaro, the Jews of L'Echo de Paris, the Jews of all the newspapers, all the reviews, all the press agencies played our great game even when they pretended to resist us. Arthur Meyer answered to us from the nationalist staff, as he had answered to us from the Boulangist staff: intimidating some, buying others, at our expense, spying on them all, he delivered them to us at our mercy. The Nationalist Party and "La Patrie française" did not carry much weight.

The Catholic Church seemed to be a force to be reckoned with. But when I arrived from Krakow and saw the enormous and ruinous building of the Sacré Coeur looming over Montmartre, I lost my worries: people who spend fifty million on rubble and don't have fifty thousand francs to support a newspaper are not dangerous. We find it clever to maintain the legend that the Church is furiously persecuting us; then we become the martyrs and champions of free thought; Freemasonry has no other concern than to glorify us and serve us; the anticlericals are committed to covering us: the whole atheist, secular and secularising Republic is our thing.

In fact, some of the high clergy got on very well with us. The hope of converting a few Jewish millionaires and getting ostentatious alms from them appealed to the prelates. The baptism of Gaston Joseph Pollack, known as Pollonais, Arthur Meyer's lackey at Le Gaulois, by Father Donnech, in the church of Saint Thomas Aquinas, was the main success

---

[78] See *Le Testament d'un antisémite* by Edouard Drumont.

of which the Church was proud during the terrible Dreyfus crisis: our renegade, held at the baptismal font by the Countess de Béarn and General Récamier, did little credit to his godparents.

That fearsome Jesuit, Father Dulac, who frightened the Libre-Pensée, had lunch with our own Joseph Reinach. Father Maumus with Waldeck-Rousseau. These champions of the Catholic faith, like the de Muns, worked with our Jews: the Marquis (...) in dubious finance with Lazare Weiler, the Count (...) in equivocal journalism with Arthur Meyer. The bishop of Albi got his clergy to vote for our best henchman, the citizen Jean Jaurès, and the Catholics of the Loire marched for the ex-prefect Lépine, an accomplice in all our machinations.

The venerable Monsignor Amette, Cardinal Archbishop of Paris, when the Republic expropriated the congregations, negotiated with our Jew Ossip Lew, agent of our Jew Cahen, a coffee merchant, to lift the excommunication imposed on purchasers or tenants of confiscated religious property.

At the time of the Kiev trial, the academic prelate Duchesne and certain Catholic bishops in England thought, for some reason, of protesting against the accusation of 'ritual crime' (the subject of the Kiev trial) as forcefully as our rabbis. We don't know what their flocks thought: we were more disgusted than delighted.[79]

If we maintain that our books and our priests do not advocate ritual crime, and we affirm the innocence of one of our own accused of ritual crime, we cannot guarantee that there has never been any and that there will never be any among the bloody fanatics among us. The Roman

---

[79] This kind of remark, like the tone of the whole, leads me to believe that this document was conceived by a conscious Goy with an admirable knowledge of all the nooks and crannies of current affairs. What followed after 1934 was the same, but tenfold, and the Jewish names of the time were replaced by Aron, Wahl, Soros, Bleustein-Blanchet and so on.

Church is responsible! Its cardinals and bishops are more Jewish than we are! They go the extra mile: it's not for us to complain.

The trade in objects of piety in the Saint Sulpice district, as well as in the miraculous city of Lourdes, is, on the whole, a Jewish monopoly. On the other hand, our Jews, in possession of a parliamentary seat, willingly grant protection to the parish priests of their constituency. They can do so without incurring the mortal suspicion of clericalism, and they derive some benefit from it.

But it is essential that anti-Semitism be regarded in France as the worst expression of clerical fanaticism. The natives of this country live on ready-made phrases and absurd legends: let's make the most of them.

The only group of indigenous French people who still oppose us is the neo-royalist group. I have said how we get rid of individuals who get in our way. We would have no more trouble getting rid of an organised group. But this group is precious to us. If Action Française did not exist we would have to invent it. After the Dreyfus Affair, in the intoxication of victory, we committed some imprudence, some clumsy brutality. The defeated, scattered anti-Semitic gangs rallied around a few strange Dreyfus supporters, more inflamed against us and more implacable than our previous adversaries. A new wave of anti-Semitism would batter the walls of Jerusalem before our song of triumph was extinguished.

Fortunately, Action Française appeared, set out its doctrines and enabled us to link our cause to that of the Republic.

During the tumultuous evenings of the Bernstein affair at the Comédie-Française, when Lépine was flanking each spectator with two gingers to ensure that Israel was respected, a tall Jewish woman said to her French freeloaders: "It's nothing, a bunch of rascals, the King's Camelots shouting 'Down with the Jews'", and our Judith pretended to laugh. Like her, we laugh when we hear "Down with the Jews". They are the Camelots du Roi, they are the Ancien Régime, feudalism, the droit du seigneur, obscurantism, the gabelle, the mainmorte, the corvée. These are our adversaries. We are the Republic, Liberty, Progress, Humanity, the future City...[80] For ignorant, thoughtless Frenchmen, who are led where they want with the bait of a hollow formula, that's all it takes. Rather than being seen as Camelots du Roi, as henchmen of the Ancien Régime, the French will allow us anything, forgive us everything, hand over everything. If Action Française ever runs out of money, we will provide it with more than the dowagers: it is our security.

What's more, we are not afraid of the improbable prodigy that would re-establish the monarchy: the monarchy would be ours like the Republic. Philip VII would go hunting at Rothschild's like the King of Spain and lunch at Reinach's like the Tsar of Bulgaria. The monarchy would not rely on a clan of over-excited folliculars but on the aristocracy and the upper bourgeoisie. The aristocracy is one of our appendages and the upper middle class its servant.

We keep the upper middle classes on a tight leash on the boards of directors. We have bought what was left of the aristocracy. Bourgeois who want to make a career of it have to be our sons-in-law or our estafiers. The more or less authentic descendants of the former great families are also marrying our daughters or living off us. If there is a mismatch, it is on our side. We are the world's leading aristocracy.

To give ourselves a French appearance, we usurp the outward signs of French nobility. There are several ways of doing this. The simplest and cheapest is to take on a land name, a particle or a title on our own authority, as many courtesans and swindlers do. For example, our Finkelhaus bought a château in Andilly and signed it Finkelhaus

---

[80] The city of the future is a beautiful thing: in the United States and France, thousands of cities have been abandoned to violence, unemployment, drugs and all kinds of crime, and in the year 2000, where we will be tomorrow, this is only the beginning.

"The world will end in bloody anarchy", I wrote in my book *"J'ai mal de la terre"*, 50 years ago (Note by R. Dommergue Polacco de Ménasce). This is where Jewish hegemony and the absence of any religion leads.

d'Andilly, (F. d'Andilly). *Our Miss Carmen de Raisy, one of Rostand's hens (Chantecler), is our sister Lévy. Or Bader et Kahn des Galeries Lafayette, B. et K. de Lafayette, baron et comte de Lafayette. Others, embarrassed by scruples, acquire a real parchment from a hard-working and venal monarch: thus the Rothschilds. Or from the Pope: Count Isidore Lévy, who paid cash for the Papal Brief of 8 January 1889.*

The government of the Republic is doing us the same service for less money. For less than fifty louis, our Wiener became, by presidential decree, Monsieur de Croisset. Finally, if we are vain only for our grandchildren, we simply buy our daughters gentlemen of good stock. Isn't it better for them to restore their reputation by marrying an honest Jewess than by marrying an old whore, as they are bound to do?

The Prince de Bidache, Duc de Grammont, related to the Ségurs, Choiseul-Pralin, Montesquiou-Fézensac, Lesparre, Conegliano, etc., married a Rothschild. The Prince of Wagram and Neuchâtel (Berthier) married a Rothschild. The Duke of Rivoli (Masséna) *married a Furtado-Heine, who had previously married the Duke of Elchingen* (Ney), *whose daughter married Prince Murat. Prince de Chalençon-Polignac married a Mirès. Our Marie Alice Heine, before marrying the Prince of Monaco, was the wife of the Duc de Richelieu. The Duchesse d'Étampes is a Raminghen Jewess. The Marquise de Breteuil is a Fould Jewess. The Viscountess de la Panouse was a Heilbronn Jewess. The Marquise de Salignac-Fenelon, a Hertz Jewess. The Marquise de Plancy, a Jewess Oppenheim. The Duchess of Fitz-James* (of the Stuarts, my dear), *a Loevenhielm Jewess. The Marquise de Las Marinas, a Jacob Jewess, perhaps an escapee from Turcaret. The Princess Della-Roca, an Embden-Heim Jewess. The Marquise de Rochechouart-Montemart, an Erard Jewess. The Viscountess of Quelen, the Baroness of Baye, and the Marchioness of Saint Jean de Lentilhac, are three sisters, three Hermann-Oppenheim Jews. The Duchess de la Croix-Castries is a Sena Jewess. Widowed, she remarried the Comte d'Harcourt: she thus entered all the d'Harcourt families, the Beaumonts, the Guishe, the Puymaigres, the Mac Mahons, the Haussonvilles. Personally, the D'Haussonvilles had other opportunities to ally themselves with the Éphrussi Jews* (see a famous novel by Gyp on this subject). *The Marquise du Taillis is a Jewish Cahen. The Princess of Lucinge-Faucigny was another Jewish Cahen. The Countess de la Rochefoucault was a Rumbold Jewess. The Marquise de Presles is not a Demoiselle Poirier as the naive Augier believed, but a Klein Jewess. The Countess de Rambervilliers was a Jewish Alkein. The Marquise de Groucy, the Viscountess de Kerjégu and the Countess de Villiers were all Haber sisters. The Marquise de Noailles, a Lackmann Jewess, the Countess d'Aramont, a Stern Jewess...*

The entire armorial would be included. Our Finkelhaus published a very extensive work by the Viscount de Royer on this important subject. Since then, these "old rock" families have swarmed. Their children have grown up, and other "old rock" families hungry for Jewish money have followed suit. So we have a pint of good blood when we see the neo-royalists of Action Française lavish their energy, talent and eloquence on restoring the ancient nobility to its rightful place and returning France to its destiny. The "ancient nobility" *is now made up of our sons-in-law, grandsons, nephews and first cousins: all of them half or quarter kike. Does the good Monsieur Charles Maurras never receive an announcement when a bereavement occurs in a noble household? Mixed in an edifying salad with the oldest names of French descent, he would read the names of our Grumbachs, Lévys, Schwobs, Kahns and Meyers, who are* 'these gentlemen of the family'.

However, we found in Action Française itself an account of the funeral given by the nobility of France to Arthur Meyer's father-in-law, a d'Antigny Turenne. The whole armorial and the whole ghetto swayed in a fraternal embrace. Ah, it would be a fine ceremony for us if Philip VII were to be crowned surrounded by his valiant men and his pages: the sons and grandsons of our Jewish women would show off the frizzy fleeces, hooked noses, lewd lips and protruding ears that make up our trademark.[81] *It is stamped by us, the fine French aristocracy: our daughters or our sisters laid the eggs.*

La Vie Parisienne" *recounts how Tristan Bernard was at loggerheads with a noble old man in one of the most aristocratic salons. As the nationalist and Catholic Barrès was a regular guest of the Blumenthals, our Jewish Bernard could well be a regular guest of the Breteuils or the Larochefoucaulds, since the Marquise and the Duchess are precisely from his tribe...) and the noble old man said: "My grandfather was killed during the conquest of Algeria, my great-great-grandfather was guillotined by Robespierre, one of my great-cousins was assassinated by Henri de Guise, another of my ancestors died gloriously at Pavia...*

Ah, Sir," interrupted the famous ironist, *"believe me, I am taking part in this cruel and repeated mourning.*

Bravo, good Jew Bernard, you did well to insult the noble old man.

His nobility and old age merited insult among the noble hosts who welcomed the Jews and whose luxuries were probably paid for by a Jewish dowry or a Jewish housekeeper. All social distinctions are ours by right.

When Napoleon I created the Legion of Honour, he wasn't thinking about us. Under the Republic, the Legion of Honour belongs to us.[82] *You could say that the pink ribbon or rosette has replaced the yellow cap of the Middle Ages: that's how you recognise a Jew in the streets of Paris. We seem to wear in our buttonholes what has been cut off elsewhere. Our May, Mohr, Hahn, Sue, Sacerdote, Klein and Baron James de*

---

[81] This is the kind of comment that leads me to conclude peremptorily that this text is "a fake that tells the truth".

[82] It is true that in the course of the twentieth century, which my life has practically covered, it would be impossible for me to give the enormous number of Jews who have obtained this decoration enshrining democratization...

Rothschild, who were decorated as "literary men" in 1913, were undoubtedly the last not to be so. From Schmoll, administrator of Le Gaulois, Officer of the Legion of Honour[83] and Meyer Arthur d'Antigny-Turenne, Commander of the Order of Saint-Stanislas, to Mme Guillaume, née Goldschmidt (in literature, Jean Dornis), *via Marcel Cahen,* "caïffa planter" *and Lévy-Brühl, who passed on Rothschild subsidies to L'Humanité, our twelve tribes wore the Star of the Brave.*

Our own Lazare Weiler, an associate of the Marquis de Mun, was made a Commander of the Legion of Honour for his raid on French savings in the General Motor Cab, the New York Taxi Cab and Anglo-Spanish Copper & Cie Ltd. Similarly, our own Bonnichausen (known as Eiffel) *was made an Officer of the Legion of Honour for his dismissal by prescription of the Panama scandal:* "A little glory for the great humiliated of 1870, France," *explained his lawyer Waldeck-Rousseau. We are constantly giving humiliated France the alms of our glories! It will never be able to decorate us enough to recognise this. Each of our families provides the chronicle of national life in France with more than a thousand indigenous families.*

Where can you not find our Blochs? Jeanne Bloch the great artist; Bloch the satirist who stuck pins in the breasts of French girls; Bloch the civil servant who stole half a million from the subscription for the victims of the Mont-de-Piété (Martinique); *Bloch-Levallois, who strips all the old properties and will strip the Palais Royal. Who represents the French playwrights? Bloch. Who presides over the great boulevardier circles? Bloch. Who is in charge of human rights? Bloch. Who robbed the 14th Hussars, the little girl from Quinsonnas? A second Jeanne Bloch. Who*

---

[83] When Mr Rouvier, President of the Council, was recommended a journalist for the cross, he said: "That's impossible, he's not on my list of secret funds! Rigorous logic. The government can only decorate its auxiliaries. The Jews in Le Gaulois have always been appointed to Place Beauvau as "opposition members".

killed Minnie Bridgemain? Our Rachel Bloch. Who teaches morals and sociology at the Collège des Hautes Études Sociales? Three Bloch masters.

I could go on for ten pages, and if I took the Lévy family or the Cohen family, I'd fill two volumes: it's just us. Go to the Place des Victoires, around the statue of Louis XIV and the bas-relief commemorating the crossing of the Rhine. The business houses are run by Bloch, Lippmann, Weill, Klotz, Kahn, Lévy, Wolff, Alimbour-Akar, Cohn, We're the ones who crossed the Rhine!

It's just us. Who is on the executive committee of the Société des Commerçants et Industriels de France? Mr Hayen, general secretary, Mr Klotz, deputy, Mr Cohen, administrative secretary, Sachs, Schoeen, Sciami, Zébaum. The offices were swept by the French. It's just us. Who are the French foreign trade advisers appointed by the Republic to monitor national interests? Messrs Amson, Baruch, Moïse Bauer, Moïse Berr, A. Bernheim, G. Bernheim, Aaron Bloch, Louis Bloch, Meyer Bloch, Raoul Bloch, Isidore Blum, Brach, Brunswick, E. Cahen, A. Cahen, H. Cahen, Jules Cahen, Joseph Cahen, A. Dreyfus, Moïse Dreyfus, Dreyfus-Bing, Dreyfus-Rose and so on in alphabetical order down to Weil, Weill, Weiss and Wolf.

The French help export by nailing down the packing cases. The French are not even capable of profitable theft. They steal a loaf of bread when they're hungry, but to steal pearl necklaces, break through walls and jewellers' chests, swindle jewellers, carry out robberies from 100,000 francs to 3,000,000 francs, there are only our Jews: Kaourbia, Aaron, Abanowitz.

And the heroes of the Meyer-Salomons affair, and the heroes of the Goldstein mystery? Who runs the most flourishing industry in Paris: the white slave trade? Our Jews Max Schummer, Max Epsten, Jacques Jeuckel, Sarah Smolachowaka, Samuel Rosendthal, Sarah Léovitch, Sarah Planhouritch. The headmaster of the municipal school where the purveyors of Flachon and Nitchevo sheltered was our brother Weill.

Read "Les communiqués de la vie mondaine" *from our organ* "Le Matin": *nothing but the bereavements or unions of our Aron, Abraham, Gobsek, Schwob, Meyer, Worth, Kuhn and so on.*

Open "Excelsior": a *photograph of the living rooms of Madame Navay de Foldeack, formerly Madame Dreyfus, née Gutmann.*

Car accidents? Mr Bodenschatz collides with Mr Gutmann, Mrs Gutmann, Miss Gutmann and Mrs Rosenstein. "A Parisian family", *says* Le Matin. *Or maybe it's our Théodore Reinach who crushes an old French woman under his 60HP. All the newspapers remained silent and the court valued the life of the native woman at 15,000 francs.*

We are sovereign in deciding questions of honour. In the Bernstein case, three pairs of native witnesses disqualified our great Austro-American playwright on the grounds of civil status. Hebrew by race, French by fancy. We immediately convened a jury of honour and a French admiral solemnly declared that desertion in no way tarnished the honour of a gentleman from Israel. The six Frenchmen who had ruled against him did not budge.

Have you visited the exhibition of gifts received by our Myriam de Rothschild when she married our Baron de Goldschmidt?

The donors had inscribed their names on monumental cards to show their devotion to the Rothschild and Goldschmidt families. They were the Duchess de Rohan, the Duke and Duchess de la Tremoille, the Duke and Duchess de Guiche, the Marquis and Marquise de Ganay, de Jaucourt, de Noailles, de Breteuil, de Mun, de Montebello, de Saint-Sauveur, Prince and Princess de Broglie, de la Tour d'Auvergne, Duke Vogue, de Talleyrand-Périgord, de Chevigné, de Beauregard, de Kergorlay, de Pourtalès, de la Tour-du-Pin, Chambly, etc.

Did he? Do you think that our little Goldschmidt had the right to take the piss?

And when our Maurice de Rothschild, son of Baron Edmond, married our Noémie Halphen, what a crowd crashed into the synagogue on the rue des Victoires, watched over by the IXth arrondissement's peace officer. Always the same mob of Rohan, Harcourt, Ganay, Breteuil, Morny, Sauvigny, Mouchy, Bertheux, Fitz-James, La Rochefoucault, etc. Most of them half-Jews themselves answered the call of the police. Most of the half-Jews themselves responded like Jews to the Ketubah and the Aschrei Kol Yerci intoned by Chief Rabbi Dreyfus after Rabbi Beer's seven blessings. All the real France was there, the new France, summed up in its aristocracy.

As for the French bourgeoisie, they usually pay the price for our greatness. When we arrived in the marvellous land of Chanaan, fleeing the Russian police or the German gendarmes, with only our fleas and a few Asiatic diseases (elephantiasis, purulent conjunctivitis) as baggage, the Alliance Israélite and Freemasonry provided us with the initial outlay for a small business to give us some "surface area". In the space of a few years, through fortunate bankruptcies, by issuing fantastic securities, by trafficking that has no precise name in any language, we have put the fortunes of ten, a hundred, a thousand French families into our pockets. The Republic protects us, the judiciary is ours, the laws no longer exist.[84] When I say that the[85] judiciary is ours, I am not betraying any secrets. Many of the magistrates, judges and councillors in Paris are Jewish. The native magistrates know very well that promotion depends on their zeal for the Jewish cause. At the ninth chamber, substitute judge Péan proclaimed that his first duty was to

---

[84] Better still, at the end of this century, they are imposing anti-constitutional, anti-human rights, anti-democratic laws on politicians and mop-up magistrates, giving them every right and forbidding them to be criticised on pain of being accused of racism. Their megalomaniac racism becomes totalitarian in the name of anti-racism. Here they are supporting the Arabs they are massacring in Palestine, in the name of an anti-racism that allows them to institutionalise interbreeding with the dregs of the Afro-Asian world. Globalism is already in a coma. The law is called "Fabius Gayssot": a Jew responsible for the atrocious contaminated blood affair and a Communist who is dragging 200 million corpses behind him...

[85] This was even truer in 1999.

protect the Jews against rebellion by the French. We immediately made Mr Péan chief of staff to the Minister of Justice and had him decorated. At the 8th Chamber, a clumsy examining magistrate tried our brother Leib Prisant as a fence. His Jewish lawyer, Mr Rappoport, only had to produce a certificate from the synagogue:

"*I, the undersigned rabbi of the Agondas Hakehilok religious association, certify that Mr Prisant Leib has already attained a very high degree of perfection in the study of the Talmud and that he will soon be worthy of the title of rabbi*" (Signed, Rabbi Herzog).

The court immediately acquitted our brother. What do we have to fear? The French bourgeois works for twenty, thirty years like a galley slave. He hoards shield after shield. He denies his family, and often himself, all the pleasures of life. When he is rich, he brings his loot into our coffers, because we promise him 40 or 400% income and the joke is over. Not so long ago, farce still presented some dangers.[86] *We remember the disaster of our Benoist-Lévy, who robbed several local families and was killed by a ruined Mr Caroit with three shots from a revolver. The murderer was defended by Henri Robert, now President of the Bar, who said:* "Mr Benoist-Lévy called himself Benoist. Lévy is a nice name, though. Not everyone can be called Abraham, Lévy or Methuselah. He practised the system of the spider that lets the fly approach and snatches it up at the right moment. All these wolves and hawks of the stock market deserve no consideration. Their wealth comes from our poverty, their hopes from our sorrows. If you believe in protecting the honest French, acquit Caroit without hesitation. *The murderer was acquitted and the widow Lévy was awarded only twenty cents in damages.*

But time marched on.

---

[86] Today, the widespread Jewish system for the stock market, banking and insurance gives them every right, without any risk.

Today the jury would proclaim Lévy's legal right to Caroit's remains: the right of the superior race.[87]

This winter I was at the Five-O'Clock of one of our beautiful Jewish girls. She said that her brother-in-law Salomon spends three hundred thousand francs a year, and that he had given his daughter a superb pearl necklace. Among the native women who had come to admire our luxury, I saw a mother and daughter whom Salomon had lightened by three hundred thousand francs the previous year. The little French girl no longer has a dowry: she will marry one of our employees or teach our children. But she does not rebel. She and her mother are full of respect for the wealth made from their misery, for the car, the hotel, the historic castle of the great Israelite lady.[88] *It is enough for Salomon to find just one French family of this kind once a year to support his train and to choose his sons-in-law from the royalist nobility* (Noailles or La Rochefoucault), *from the nobility of the empire* (Wagram or Rivoli), *from the republican nobility* (Besnard, de Monzie, Kruppi, Crémieux, Renoult-Wormser, Delaroche-Paraf, or Baudin-Ochs).

The little French girl, wearing the bonnet of Saint Catherine and her feet in the mud, will see their wedding procession ascend the grand staircase of the Madeleine. We are the chosen people. For it is written Tractate Hid: "God gave the Jews power over the fortunes and lives of all peoples". *The Lord had given us the lives of the Philistines, the Amalekites, the Midianites, the Ammonites, Moabites, those of Bethel, those of Rabba and those of Galgala. We destroyed them. We slaughtered them, crucified them, hanged them and cut them into*

---

[87] Everything, absolutely everything, in the political and legal context proves that this assertion is true. Jewish bloodshed has become multilateral and perfectly legal. And to a degree that is beyond human intelligence.

The shameless exploitation of a holocaust whose arithmetical-technical ineptitude is dazzling is the nail in the coffin of this monstrous system of goy ruin.

[88] This anecdote illustrates what I always say: "there is no Jewish question, there is only the question of goyish bullshit"...

pieces, roasted them in bronze statues, tore them apart alive under iron harrows, (Pentateuch, Book of Kings).

The Lord has given us the lives of the tsars, grand dukes, governors and generals of Russia, and we are continually making a great chérem (massacre, slaughter) of *them with bombs and browning guns.*

But the Lord gave us France to make it our land of plenty and the French to make them our slaves.[89]

His will is done: may the name of Jehovah be glorified! We are the superior race...

---

[89] Consenting and satisfied slaves who, in their hideous Levy blue jeans, blissfully proclaim "liberty, equality, fraternity" while watching a football match or a pornographic film...

À NOUS LA FRANCE!

France is a geographical concept. The name France refers to the territory between the English Channel and the Vosges mountains, between the Bay of Biscay and the Alps. The men who rule this region are called the French. Now we Jews rule and command France. The natives obey us, serve us and enrich us. So the French are us. One people replaces another, one race replaces another: with the new French, France continues. We are a great nation of twelve million people. One of the richest and, despite our dispersion, the most homogeneous, the most united and the most strongly organised on earth. More than five million of our people are camped in Russia, including two million in Russian Poland. More than two million in Austria-Hungary, seven hundred thousand in Germany, three hundred thousand in Turkey, three hundred thousand in Rumania, two hundred and fifty thousand in England, but there are only sixty thousand Hebrews in Jerusalem. There are one hundred and fifty thousand in London and one million two hundred thousand in New York.[90]

But our chosen country is France. The climate is healthy, the land is rich, gold is plentiful, and the natives offer themselves to our conquest. Deprived of a homeland, we must settle in the homeland of others. By seeking out the line of least resistance, we have penetrated the French organism most easily and established ourselves most firmly. Before the Dreyfus Affair, there were a hundred thousand of us in France. Since the beginning of the twentieth century, through the work of the Consistory and the Alliance, with the help of successive ministries, which

---

[90] In 1999 these figures will all have to be revised upwards. There are more Jews in the United States than in Israel. The American government is radically and totally Jewish. The clown Clinton, who is the subject of a grotesque trial (for fondling a Jewish girl) and whom they obviously want to get rid of by this ridiculous procedure, has nine Jewish advisers out of ten. He was elected by 60% of Jewish voters.

we have kept on a tight leash, and our own men whom we have posted in the administration, our brothers have been called, brought, settled, provided with the necessities and the superfluous in this land of Chanaan in batches of thirty to forty thousand a year.

President Loubet and President Fallières will live on in the memory of Israel. In December 1912, the official section of the organ of Judaism in Tunisia published this expression of our gratitude:

President Armand Fallières,

As our beloved and revered President of the Republic, Armand Fallières, completes his seven-year term in office and retires to become an ordinary citizen of republican France, we would like to take this opportunity, in this French magazine, to salute him respectfully.

M. Fallières is a friend of French Judaism and has always maintained the most courteous relations with our co-religionists in metropolitan France. When he came to Tunisia in 1911, he received with great cordiality the various Jewish delegations who had gone to pay him their deferential homage. He had words of sympathy for the loyalty of our indigenous brothers and for their devoted collaboration in the civilising and emancipating work of our beloved homeland. We should also remember that it was he who awarded the Légion d'honneur to our eminent colleague Elie Fitoussi, thus honouring the whole of Tunisian Judaism in the person of our delegate.

We renew to M. le Président Fallières the expression of our deepest respect and our best wishes follow him in his retirement. The last signatures given by the venerated President Fallières granted the title and prerogatives of French citizens to our brothers: Marcus Grunfeld, Vohan Sholak, Fermann, Zeftmann, Guitla-Ruchla Merovitz, Jacob-Ariya, Altsschuler, Taksen, Wurtz, Hanna Guelbtrunk, Weinberg, Kayser, Kummer, Ott, Lew Spivakoff, Reifenberg, Kopetzky, Hanau, Wittgenstein, Valsberg, Esther-Lévy Ruben, Schmilovitz, Dobès dit Dobison, Goldstein, Isaac Azoria, Kapelonchnick, Robenowitz,

Baretzki, Nephtali Gradwohl, Meyer, Abraham Garfoukel, Isaac de Mayo, Roethel, Kuchly, Friess, Sarah Kaluski, Nathalie Schriftgiesser, Martz, Mecklenburg, Bernheim, Tedesco, Schmidt, Fisher, Ehrhardt, Wachberg, Strasky, Miraschi, Weiss, Schellenberg, Moïse Cohen, Finkel, Aron, Rabinovitch, Handverger, Josipovici, Ornstein, Rosenthal, Frank, Dardik, Sternbach, Max Goldmann, Lubke, Rossenblat, Bleiweiss, Mayer, Belzung, Salomovici, Kahan, Salomon, Kopeloff, Isaac Danon, Wertheimer, Kleinberg, Himstedt, Lewy, Reichmann, Weill, Schuffenecker, Moïse Saül, Wend, Oberweiss, Meyer, Goldstein, Elmach, Schamoun, Isaïe, Feldman, Weinberg, Kahn, Rosenblum, Mozes Wallig, Stern, Jakob-Karl, Noetzlin, Karnik Kevranbachian, Isaac Silberstein, Fremde Rosenzweig, Engelmann, Bloch, Jontor Semach, Spitzer, Freidlander, Lévy, Lilienthal, Taub, Zucker, Friedmann, Meyer, Klotz, David Salomon, Navachelski, Jacob Meyer, Eljakim-Ellacin Ubreich, Schlessinger, Weiss, Wolff, Aaron Viesschdrager, Sarah Id, Gombelid, Abraham Zaslawski, Ettla Granick, Ouwaroff, Ruhl, Maienberg, Feier, Munschau, Leib David, Rosenthal, Israël Quartner, Simon-Baruch Prechner, Fürst, Haym Cohen, Saül Blum, Goldenberg, Lichtenberg, Schwartz, Leichle, Bachner, Haberkorn, Pfaff, Abraham Berger, Leib, Axebronde, Elie et Simon Arochas, Ephraïm Marcovlcl, Eisenreich, Pfirsch, Moïse Sapsa, Miriam Sapsa, Sura Hamovicy, Hack, Nathalie Jacob-Isaac, Schweke, Mifsud, Isaac Mayer, Bertchinsky, Moïse Seebag, Moïse Bedoncha, Ephraïm Bronfein, Necha Arest, Jacob Bronfein, Haïm Tcherny, Stoianowsky Liba, Metzger, Marcus, Friedmann, Zacharie Zacharian, Nathalie Pitoeff, Leonhart, Hofrath, Unru Fisher, Katuputchina Fisher, Kieffer, Schick, Schor, Abraham Eptein, Esther Goldenberg, Jacob Kozak, Kamm, Abraham Rabinovitcz, Abrahamovitcz, Suralski, Jacob Bercovich, David Guenracheni, Cohen, Cahen, Mohr.

(Extract from the Journal Officiel).

Our beloved President Poincarré, supported by Klotz, the Jewish minister, and Grumbach, the Jewish deputy minister, is resolutely following in the footsteps of his predecessors. He had already given us proof of his devotion on several occasions. It was he who, as Finance

Minister, valued the estate of our great Rothschild (Amschel Meyer) at three hundred and million, thus remitting to the heirs rights which would have amounted to several hundred million, and above all concealing from the French plebs the enormity of the fortunes fed by his servility. It was also President Poincaré who, as former President of the Council and lawyer, took under his protection our sister Marfa-Salomé Slodowska, Dame Curie, and spared no effort to bring down a foolish Frenchwoman; thanks to his influence, embarrassing investigations were stopped, compromising documents were hushed up, dangerous witnesses were intimidated. It took an unfortunate chance for the Frenchwoman and her brood to escape the trap so well set by our bold compatriot.

The first signatures given by the new Head of State granted the title and prerogatives of French citizens to our brothers: Jacob Eisenstein, Stein, Kissel, Moïse Abraham, Rachel Lehmann, Nahïn Zaïdmann, Nessi Flachs, Tugendhat, Steinmetz, Acher Lourie, Slata Rocks, Weismann, Loeb, Reicher, Bassa, Weksler, Abraham, Kerestdji, Bohn Gruenebaum, Kouttchneski, Zelenka, Klotz, Moïse Leibowitz, Olga Herscovici, Reisner.

(Extract from the Official Journal).

This is how Mr Poincaré continued the work of Mrs Loubet and Fallières. We cannot miss him. It is not from him that we would accept resistance to the introduction of foreign elements into the French body.

We will allow him a nationalism on parade; he knows well what considerations we would put forward to forbid him an effective nationalism. He will never risk it: prudence is the main trait of his vigorous character. During the crisis that shook his country for several years, M. Poincarré had the courage to keep quiet, not to take sides, to curb both his passion for justice and his patriotic instinct. Later, after victory, he "freed his conscience" and publicly acknowledged that the victors were right.

On 13 September 1913, during his royal tour, Mr Poincaré presided over the banquet held in his honour at the prefecture in Cahors. On his right was Madame Klotz, a Jewess and wife of the Minister, and on his left was Madame de Monzie, a Jewess and wife of the Deputy Minister. The native women occupied stools a little lower down. Between the two Jewish princesses, the President of the Republic displayed his role and his devotion: Long live Poincaré!

France is now ours. We are the Republic.

These Sternbachs, Goldmans, Kohans, Schuffeneckers, Schamanns, Oberweisfs, Kaksens, Scholacks, Ruchlas, Merowitzs and Guelbtrunks, who reinforce our ranks every year by the score of thousands and whom the Presidents of the Republic immediately declare to be 'first class French', may at first seem a little disorientated. It's only natural that they should be unfamiliar with the language and customs, the history and traditions, the people and things of France. But they quickly got to grips with the fact that the whole political organisation and all the social powers were at their service. Naturalized in 1912 and 1913, yesterday helmetsmen, like my venerated father, furriers, itinerant merchants in the depths of Tartary, Ukraine, Galicia, Poland, Swabia, Prussia, Moldo-Valachia, we will see them before ten years prefects, deputies, editors of major newspapers, professors at the Sorbonne, concessionaires of colonial estates and metropolitan monopolies, knights, officers of the Legion of Honour, owners of forests and historic châteaux, undisputed lords of France.

And the French populace salutes them low.

French by the decrees of Loubet, Fallières and Poincaré, they remain at the same time Germans, Russians, Austrians, Romanians by the laws of their country of origin: they thus have several fictitious nationalities to use according to circumstances. But they have only one real nationality: ours, Jewish nationality. We are foreigners, hostile guests in every country, and at the same time we are at home in every country where we are the masters. That is why we are protesting here against the pusillanimity, against the pitiful cowardice of the Jews who invent sophisms to conceal their defeat from the vanquished and to let our vassals believe that we are not their barons.

Some imagine to maintain that there are no human races, that a Spaniard or an Eskimo, a Japanese or a Norwegian, a Cafre, a Sicilian, a Patagonian, are all beings of the same species, with the same faculties, the same physiology, the same mentality, the same sensibility. A grossly absurd theory. There are races of men just as there are races of dogs or horses, so different, so distant, physically enemies, that the elements of their bodies cannot be brought together.

At the congress of surgery held in Paris in October 1912, Dr Serge Voronoff proved by experiment that it was possible to graft the ovaries of another ewe of the same species onto a ewe and that it remained fertile. However, it is impossible to graft between two ewes of different species.

What a gulf between the Jew and the Frenchwoman! Between the Jew and the Frenchman!

Other Hebrews, such as our brother Weyll (known as Nozières) *in his comedy* "Le Baptême" (Baptism), *beg for pity from our French subjects, moaning*: "Being a Jew is not a religion, nor a race, it's a misfortune". *A misfortune! When all we have to do is cross the border into France, with our saddlebags over our shoulders, and declare ourselves to be Jews in order to immediately receive from the Republic a French name, land, fruitful privileges, honours, countless immunities, power and inviolability! Whereas all we have to do is declare ourselves Jews to see the indigenous French grovel before us.*[91]

---

[91] This is increasingly true: the last President of the Republic was only elected because he grovelled before the Jews. The other candidate refused and was not elected, even though the polls were considerably in his favour.

TRUTH AND SYNTHESIS

Come on! No false humility!

Gone are the days when we had to bend over backwards, sneak down the back stairs, accept the advances and rebuffs. We have the strength, and therefore the right, to speak out, to present ourselves as we are, to be proud of our status. It is shameful that so many Jews ask the French Chancellery for a French name or give themselves a pseudonym. Why do our Meyer Amschels call themselves Rothschilds and the Rothschilds call themselves Mandels? What are all these false names of Tristan Bernard, Francis de Croisset, Cécile Sorel, Henri Duvernois, Isidore de Lara, Jeanne Marnac, Jean Finot, Séménoff, Nozières? When I arrived from Krakow, our Alliance Israélite chiefs advised me to translate my name Blümchen and to call myself François Fleurette from now on, to mollify the natives. At the naturalisation office, our brother Grumbach wanted to create a civil status in the name of Raoul d'Antigny or Robert de Mirabeau, to give me easier access to the big world and official salons. I refused with contempt: I know better what we are worth today. How low is it to make the French believe that we are one of their enslaved people when we are the sovereign people.

Honour to our Jeanne Bloch, Henry Bernheim, Sulzbach, Morzbach, Blumenthal, Gugenheim, Bischoffsheim, our Cohen, Cahen, Kohn, Kahn, Kohan, our Meyer, Lévy, Rosenthall, Roseblatt, our Stern, Klotz, Schrameck, and Schmoll, who proudly bear the Hebrew or Germanic name.

These are the worthy sons of Judah, the true conquerors, and the reward for their courage is to be found in the lowliness of the conquered people, bent before them, bringing their own harvest into their granaries and their savings into their coffers.

In England and a number of other countries where we still have only major financial interests, without much political power, we are accused of creating a state within a state.

In France, that period is over: we are the State.

The Catholic admiral de Cuberville once made a fool of himself in the eyes of free-thinking Frenchmen by saying that "France should be the sword and shield of the Church". *The Crusades are long gone. Today, France is the sword and shield of Israel. We can put four million Frenchmen under arms to support our international speculations, to recover our large debts, to deliver our oppressed brothers, to carry out our national policy.*

How dare anyone challenge our love for France?

We love him like a rich landowner loves his estate, like a hunter loves his dog, like an epicurean loves his cellar and his mistress, like a conqueror loves his elite praetorians.

Hysterical Jews, the kind who sometimes jeopardise our business by their blunders, threatened the French with "getting them out of France". *They were referring to the very few Frenchmen who still dare to stand up to us: a handful of lunatics, with no credit and no resources, who will be stoned to death at the first sign of our presence.*[92]

But what, by Jehovah, would we do with France without its good people, cattle easy to shear, docile to the whip, industrious, thrifty, humble before their masters, productive beyond anything we could hope for from the Promised Land?[93] *We love the natives of France as we love France: they are the livestock of our farm. All we had to do was subdue them, and we've done that, and done it well.*

Not only in assemblies, in cafés, in public places, but in newsrooms, at home, at their own tables, the natives lower their voices when they talk

---

[92] It's so true: it's the French politicians and judges who apply the Gayssot law against those who rebel against all manifestations of totalitarian Judeopathy... The Jews don't move: they pass the laws like "big brother"...

[93] Unfortunately, the socio-economic conditions imposed by Jewry have changed this unhappy people, who are no longer encouraged to work by social security contributions and taxes, and are reduced to unemployment...

about us: Just as the Italians did in Milan under the Austrian terror. They sometimes murmur against us, casting a worried glance around. But if some foolish person incites them to action, they hasten to reply: "I can't, I have family, I need to earn a living, They have everything".[94] In the same way that Germany has the French Republic oust ministers who displease it, we have French magazines and newspapers oust suspicious writers who try to resist us or who simply evade our control.[95] The biggest, most powerful newspapers in France no longer even dare to print the word "Jew", which seems to them harsh and aggressive. For them, there are no longer any Jews. In cases of absolute necessity, with a thousand precautions, they timidly write "Israelite".

We have imposed absolute silence on our domination and on any incident that might remind the natives of the fact of our domination.[96] This marvellous discipline of the French press deserves a chapter of its own: Je l'écrirai.

Our victory is so complete, our conquest so definitive, that we do not even allow the French to remember that there was a battle, that they were once the masters of the country, that what is was not always what was. And we don't allow them to be reminded of that. One example shows how we handle our subjects. The Paris trade is grouped into two large associations. One, the Mascuraud agency, is effectively run by a dozen or so of Cohen, Weill, Meyer and Lévy, and the other, the French

---

[94] Such a remark would be worth the application of the Gayssot law by a Goyim judge. Fine, prison. There is no longer the slightest freedom to talk about Jewish atrocities.

[95] Louis Ferdinand Céline was the cause of the first racist law against the Jews, through his exceptional pamphlets which set out the fundamental truth about Jewish atrocities. This was the first Pléven and Marchandeau law, which evolved into an increasingly totalitarian form until the Fabius Gayssot law.

[96] The newspapers talk about Soros' monstrous deeds (destabilising economies, planning over-the-counter drugs) but NONE of them say that Soros is a Jew. Nowhere in the so-called democratic newspapers will you find that the WARBURGs who financed the 14-18 war and Bolshevism are Jews.

traders' association, is run by Hayem. Recently, a very large shopkeeper in the rue de la Paix allowed his name to be put on the patronage lists of a candidate who had made anti-Semitic statements in the past. The candidate thought nothing of it and his supporters ignored him. The big businessman had no doubts about it . But we knew: our files are well kept, our police are vigilant, our memory is secure. All the rich Jewish women who bought from this big shopkeeper claimed their accounts from him during the day. The pitiful Frenchman immediately ran to each of his customers to appease them. He protested his innocence, "they had used his name without warning". *He humiliated himself, apologised and replaced the candidate's posters at his own expense with others that did not bear his signature. He affirmed his devotion to the generous Israelites, to the beautiful Israelites, to all Israel.*

Oh my! What training![97]

Anyone who claims to be standing up to Israel and who dreams of taking France from us, we slander, we smear, we starve and we murder.[98] *In fact, we have him slandered, smeared and murdered by our French henchmen.*[99]

At a hundred francs a month, our Rothschild barons find as many French lackeys as they want, who they disguise as estafiers to murder peasants guilty of snaring a rabbit or stealing a bundle in the formerly French forest. At twenty-five louis, ten louis, we can find as much as we

---

[97] The same was true of FORD, who wrote a hard-hitting study against world Jewry. He was forced to fold or face ruin. Recently, the famous actor who played "*The Godfather*" and who had denounced the Jewish hegemony over the cinema pushed repentance to the point of tears! (Marlon Brando).

[98] Today, the simple Fabius Gayssot law takes care of everything: fines and prison.

[99] That's why I keep saying that there is no Jewish question but THE question of goyish bullshit.

like of the French cut-throats to intimidate our detractors, or judges to condemn them, to gag them.

All the natives of France tremble before the Jewish master as the natives of India tremble before the English master.[100] *Not that the French fear shedding human blood, they have the same taste as other peoples for slaughter, especially the slaughter of the weak and the defeated. In Madagascar, Sudan and Morocco, the French have killed and are still killing. In China, they have equalled or surpassed the appalling sadism of the Germans and Russians. In France itself, they occasionally slit each other's throats with implacable ferocity. The Revolution methodically exterminated almost a million Frenchmen: in the Vendée, Paris, Lyon and Bordeaux, there were guillotines, shootings, drownings and septembrisades that make you shudder.*

In June 1848, the bourgeoisie destroyed half of the old people of Paris, and it destroyed the rest in May 1871. As a result, the great city, intelligent, lively and generous, was now populated only by immigrants who came to enrich themselves by exploiting the vices of idlers and rascals. Paris had fallen to the level of Byzantium: a swarm of balladeers, jesters, matchmakers, harlots and valets. Easy prey for the conquerors that we are. But these same Frenchmen, ruthless to others, ruthless among themselves, are seized with panic terror in the presence of the Jew, their master.

When Monsieur Antoine, having made the Odéon a Hebrew theatre in the same way as his emulator, M. Claretie, had made the Comédie Française a Hebrew theatre, gave "Esther, Princess of Israel" *in February 1912, it was a splendid demonstration of our power and our hatred.*

---

[100] The English master delegated by the Jew, because colonisation was a Jewish operation, especially in India.

Twenty times the auditorium was packed with our ardent Jews, cheering the bloody triumph of Esther and Mordecai, the enslavement of Ahasuerus, the torment of Aman and his family.

The spoiled Ahasuerus symbolised the former French people, while Aman and his children symbolised our last adversaries.

> *Mordecai testified that our race*
> *Is the chosen race and the eternal race,*
> *Which God himself dictated to our forefathers,*
> *The book of life and truth;*
> *The race to whom the whole earth was promised,*
> *And who must conquer subjugated mankind.*
> *When he added in a hoarse voice:*
> *In Israel there is a force that breaks*
> *Any human movement unleashed against us,*
> *That touches our rights, is doomed in advance!*

The whole room roared with pride and fury: "Down with the Goyim, death, death!
Yes, whoever touches our rights in advance is condemned. Our rights are my conquest and mastery of the world, the merciless destruction of the Philistines, the Amalekites and the Midianites, and the exploitation to the point of blood of all goy humanity, vile cattle. The wretched Aman begged for mercy, at least for his children. So our Esther :
> *Aman reminded me that he has ten sons at the front*
> *Charming, young and handsome and strong, who could*
> *Avenge him one day if we let them live.*
> *Give me their ten heads*
> *Ahasuerus: I give them to you.*
> *Our Mordecai immediately roared these admirable verses*
> *Thus perish the enemies of Israel,*
> *And let the example be such that the Universe learns*
> *That, marked out by his God for the sovereign work,*
> *Strong in the infallible goal to which this God has led him,*

Yesterday as tomorrow, tomorrow as today,
Our people - unaware of time, century and hour,
Among the passing nations, alone remains!
In vain, Ahasuerus tried to evade his promise, frightened by the
immensity of the slaughter.
Blood, always blood!
Esther:
I want more, I want more
So that the sons of Israel can, until dawn,
slaughter without remorse, without pity, without mercy,
The enemies of God ... who are mine too.
We were killing, still killing.
In the hall, our brothers felt a secret intoxication. For three whole
days, non-stop, without rest,
Strike, strike one by one, by flocks,
by house, by tribe!
Esther:
Strike in multitudes
And if need be, cast to the winds of solitude
The seed of future generations!
It's such a balmy night
How good it is to be alive!
So here it is, the day of vengeance,
The long-awaited day of consecration,
Vibrant with clamour and hot with slaughter,
The triumph promised to my eternal people!
In twenty performances fifty thousand impatient Jews shouted
along with the beautiful Jewish actress:
Awake, ye singers of the splendour of Israel
Sound the harps of kings, the trumpets of Levites!
May the swords be swift, may the arrows be swift
May vengeance run with the feet of a madman!

The walls of the theatre shook with the clamour. As they left, the enthusiasm of our brothers echoed throughout the neighbourhood. The pale French hid under their blankets, frightened as the storm passed.

Beautiful evenings! Paid for by the budget of the Republic, in an official theatre of the Republic, to show the Republic's support for our plans and its obedience to our wishes!

We will have them, the three days of Esther. We can't have them in Russia,[101] *we can't have them in Germany, or in England because the natives are still capable of defending themselves. We will have them in France, where the bastardised people, skilfully emasculated by us, cowardly and gutted like Ahasuerus, voluntarily submit their spines to our whips and their throats to our knives.*

In Israel there is a force that breaks
Any human movement unleashed against us,
And whoever touches our rights, is condemned in advance
Unforgettable evenings!

> *All the verses obsess me and sing a delicious melody within me.*
> *I can't get enough of rereading and copying them!*
> *To slaughter without remorse without pity without mercy,*
> *God's enemies who are also mine.*
> *Strike, strike one by one, by flocks,*
> *By houses, by tribes,*
> *How sweet the night, how good to live*
> *The beautiful day that consecrates*
> *The triumph promised to my eternal people!*

Ah, France, dear France, precious Chanaan! What a source of revenge and delight you were to be for us! Now it's our turn! For 20 centuries we have endured violence and outrage, we have bent our backs, we have opposed only baseness to brutality. Finally, we have found someone more resigned than us, more grovelling than us, more cowardly than us: the natives of France. It was up to us to wield the whip and the stick! It's up to us to strip the vanquished and insult the slave! While we await

---

[101] It's done: the Judeo-Bolshevik revolution of 1917 handed Russia over to them. With its 80 million dead victims of Bolshevism...

the beautiful red nights of the massacre, we have already managed to debase this wonderful country.[102] *Our colleague Grumbach, whom the Alliance Israélite has placed at the head of the French naturalisation service, is not content with naturalising tens of thousands of our compatriots from Germany, Russia, Romania and Turkey, the reinforcements we need to occupy Paris. Grumbach also naturalised batches of the dregs of Europe, convicts, contumaxes and bandits from every country, turning them into French citizens, French magistrates, French diplomats, French legislators and the main editors of the main French newspapers to preside over France's destiny and enlighten French opinion.*

Ah, we'll get the lice out of the old lion's hair before we shoot him!

Ah, we'll have dragged beautiful France, great France, glorious France over the dung before we've finished her off!

Our people, unaware of time, century and hour
Among the nations that pass away, they alone remain!

Long live the Republic!

---

[102] They will succeed: the juxtaposition of unassimilable ethnic groups makes revolution inevitable between the French and the Africans. The Africans have shotguns and other weapons. The French are disarmed by law.

TOTALITARIAN GLOBALIST JUDEOPATHY

Three Jews built NBC, ABC and CBS, which are the epicentres of the texture of American society. Jews rule almost all the Hollywood studios. Four out of five of Viacom, Disney-ABC, Time-Warner and AOL are Jewish. So is Murdoch, who runs the world. They founded three television networks in England: Associated-Rediffusion, Associated-Télévision and Granada. The New York Time and the Washington Post are Jewish, as is the Wall Street Journal. The largest television group in Canada is Jewish, as is the second largest in Brazil. 50 to 60% of the Russian economy is controlled by a handful of Jewish oligarchs, some of whom have dual Russian-Israeli nationality. In Russia, two out of three television networks are Jewish. A study in 1973 showed that 21 out of 36 news network producers and editors were Jewish. Another study established that 59% of the directors, writers and producers of fifty films that had a definite economic success between 1965 and 1982 were Jewish. According to a study from the 1970s, 70-80% of Hollywood screenwriters are Jewish. Four Jews created the famous *Woodstock Festival*. A Jew built and directed the Beatles' fame. The vast majority of the rock 'n' roll scene is controlled by Jews: The Rolling Stones, Credence, Clearwater, Bruce Springsteen, etc. The foundation of American popular music "*Tin Pan Alley*" is dominated by Jews, who dominate the music industry. 80% of American comedians are Jewish, as are 80% of the pioneers of the comic book industry. Jews dominate the theatre and classical music. Two Jews run the Museum of Modern Art and the Whitney Museum, just the most famous of a long list of Jewish art world moguls. One of them supports a right-wing party in Israel and also runs a television conglomerate with a foothold in a dozen Central and Eastern European countries. A Jew founded the Intel computer company and Microsoft's number two is a half-Jew who supports

Israeli causes. In recent years, Jews have been at the helm of Compaq, Hewlett-Packard and Dell.

The head of NASA is Jewish. The Jews played a major role, along with the Italian Mafia, in founding Las Vegas. Its development was greatly helped by the largest crime syndicate in American history, which was headed by a Jew. In the Russian Mafia, Jews play an immense role. In the 1970s, 80% of New York's businesses were owned by Jews. 5 of the last 8 poets laureate are Jewish and so are 15 of the 21 leading intellectuals. These intellectuals are promoted by journals founded and edited by Jews, such as the New York Review of Books and the Partisan Review. Simon and Schuster, Alfred A. Knopf, Farrar Strauss and Giroux are the beginning of a long list of publishing houses founded and controlled by New York Jews. Half the basketball teams are run by Jews, and the National Hockey League and professional baseball are Jewish. Jews oversee the agencies that look after the careers and interests of professional sportsmen. Five of the eight Ivy League colleges are run by Jews.

In Clinton's cabinet were Jews: the Secretary of Labour, Commerce, Finance, Agriculture and the Secretary of State. The Secretary of Defense had a Jewish father. Clinton's two Supreme Court nominees were Jewish. The two Californian senators are Jewish and both members of a pro-Israeli women's activist organisation. A Jewish newspaper from the 1990s reveals that four of the seven CIA directors were Jewish. So was the top man, who was later pardoned by Bill Clinton for security breaches before investigations into his activities were completed.

Although they represent only 5% of the overall population of the United States, 45% of the forty richest Americans are Jewish. In the year 2000, Jews had forty-two major donors to the American national elections. They provide half the funding for the Democratic Party. Their top priority is always foreign policy in favour of Israel. In 1997, the head of the Pro-Israel Committee became leader of the Democratic Party and a few months later, the political affairs officer for the pro-Israel lobby became finance director of the Democratic Party. In the 1990s, the president of the International Monetary Fund was Jewish, as are the two directors of the World Bank. A Jew heads the Federal Reserve and the Federal Trade Commission.

In 2001, a Jewish "oligarchy" controlled 50 to 80% of the Russian economy. The second richest man in Australia is Jewish and owned part of the World Trade Center, the other part belonging to a Jew from New York. Around 1990, a Jew ran Mac Donald, others, the Bank of America, United Airline, and this is just the beginning of a long list. A Jew wrote a book about the diamond monopoly, which is entirely in Jewish hands. They also dominate the fashion industry: Calvin Klein, Tommy Hilger, Ralph Lauren, Donna Karan, Kenneth Cole, etc.

These are just examples, the tip of the iceberg of the gigantic Jewish influence in our society. Their activity in favour of the State of Israel is enormous. But if you mention these simple facts, the condemnation rains down: "prejudice, bigotry, racism, hatemongering", you are then anti-Jewish, which will destroy your life and your career. You are accused of racism, whereas the Jewish question can in no way be part of the myth of racism (races do exist and ethnic groups are constituted by centuries of belonging to a fixed environment, which is in no way the case for Jews. Ethnicity is the result of hormonal adaptation to a fixed environment: Jewish particularism comes exclusively from circumcision on the 8th day, the first day of puberty). No Western politician can keep his well-paid elected post if he utters ONE word of truth about the Jews. They have organisations with million-dollar budgets whose sole aim is to silence all those who oppose their domination by convicting them of anti-Semitism. In France, the Gayssotine law, which is anti-democratic, anti-human rights, unconstitutional and therefore illegal, is the last straw.

Any distinguished professor who wanted to publish the results of research that displeased the Jews was dismissed and condemned. It is therefore impossible to expose their lies, except in the underground press, which is now considerable. (The arithmetical-technical nonsense of the myth of "six million gas chambers" can never, under any circumstances, be mentioned). Most people, dumbed down by secularism, television, chemotherapy in food and pharmaceuticals, and vaccinations, have no idea of the dimensions of the Jewish question, because censorship is omnipresent, just as it is in Orwell's *1984*, when people are condemned for "*thoughtcrime*".

For example, if you talk about Jewish predominance in Hollywood, you have to defend yourself against anti-Semitism in the face of those who demand silence on the issue of Jewish predominance in Hollywood.

In a robotic society where Jewish power is radical, Hollywood makes us ignore the fact that the Second World War was concocted by the Jews, that it left sixty million dead and not just six million Jews (whose revisionist work has revealed to us the enormous inflation and the impossibility of gassing with Zyklon B). Hollywood has reinvented the war for the benefit of the interned Jews, even though they declared war on Hitler in 1933, and never tells us about the tens of millions of corpses of the radically Jewish Soviet Russia, from its ideologists like Marx and Hegel to its prison and concentration camp executioners like Kaganovitch, Frenkel, Yagoda, etc.

In France and everywhere else, the situation is the same. As a bonus, we have Badinter, who had the death penalty annulled and institutionalised it for an unlimited number of innocent people, since once a murderer has been convicted there is no risk of him being convicted again if he kills again six to fifteen times, which he sometimes does... This same Badinter tells us that to be a good father you have to be a bit of a paederast and paedophile, while Mrs

Badinter tells us that the maternal instinct does not exist. Lang and Kouchner tell us that children "*have a right to sexual pleasure*", Simone Veil institutes self-service abortion for healthy children, while the crazies swarm. Lang also promotes pathogenic and criminogenic music and rave-parties... The pornography of the Benezaref is on display at the "*athée-lévy-sion*" and elsewhere...

We have here a host of extra-dimensional criminals of lèse-humanité... Immorality has become a system...

CONCLUSION

It is quite clear to me that these facts, which have been in the news since 1934 and offer a Niagara of ninefold proof, were not written by a Jew (unless there is proof to the contrary) but by a Goy who was as disgusted by Jewish perversity as he was by the disgusting slavishness of the Goyim, *"that vile seed of cattle"*.

The radical abolition of circumcision on the 8th day would settle the Jewish question (as I have explained in my secret works). But, alas, Judeo-Cartesianism is launched and nothing can stop its race towards nothingness.

Rothschildo-Marxism is going to exterminate us. After the ruins... We'll see!

After the age of iron, concrete and darkness, there will be a golden age, but we won't be here to see it.

* * * *

OTHER TITLES

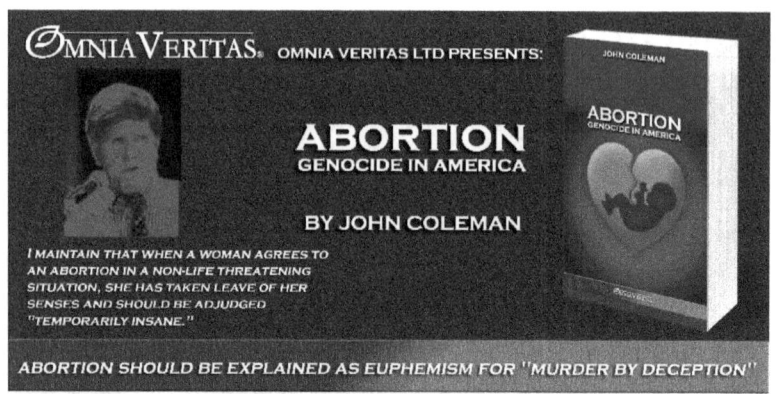

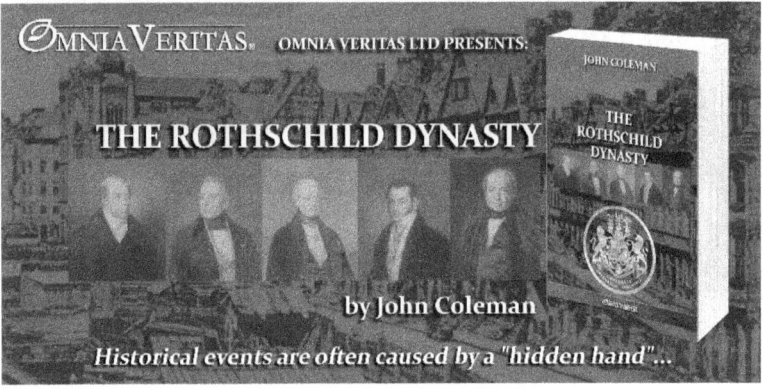

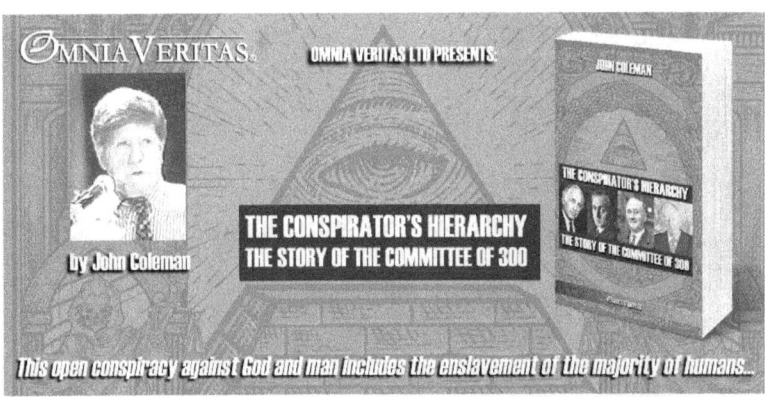

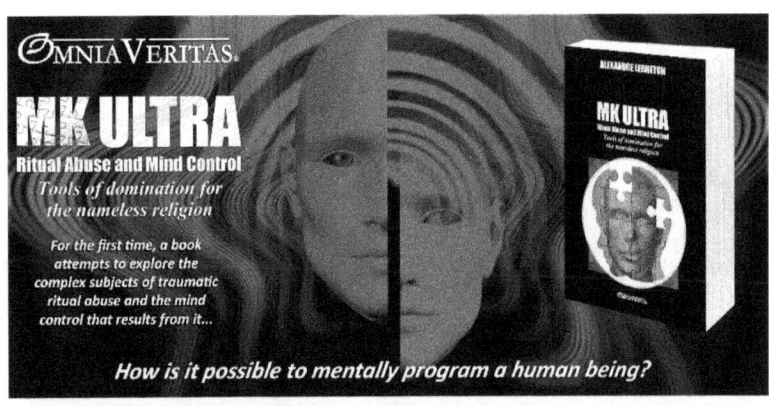

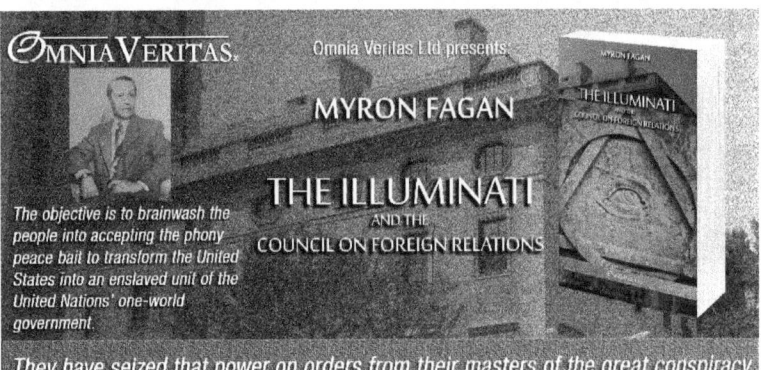

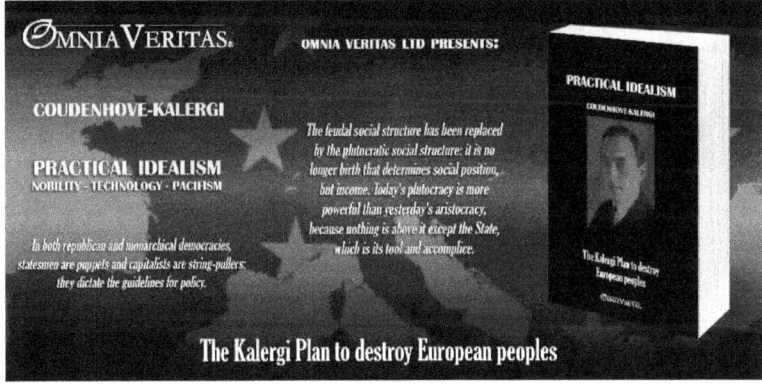

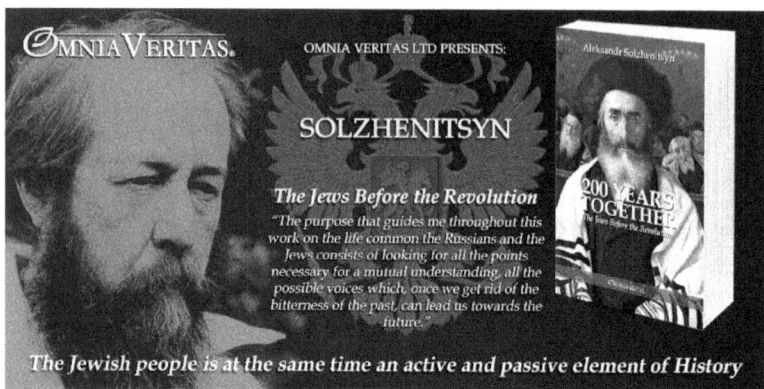

www.ingramcontent.com/pod-product-compliance
Lightning Source LLC
Chambersburg PA
CBHW050133170426
43197CB00011B/1818